endorsed for
BTEC

BTEC Level 2 Technical Diploma

Children's Play, Learning and Development

Early Years Assistant

Learner Handbook

Louise Burnham
Sharina Forbes
Katherine Stapleton
Denise Tolhurst

Pearson

Published by Pearson Education Limited, 80 Strand, London WC2R 0RL.

http://qualifications.pearson.com/en/qualifications/btec-specialist-and-professional-qualifications/

Text © Pearson Education Limited 2018
Typeset by Phoenix and PDQ Digital Media Productions

The rights of Louise Burnham, Sharina Forbes, Katherine Stapleton and Denise Tolhurst to be identified as authors of this work have been asserted by them in accordance with the Copyright, Designs and Patents Act 1988.

First edition published 2018

22 21 20 19
8 7 6 5

British Library Cataloguing in Publication Data
A catalogue record for this book is available from the British Library

ISBN 978 1 292 19708 1

Acknowledgements
The publisher would like to thank the following for their kind permission to reproduce their photographs:
(Key: b-bottom; c-centre; l-left; r-right; t-top)

123RF.com: Komdet Chanakittidecha 23c; Alamy Stock Photo: Jozef Polc 81cr, Marmaduke St. John 172bl, PhotoAlto 125b/8, Picture Partners 53tl, 70tl, 128cl, Waechter / Agencja Fotograficzna Caro 112t, Zuma Press Inc 210t; DK Images: Dave King 24tl/1, 24tr/2, 24bl/3, 24br/4, Ruth Jenkinson 51br; Food Standards Agency: Crown Copyright 2017 149bl; Fotolia.com: Alex 96tl, athomass 31bc, dglimages 101tr, 106b, lalalululala 55cr, pressmaster 186t, Robert Kneschke 56b, sheva_ua 125b/5; Imagestate Media: Bananastock 50cl (Grasping), 79bl, 122, 162; NSPCC: 12bl/1 (P), 12bl/2 (A), 12bl/2 (N), 12bl/4 (T), 12bl/5 (S); Pearson Education Ltd: Studio 8 2, 31br, 71tr, 95br, 109tl, 165tr, 166tl, 194b, 232, 256t, Carla Mestas 226tl, Stuart Cox 125b/1, 125b/2, 125b/3, 125b/4, 125b/6, 125b/7, David Kostelnik 36c, Lord and Leverett 64tl, 169b, 173b, 208t, David Sanderson 20bl (Water), 20bc (Foam), 20bc (Powder), 20br (CO2), Jules Selmes , 25b, 37tr, 46, 50tc, 50tr, 50c, 50cl (Stepping), 50cr, 50bl, 50bc, 50br, 51cl, 51cr, 51bl, 51bc (left), 51bc (right), 55br, 57b, 62tl, 75cl, 80c, 81bl, 81br, 88, 90tl, 90bl, 135bl, 145bl, 153tl, 155b, 157b, 180t, 193c, 200, 217tr, 218tl, 225tr, Ian Wedgewood 254t; PhotoDisc: C Squared Studios 53br; Science Photo Library Ltd: PAUL WHITEHALL 28tl; Shutterstock.com: chairoij 31bl, Igor Stepovik 51c (3 Months), Isantilli 53bl, Kokhanchikov 67tr, Marlon Lopez MMG1 Design 50tl, Tom Wang 176tr, vlatetal 51c (1 Month), wavebreakmedia 94cl

p.11 Figure 1.2 Gibbs' reflective cycle is reproduced by permission of Oxford Brookes University; **p.17** Figure 1.3 The NARU triage sieve is reproduced by permission of the National Ambulance Resilience Unit (NARU); **p.25** Figure 1.5 Hand-washing technique is reproduced by permission of the World Health Organisation; **p.71** Figure 2.11 The four stages of the Chain of Survival is reproduced by permission of The Resuscitation Council (UK).

Cover image: OpopO / Shutterstock.com
All other images © Pearson Education

Websites
Pearson Education Limited is not responsible for the content of any external internet sites. It is essential for tutors to preview each website before using it in class so as to ensure that the URL is still accurate, relevant and appropriate. We suggest that tutors bookmark useful websites and consider enabling students to access them through the school/college intranet.

Note from the publisher

1.
In order to ensure that this resource offers high-quality support for the associated Pearson qualification, it has been through a review process by the awarding body. This process confirms that this resource fully covers the teaching and learning content of the specification or part of a specification at which it is aimed. It also confirms that it demonstrates an appropriate balance between the development of subject skills, knowledge and understanding, in addition to preparation for assessment.

Endorsement does not cover any guidance on assessment activities or processes (e.g. practice questions or advice on how to answer assessment questions), included in the resource nor does it prescribe any particular approach to the teaching or delivery of a related course.

While the publishers have made every attempt to ensure that advice on the qualification and its assessment is accurate, the official specification and associated assessment guidance materials are the only authoritative source of information and should always be referred to for definitive guidance. Pearson examiners have not contributed to any sections in this resource relevant to examination papers for which they have responsibility.

Examiners will not use endorsed resources as a source of material for any assessment set by Pearson. Endorsement of a resource does not mean that the resource is required to achieve this Pearson qualification, nor does it mean that it is the only suitable material available to support the qualification, and any resource lists produced by the awarding body shall include this and other appropriate resources.

2.
Pearson has robust editorial processes, including answer and fact checks, to ensure the accuracy of the content in this publication, and every effort is made to ensure this publication is free of errors. We are, however, only human, and occasionally errors do occur. Pearson is not liable for any misunderstandings that arise as a result of errors in this publication, but it is our priority to ensure that the content is accurate. If you spot an error, please do contact us at resourcescorrections@pearson.com so we can make sure it is corrected.

Contents

How to use this book

This handbook is designed to support you in developing the skills and knowledge to succeed in your BTEC Level 2 Technical course. It will help you to feel confident in taking the next step and be ready for your dream job.

The skills you will develop during the course include practical skills that you'll need in your chosen occupation, as well as a range of 'transferable' skills and behaviours that will be useful for your own personal development, whatever you do in life.

Your learning can be seen as a journey which moves through four phases.

Phase 1	Phase 2	Phase 3	Phase 4
You are introduced to a topic or concept; you start to develop an awareness of what learning and skills are required.	You explore the topic or concept through different methods (e.g. watching or listening to a tutor or a professional at work, research, questioning, analysis, critical evaluation) and form your own understanding.	You apply your knowledge and skills to a practical task designed to demonstrate your understanding and skills.	You reflect on your learning, evaluate your efforts, identify gaps in your knowledge and look for ways to improve.

During each phase, you will use different learning strategies. As you go through your course, these strategies will combine to help you secure the essential knowledge and skills.

This handbook has been written using similar learning principles, strategies and tools. It has been designed to support your learning journey, to give you control over your own learning and to equip you with the knowledge, understanding and tools to be successful in your future career or studies.

Getting to know the features

In this handbook you'll find lots of different features. They are there to help you learn about the topics in your course in different ways and to help you monitor and check your progress. Together these features help you:

- build your knowledge and technical skills
- understand how to succeed in your assessment
- link your learning to the workplace.

In addition, each individual feature has a specific purpose, designed to support important learning strategies. For example, some features will:

- get you to question assumptions around what you are learning
- make you think beyond what you are reading about
- help you make connections across your learning and across units
- draw comparisons between the theory you are learning about and realistic workplace environments

- help you develop some of the important skills you will need for the workplace, including planning and completing tasks, working with others, effective communication, adaptability and problem solving.

Features to build your knowledge and technical skills

Key terms

Terms highlighted LIKE THIS, are 'Key terms'. It is important that you know what they mean because they relate directly to your chosen subject. The first time they appear in the book they will be explained. If you see a highlighted Key term again after that and can't quite remember its definition, look in the Glossary towards the end of the book – they are all listed there! Note that these key terms are used and explained in the context of your specialist subject or the topic in which they appear, and are not necessarily the same definitions you would find in a dictionary.

Practise

These work-related tasks or activities will allow you to practise some of the technical or professional skills relating to the main content covered in each unit.

> **Practise**
>
> Visit the NHS choices website to watch videos on how to put someone in the recovery position and how to perform CPR.
>
> Work with a partner and practice putting each other in the recovery position.

Skills and knowledge check

Regular 'Skills and knowledge check' boxes will help you to keep on track with the knowledge and skills requirements for a unit. They will remind you to go back and refresh your knowledge if you haven't quite understood what you need to know or demonstrate. Tick off each one when you are confident you've nailed it.

> **Skills and knowledge check**
>
> ☐ I can contribute to monitoring children's development through observation.
> ☐ I can track a child's development based on the established milestones.
> ☐ I can look out for atypical development and understand its possible impact if not identified.
>
> ○ I can name the five areas of development.
> ○ I know the impact of a 2-year-old's emotional development and why this means that they may have tantrums.
> ○ I can name three things that are developmentally 'normal' for a 4- to 5-year-old.
> ○ I know that children's development is holistic and what this means.

What if...?

Employers need to know that you are responsible and that you understand the importance of what you are learning. These 'What if...?' scenarios will help you to understand the real links between theory and what happens in the workplace.

What if...?

Imagine a 9-month-old baby in your care had diarrhoea this morning and has since been sick. This has been dismissed as nothing to worry about as he is teething. The baby remains in the setting for the rest of the day. The following day another baby is not in nursery as they have picked up a sickness bug.

1 Do you think the two incidents are related?

2 What should the setting have done the previous day when the 9-month-old was sick?

3 What hygiene practices should the setting follow to prevent the sickness bug spreading further?

Link it up

Go to Unit 5, B3 to learn more about suitable resources and equipment for play and learning activities.

Link it up

Although your BTEC Level 2 Technical is made up of several units, common themes are explored from different perspectives across the whole of your course. Everything you learn and do during your course will help you in your final assessment. This kind of assessment is called 'synoptic'. It means that you have the opportunity to apply all the knowledge and skills from the course to a practical, realistic work situation or task.

The 'Link it up' features show where information overlaps between units or within the same unit, helping you to see where key points might support your final assessment or help you gain a deeper understanding of a topic.

Step-by-step

This practical feature gives step-by-step descriptions of processes or tasks, and might include a photo or artwork to illustrate each step. This will help you to understand the key stages in the process and help you to practise the process or technique yourself.

Checklist

These lists present information in a way that is helpful, practical and interactive. You can check off the items listed to ensure you think about each one individually, as well as how they relate to the topic as a collective list.

Features connected to your assessment

Your course is made up of several units. There are two different types of unit:

- externally assessed
- internally assessed.

The features that support you in preparing for assessment are below. But first, what is the difference between these two different types of unit?

Externally assessed units

These units give you the opportunity to present what you have learned in the unit in a different way. They can be challenging, but will really give you the opportunity to demonstrate your knowledge and understanding, or your skills, in a direct way. For these units you will complete a task, set by Pearson, in controlled conditions. This could take the form of an exam or onscreen test, or it could be another type of task. You may have the opportunity to research and prepare notes around a topic in advance, which can be used when completing the assessment.

Internally assessed units

Internally assessed units involve you completing a series of assignments or tasks, set and marked by your tutor. The assignments you complete could allow you to demonstrate your learning in a number of different ways, such as a report, a presentation, a video recording or observation statements of you completing a practical task. Whatever the method, you will need to make sure you have clear evidence of what you have achieved and how you did it.

Ready for assessment

You will find these features in units that are internally assessed. They include suggestions about what you could practise or focus on to complete the assignment for the unit. They also explain how to gather evidence for assessment from the workplace or from other tasks you have completed.

Ready for assessment

You will be observed carrying out physical care routines and supporting meals or snack times in your setting. Start by considering which care routines and activities you can be involved in. Remember, you will need to demonstrate a consistently high standard and quality of support – not just on one occasion. As well as supporting children, you will need to demonstrate how health and safety practices are identified and followed.

So, it is important to remind yourself of all the essential behaviours and practices in this chapter. You should also make sure you have completed Section B, Unit 4 of form CPLD 1 in your Placement Experience Assessment Portfolio of Evidence. Complete the self-assessment form in your booklet and include ideas about the different skills you have developed when completing the activities for this unit. Make a note of things you could do to keep improving on these skills.

You will need to collect evidence to show how you have supported children's routines in the setting. This should include:

- daily routine logs
- witness statements from your setting supervisor or your college assessor
- menu plans and snack preparation accounts to demonstrate how you support healthy eating in the setting
- reflective summaries (these show how you have evaluated the effectiveness of the support you offer to young children during care routines).

Assessment practice

These features include questions similar to the ones you'll find in your external assessment, so you can get some experience answering them. Each one relates to one or more Assessment Outcomes, as indicated in the top right-hand corner of this feature box. Suggested answers are given at the back of this book. Where Assessment practice features require you to carry out your own research or give individual answers or opinions, however, no answers are provided.

Assessment practice 1.4   AO1 AO2 AO4

It is common for early years practitioners to notice marks and bruises on children that have happened accidentally through everyday life. However, some injuries can be a sign that a child has experienced physical abuse.
1 Identify two injuries from the choices below that may cause you concern.

- Scrape to knee
- Burn on stomach
- Bruise on buttock
- Bruise on shin
- Scab on elbow
- Bruise on neck

2 Explain what you would do next if you had a concern that a child had experienced physical abuse.

Getting ready for assessment

This section will help you prepare for external assessment. It gives information about what to expect in the final assessment, as well as revision tips and practical advice on preparing for and sitting exams or a set task. It provides a series of sample questions and answers that you might find, including helpful feedback, or 'verdicts', on the answers and how they could be improved.

Features which link your learning with the workplace

Each unit ends with a 'Work focus' section which links the learning from the unit to particular skills and behaviours that are required in the workplace. There are two parts in each Work focus section:

1. **Hands on** – gives suggestions for tasks you could practise to develop the technical or professional skills you'll need on the job.
2. **Ready for work?** – supports you in developing the all-important transferable skills and behaviours that employers are looking for, such as adaptability, problem solving, communication or teamwork. It will give you pointers for showcasing your skills to a potential employer.

HANDS ON

For this internally assessed unit, you will need to show that you are able to make the link between the knowledge you have gained and the skills you are showing as part of your work placement. There are also some transferable skills to practise, which relate to this unit and that could help you to gain employment as an early years assistant.

1. Communication

- Show how you communicate effectively with others, both when working with children and as part of the early years staff. Remember to use positive facial expressions and body language as well as thinking about how you can communicate clearly.

- Develop your confidence when communicating with others in different ways and think about how you do this in different situations, such as with parents, colleagues and children of different ages.

2. Preparing for work

- Plan activities carefully and review what you have done afterwards to develop your awareness of your own practice.

- When carrying out activities with children, show how you are applying your knowledge and understanding of their communication skills so that you can relate this to your interactions with them.

3. Demonstrate thinking skills

- Show that you can assess situations quickly so that you can adapt how you communicate with others. Remember that some children may have communication issues which are as yet undiagnosed.

- Use **INITIATIVE** when working with children and show that you can think independently, but *do check* if there is anything you are not sure about.

Ready for work?

Answer the questions below to find out if you've got what it takes to be a great early years assistant. Some questions have more than one correct answer, so tick all that apply.

1 When working in an early years setting, which of the following should you do?

- [ ] A Always work closely with others and share information.
- [ ] B Talk to parents as much as possible.
- [ ] C Do your own thing.
- [ ] D Keep out of others' way.

2 Which of the following should you do when planning activities?

- [ ] A Plan the kinds of things you enjoy.
- [ ] B Plan the kinds of things the children enjoy.
- [ ] C Change the activities when you feel like it.
- [ ] D Make sure all areas of learning and development are included.

3 When you are preparing learning activities, which of these will support children's development?

- [ ] A Most activities will be okay.
- [ ] B A mixture of creative, imaginative, physical, sensory and construction activities would be ideal.
- [ ] C Choose activities that the children enjoy and use.
- [ ] D Focus on allowing the children to use their imagination.

4 How would you support a child who has atypical development and is not reaching their developmental milestones?

- [ ] A Talk to their key person and find out more about them.
- [ ] B Observe them over time and gather information about different areas of their development.
- [ ] C Make sure they are okay by having a chat with them.
- [ ] D Speak to others in the setting about putting a plan together.

Answers: 1 A/B=5, C/D=2; 2 A/C=2, B/D=5; 3 A/D=2, B/C=5; 4 A/B/D=5, C=2

If you have scored 12 or less, you need to go over the requirements for this unit. Make sure you have understood each of the areas of development and how they relate to the areas of learning in the EYFS.

1 Policy and Practice for Working in Early Years Settings

Everyone working in early years settings should know about the legislation in place to keep children safe and well. Legislation is important as it makes sure all settings have policies and procedures to protect children from harm and to keep them healthy. Legislation gives guidelines on how to provide a safe and inclusive environment.

Imagine there were no legislation that early years settings had to follow. Would you be able to care for children effectively without a clear set of standards and guidelines?

An understanding of legislation and policies is key to safeguarding and promoting the welfare of children.

How will I be assessed?

This unit is assessed using an onscreen test, containing different types of questions, which is set and marked by Pearson.

You will need to show that you know and understand the policies and legislation designed to keep children safe and to promote their welfare. Another important skill you will need to demonstrate is that you know how to apply that knowledge and understanding to your work with children in an early years setting.

Assessment outcomes

AO1 Demonstrate knowledge of principles of safeguarding and welfare of children in the early years setting.

AO2 Demonstrate understanding of the significance of legislation, policies and procedures, and practice relating to safety and wellbeing of the child in promoting safe environments in early years settings.

AO3 Evaluate the application of policy and procedure in maintaining the welfare of the child in the early years setting.

AO4 Make connections between the wellbeing of the child and the working practices in the setting that promote safeguarding, inclusion and health and safety.

What you will learn in this unit:

A   Safeguarding children in early years settings

B   Promoting safe environments in early years settings

C   Child health

D   Anti-discriminatory practice in the early years setting

A Safeguarding children in early years settings

A1 Child protection legislation in early years settings

There are a number of pieces of legislation that underpin your setting's SAFEGUARDING POLICIES AND PROCEDURES – the methods used to protect children from harm and abuse.

Safeguarding legislation in the early years setting

You should be aware of the following key pieces of safeguarding legislation. Settings have a STATUTORY DUTY to follow legislation; this means it is a legal requirement.

Table 1.1: Key safeguarding legislation

Key legislation	Purpose of legislation	Main features
Children Act 1989	This Act was designed to help keep children safe and well and, if necessary, help a child to remain living with their family by providing services to meet the child's needs	• The welfare of each child is paramount when decisions are made about their upbringing. • The Act sets out systems to keep children safe and the roles that different agencies play
Children Act 2004	This Act has a child-centred approach and was designed to make sure services work together, rather like fitting all the pieces of a puzzle together to see the bigger picture	• The Act warrants that agencies such as social services, the police, the NSPCC (see page 8) and health services work together to support children. • It provides the legal basis for how local authorities and their partners should work with each other
Children and Families Act 2014, Part 3	This Act puts legislation in place to ensure children and young people with Special Educational Needs and disabilities have access to education	• The Act sets out the help children and parents can get from health-care services, social-care services and support in education

United Nations Convention on the Rights of the Child 1989	This Convention recognises that children worldwide have their own rights and sets out how these should be respected. It is a legal framework put in place to support the education, care and development of all children	• The Convention's key features are that all children have fundamental rights, including the right to:
		  – life, survival and development
		  – protection from abuse, neglect or violence
		  – an education enabling them to fulfil their potential
		  – be raised by, or have a relationship with, their parents
		  – be listened to and express their opinions

Childcare Act 2006	This Act makes provision about the powers and duties of local authorities and other bodies in England in relation to the improvement of the wellbeing of young children	• The duties on local authorities • The systems of regulation and inspection of childcare in England • The need for children's centres
EARLY YEARS FOUNDATION STAGE (EYFS) 2017 England	The statutory safeguarding and welfare guidance in the EYFS sets out the legal responsibilities of early years settings to promote children's health, safety and wellbeing	• Guidance on child protection, suitable people to work with children and disqualification

Assessment practice 1.1	AO2 AO3 AO4

Choose one of the pieces of key legislation listed above. Spend some time researching the legislation on the internet.

1   State the main features of the legislation.

2   Discuss the purpose of the legislation.

A2 Policies and procedures in early years settings

Your setting will have a range of safeguarding policies and procedures which everyone must follow by law. These stem from the key pieces of safeguarding legislation and are necessary to keep children safe from abuse and harm. The policies and procedures cover many different aspects of your work with children, and the main ones are described below.

Child protection and safeguarding policies

Legally, each early years setting must have a Child Protection Policy, so as to meet the requirements of the statutory safeguarding and welfare guidance in the EYFS. The policy must state which practitioner has been designated to take lead responsibility for safeguarding children.

Spend some time looking through your own setting's policies. Can you see how they link to the pieces of key legislation?

Assessment practice 1.2	AO2

Ask for copies of the following policies and procedures from your setting.

Read each policy and use a highlighter pen to show the main points that relate to you as an early years assistant.

- Child Protection Policy
- Staff Protection Policy
- Physical Intervention Policy
- Anti-bullying Policy
- Attendance Policy
- Missing Child Policy
- Prevent Duty Policy
- Confidentiality Policy

- e-Safety Policy
- Staff Conduct Guidance
- Record Keeping Procedures
- Safer Recruitment Policy
- Allegations Against Staff Procedures
- Whistleblowing Policy
- Mobile Phone Policy

Mobile phones and camera safety

All settings must have policies on the safe use of mobile phones and cameras in the setting. This is to stop people taking inappropriate photographs of children. Key points usually include:

- Mobile phones should not be used in a room with the children; practitioners should leave mobile phones in their locker or in the staff room. Settings should have a policy requesting that visitors do not use mobile phones in the setting.
- Only use DESIGNATED CAMERAS to take photographs. These are cameras that are for use in the setting only.

Link it up

Unit 2, A2 mentions the use of photographs of children in cognitive development. Why is it important to have policies regarding the safe use of cameras?

- Parents are usually asked to give written permission for pictures to be taken of their children. Some settings will allow parents to take photographs of their own children at family events, such as sports day, but there are requirements that these are not shared on social media. Other settings will have a policy that strictly no photographs are taken.

Safe working practice

As an early years assistant, you need to be clear on your own roles and responsibilities to ensure safe practice when working with children. Practitioners can be vulnerable to allegations of abuse as they are often caring for children intimately, for example when supporting toileting.

Who supervises you in the setting to make sure you are working safely? Are there any tasks you are not allowed to do, for example changing nappies? Look at your setting's Staff Protection Policy for clear guidance on roles and responsibilities.

Your setting should have further measures in place to ensure safe working practice.

- You, and all staff members, should have an induction before you join a setting. This will introduce you to your setting's safeguarding policies – you should also have more detailed safeguarding training throughout your career.
- Your setting's Safer Recruitment Policy should make sure that references and employment history are thoroughly checked before new members of staff are employed.
- All staff must have a current **DISCLOSURE AND BARRING SERVICE** (DBS) check. The DBS check is the record-checking process that ensures people who work with children do not have a criminal record.

What if...?

Charlie has applied for the position of Room Leader at Rocking Horse Nursery. Charlie is asked to provide two references. She gives the name of a nursery she left three years ago and her childcare tutor from college. Charlie hands over a copy of her old DBS certificate.

Both references come back and are very positive – Charlie gets the job.

A concerned parent tells the manager that Charlie was dismissed the previous month from her job at the local crèche for coming to work drunk and shouting at the children.

1 What are the potential consequences of not checking references and employment history thoroughly?

2 Why do all staff need to have a current DBS check?

Dealing with allegations or suspicion of abuse

Safeguarding is *everyone's* responsibility. If you have a concern, it is your job to report it.

Refer back to your own setting's Child Protection Policy so you are clear on reporting procedures.

Every setting should have at least one **DESIGNATED SAFEGUARDING LEAD**. This is the person who has further training on safeguarding issues and to whom you should report concerns. Make sure you know who that person is in your setting.

The designated safeguarding lead may then contact your LOCAL SAFEGUARDING CHILDREN BOARD – the statutory body that works to safeguard children in your area.

Remember, you should only report concerns to your setting's designated safeguarding lead; do not be tempted to discuss concerns with other staff members or the child's family.

Government guidance documents

The government is continually working to keep children safe from harm. One example of documentation is 'Working Together to Safeguard Children' (March 2015), which is statutory guidance on how agencies should work together to promote children's welfare and keep them safe. Another example is 'Keeping Children Safe in Education' (September 2016), which gives staff working in maintained nurseries, schools and colleges, and independent schools, information about a co-ordinated and child-centred approach to safeguarding.

What to do if a child discloses information

At any time, a child may open up to you and start to tell you things that concern you. When a child tells you that they have been abused, this is called a DISCLOSURE. You may feel shocked or upset by what the child is saying, but it is vital that you act in the correct manner. See the ten recommended steps below.

STEP BY STEP | **RESPONDING TO A DISCLOSURE**

- ☐ Remain calm – do not act shocked
- ☐ Listen to the child carefully
- ☐ Let the child lead the discussion – do not ask leading questions or prompt them
- ☐ Reassure them that it was right to tell you
- ☐ Reassure the child that you believe them
- ☐ Do not make promises you cannot keep (never promise to keep it a secret)
- ☐ Report immediately to your setting's designated safeguarding lead
- ☐ Write down exactly what the child said to you
- ☐ Make sure you sign and date any required paperwork
- ☐ Do not discuss the disclosure with anyone else, not even other staff members

---

Effective practice

If you follow the safeguarding policies and procedures in your setting, this will help to ensure best practice and that children are cared for safely. Refer back to the list of child protection and safeguarding policies in this chapter. Make sure you have read and understood them. Raise any queries with your supervisors and make sure you promptly re-read them when you are told they have been updated.

Reporting concerns of unsafe practice

Imagine you see another staff member in your setting behaving towards a child in a way that concerns you. This could include handling a child roughly, talking unkindly or not supervising children safely. This may feel like a difficult situation, especially if it is a senior member of staff, or the staff member is your friend. However, it is your duty to report your concern to your designated safeguarding lead. This is called **WHISTLEBLOWING**, when you report concerns about fellow practitioners. You should never turn a blind eye.

If concerns you have reported to your designated safeguarding lead are not addressed, or there is a situation where it is the designated safeguarding lead who shows unsafe practice, you should report directly to your Local Safeguarding Children Board.

Assessment practice 1.3   AO1 AO2

Sally is a new member of staff in your setting. You notice that Sally keeps her mobile phone in her pocket and takes it with her when she changes nappies.

- State how this goes against your setting's safeguarding policies.

- Explain what you would do next and why.

Understand the role of the NSPCC

The **NATIONAL SOCIETY FOR THE PREVENTION OF CRUELTY TO CHILDREN** (NSPCC) is a charity that has the legal power to intervene if a child is in danger. The NSPCC can apply for a court order to protect the child, for example, an emergency protection order to take the child to a safe place if they are at immediate risk at home.

Understand the role of Ofsted

OFSTED (the Office for Standards in Education) has the role of inspecting childcare settings in England. Ofsted checks that statutory requirements are met, oversees the quality of care and education provided in settings, and puts measures and recommendations in place to improve standards.

Early years settings undergo Ofsted inspections, where the inspector spends time observing practice and checking the setting is meeting all legal requirements. It is useful to look at your own and other settings' Ofsted inspection reports to see how judgements are made about children's care and education.

Roles of other professionals in the protection of children (safeguarding context)

The diagram below shows the key professionals who support children and families.

Figure 1.1: Do any professionals work in partnership with your setting to support children's wellbeing?

Many different professionals have the job of protecting children from harm.

- Social workers have a legal duty to support children and families identified as being in need, for example if a child has a disability or when adults need help with parenting skills.
- The police have the power to arrest, prosecute and detain people who harm children. Through their work in the community, they may identify children at risk, for example if responding to a report of domestic violence or drug misuse.
- Health visitors and other health professionals support children in the community, offering advice and guidance on development, behaviour and health issues. During their work, they may identify signs that a child is at risk of harm.
- Teachers and other education professionals work in education services to provide a safe learning environment for children. Teachers get to know children well and may become trusted adults, ones who children may disclose to.
- SPECIAL EDUCATIONAL NEEDS CO-ORDINATORS (SENCOs) work closely with children who have additional needs, and offer support and advice to their families. The SENCO can give guidance when children have behavioural difficulties, physical disabilities or other issues such as Autism Spectrum Disorder. Statistically, children with disabilities are more vulnerable to abuse or neglect than children who do not have a disability.

Safeguarding lead

Your setting's designated safeguarding lead plays a key role in supporting your understanding of safe working practices and child protection policy and procedure. Refer back in this unit for more information about how to report any concerns regarding a child to your setting's designated safeguarding lead.

Partnership working

When there are lots of professionals involved in a child's life, it is vitally important that they work together to support the best interests of the child. You may have seen in the news upsetting stories of child abuse and neglect. Unfortunately, tragedies could have been avoided in some cases if agencies had worked in partnership and shared information.

Partnership working can take place if there are concerns over a child's safety. Professionals such as social workers and health visitors may work with the parents and the early years setting to ensure a child is not at risk of harm. Likewise, if a child has additional needs or a disability, professionals such as the SENCO, physiotherapist or speech and language therapist can offer support to the child, their family and the setting.

The benefits of a multi-agency approach

Professionals from different agencies can support children and their families with their differing areas of expertise. When this knowledge is combined it supports positive outcomes.

Child-centred planning

Professionals should always put the needs of the child first. This means planning support to meet each individual child's needs and avoiding a 'one size fits all' approach. Putting the needs of the child above everything else should ensure that children are given the correct support and resources to help them achieve their individual goals.

Joined-up working with other services

Information should be shared between agencies, within the boundaries of confidentiality, to keep each child safe. When professionals work in a 'joined-up' manner, it helps parties to see the bigger picture and to work more effectively in partnership for the benefit of the child.

Involving families and children in planning and decision making

Parents are children's first and central carers. Families should be listened to, their choices respected and their needs for support recognised. Each child should also have the opportunity to make their voice heard and be included in decision making, within their capabilities. By engaging children and families, this ultimately increases the chances of better outcomes for the child.

A3 Types of abuse

It is extremely important that you are aware of the different types of child abuse and can look out for signs that may indicate abuse. You should know how to help a child if they disclose that they have been abused and you should be able to give children the strategies they need to keep themselves safe.

Identifying different types of abuse

Four types of abuse are recognised in law.

1 **PHYSICAL ABUSE** is when an injury is caused to a child by someone acting aggressively towards them, resulting in non-accidental injuries.
2 **EMOTIONAL ABUSE** is treating a child in a way that can upset them and damage their mental health.
3 **SEXUAL ABUSE** is when a child is persuaded or forced to take part in sexual acts.
4 **NEGLECT** is a pattern of failing to meet a child's **BASIC NEEDS** (food, water, shelter, warmth, love).

Social factors that may increase the risk of abuse

Some children are more vulnerable to abuse due to **SOCIAL FACTORS** – situations in their family or home life, such as those in the diagram below.

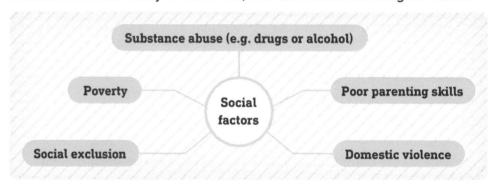

Figure 1.2: Why do you think these factors may make children more vulnerable to abuse?

Possible indicators of abuse

Look out for any of the following signs that a child may be suffering from abuse.

Physical abuse

Take note of any:

- bruising that looks like hand or finger marks, looks as if it was made by an object such as a belt buckle or is in a place where accidental injury is unlikely
- fractures
- human bite marks
- scalds or burns (especially burns that are in the shape of an object or multiple burns).

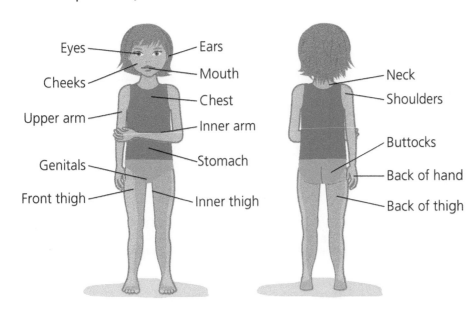

Figure 1.3: This body map highlights parts of the body where accidental injuries are unlikely to occur

Emotional abuse

Take note if any of the following apply.

- The child seems overly affectionate towards people they do not know.
- The child appears withdrawn or lacks confidence.
- The child acts aggressively to other children or animals.
- The child does not seem to have a close relationship with their parent(s) or main carer(s).
- The child does not show much emotion; they may appear unhappy.

Sexual abuse

The child may use sexual language or play in a sexualised way. They may avoid being alone with certain people. Physical signs can include a sore genital area, frequent urine infections (they may need to urinate often and it may cause them discomfort) or having a sexually transmitted disease (they may have discharge from their penis or vagina or have an itchy genital area).

Neglect

Take note if any of the following apply.

- The child is often hungry.
- The child's clothes are too big or too small, ripped or worn out, dirty or not right for the weather.
- The child has offensive body odour or nappies that are not changed regularly.
- There is a lack of supervision; the child is left at home alone.
- The child's colds, rashes or infected cuts are left untreated; the child has lots of accidental injuries.
- The child is often tired.
- The child fails to thrive – does not gain weight or grow as expected.

General indicators

You may not always see any physical signs, but you may notice a change in a child's behaviour. The way they act might worry you. Take note if any of the following apply.

- The child seems sad, withdrawn or depressed.
- The child has trouble sleeping.
- The child starts behaving aggressively or being disruptive.
- The child shows fear of certain adults.
- The child lacks confidence or has low self-esteem.
- The child is REGRESSING – behaving in a way they used to when they were younger.

Assessment practice 1.4   AO1 AO2 AO4

It is common for early years practitioners to notice marks and bruises on children that have happened accidentally through everyday life. However, some injuries can be a sign that a child has experienced physical abuse.

1 Identify two injuries from the choices below that may cause you concern.

- Scrape to knee
- Burn on stomach
- Bruise on buttock
- Bruise on shin
- Scab on elbow
- Bruise on neck

2 Explain what you would do next if you had a concern that a child had experienced physical abuse.

How to support children who have disclosed

Earlier in this chapter, you looked at how to respond if a child discloses to you. Remember that the child will need ongoing support. Take time to listen to and reassure the child.

Many children who have been abused or neglected will benefit from further professional support, such as from a counsellor or therapist. The child's social worker can co-ordinate further help.

How to support children to reduce risk of abuse

Empowering children

You should let children know that they have a right to make choices for themselves and they have the right to say, 'no'. Children who have learned that they are allowed to be involved in decision making, and who know they can choose not to take part in something, are more likely to have the tools to keep themselves safe from abuse.

Encouraging independence in personal care routines

As children's health and self-care skills develop, they are able to start to manage their own care routines. This helps children to become aware of, and value, their own body and supports their dignity and privacy.

Teaching the NSPCC 'Underwear Rule'

The NSPCC Underwear Rule helps children to understand that they have the right to say, 'no' and that their body belongs to them. It teaches children to tell a trusted adult if they feel worried. The concept encourages children and adults to talk about 'PANTS', which the NSPCC defines as:

- Privates are private.
- Always remember your body belongs to you.
- 'No' means no.

PANTS teaches children important messages.

- Talk about secrets that upset you.
- Speak up; someone can help.

A4 Confidentiality and record keeping in the early years setting

All early years practitioners need to respect and protect children's privacy. You also have to follow legal requirements to make sure that information about children and staff is treated in confidence. Effective information management and communication protect both children and staff.

The Data Protection Act 1998

DATA is personal information held in your setting. The government clearly states the legal requirements regarding how data should be used, for what reasons, how long it should be kept and how it should be handled and stored. Find out about how your setting follows the Data Protection Act.

- Is data such as children's and families' personal information stored securely?
- How long does your setting keep a child's record after they leave? Should it be kept forever?
- Is children's data ever shared with anyone else?

Following guidelines for recording information

The EYFS statutory safeguarding and welfare guidance says all settings must keep a record of necessary information for each child on the premises.

Assessment practice 1.5	AO2

Look at your own setting's Record Keeping Procedures and ask to see blank copies of the paperwork your setting uses to record different types of information.

- What information is recorded for each child?

- What information is recorded for each member of staff?

- Are any other records kept, for example, accident reports or medication forms?

Safe and secure storage of manual records

MANUAL RECORDS (paper records) need to be stored safely and securely to meet the requirements of the Data Protection Act 1998. Where does your setting keep child and staff files?

What if...?

Imagine if children's records, such as registration forms or child protection logs, were lying around in your setting – anyone could take a look and find out families' personal information. That is why manual records should be stored in a locked filing cabinet, which can only be accessed by staff and other agencies on a **NEED-TO-KNOW BASIS** (only sharing the facts that people need to know, and nothing else).

Use and storage of electronic records

Settings that store electronic information must ensure it remains secure; passwords can be used to limit access to computers. Settings must register with the Information Commissioner's Office (ICO) if records such as child and staff personal details are kept electronically.

Maintaining confidentiality to protect children and families

You should follow your setting's Confidentiality Policy. You should not discuss any information about children or families with anyone who does not need to know. Be careful when using social media that you do not inadvertently or accidentally share confidential information.

Sharing information when required

On certain occasions, your setting may legally need to share confidential information with other agencies, for example the police or Ofsted. Remember to seek advice from your supervisor if you are not sure if it is your role to share information. There may be occasions when sharing confidential information is in a child's best interests, for example if they are at risk of harm or if a crime has been committed.

Respect confidential information about children

It is important that you understand the need to respect confidential information. Consider how you would feel if others were discussing your personal issues. The welfare of each child is paramount, so always talk through concerns with your setting's designated safeguarding lead.

Skills and knowledge check

- [ ] I can respond to a child appropriately if they disclose information.
- [ ] I have the confidence to 'whistleblow' if I see a colleague acting inappropriately.
- [ ] I can teach children the NSPCC 'Underwear Rule'.
- [ ] I can keep information confidential.

- ○ I can name five pieces of legislation that underpin safeguarding policies and procedures.
- ○ I am able to explain the benefits of partnership working.
- ○ I can identify four different types of child abuse.
- ○ I know which Act regulates record keeping and safe storage of information.

B Promoting safe environments in early years settings

B1 Health and safety legislation

Health and safety legislation gives all settings a clear set of standards that must legally be met. Settings must develop suitable policies to cover these areas. The current legislation is discussed here. Settings must work in line with the most up-to-date legislation and update their policies in response to changes.

How legislation influences the early years setting

There are four laws that should be observed in early years settings.

1 Health and Safety at Work Act 1974 – This Act sets out the duties of employers to keep people safe while at work. It states that all work settings, including early years settings, must have a Health and Safety Policy. It also tells employees about their responsibility to follow safe working practices, to co-operate with their employers and to ensure the safety of others, including children, staff and visitors.

2 Reporting of Injuries, Diseases and Dangerous Occurrences Regulations (RIDDOR) 2013 – If someone in the early years setting suffers a serious injury, has a reportable disease or there is a dangerous incident at work, then this must be reported through RIDDOR. Accident and incident records must be completed.

3 Control of Substances Hazardous to Health (COSHH) Regulations 2002 – There may be lots of hazardous substances in your setting, such as cleaning fluids, washing-up liquid, correction fluid; COSHH regulations require employers to ensure these items are stored and used safely, assessments are made and information is on hand should something go wrong.

4 EYFS Statutory Framework – This document sets legal standards for staff to child ratios; safety and suitability of premises; environment and equipment; assessment of risk; and outings.

The role of the Health and Safety Executive (HSE)

The Health and Safety Executive's role is to check that employers are following current health and safety legislation. This helps to ensure environments are safe and nobody is exposed to unnecessary risk of injury or illness. The HSE can inspect and then prosecute settings that are not meeting requirements.

Assessment practice 1.6   AO1 AO2

Priya has started her own pre-school. She keeps the bathroom cleaner and anti-bacterial spray on top of the children's toilet. One day, one of the children squirts the spray into his eye.

- State which regulation Priya was not following by leaving the cleaning fluids within the children's reach.
- Discuss the possible consequences for the child.
- Explain what the HSE might do.

B2 Policies and procedures

Your setting will have a range of policies and procedures in place that help to keep children safe.

First aid

This policy tells you what to do if a child has an accident or becomes seriously ill. You can learn about basic first-aid procedures in B4 of this unit.

Link it up

Unit 4, B2 gives you lots more information about storing and preparing food safely and hygienically.

Food hygiene

Food hygiene policies cover all aspects of storing and preparing food. The policies help to ensure food is kept free from contamination, preventing dangerous levels of bacteria from developing.

Emergency evacuation

This procedure tells you about evacuating the premises in an emergency. Information about how and when to evacuate the setting are discussed in more detail in B3 of this unit.

Safe moving and handling

If you are required to lift and move equipment, you should follow these techniques to ensure both your own and others' safety.

STEP BY STEP   SAFE MOVING AND HANDLING

STEP 1

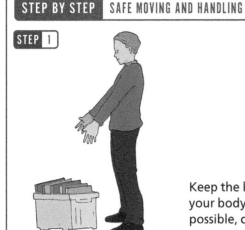

Keep the load close to your body for as long as possible, close to your waist

STEP 2

Your feet should be apart with one leg slightly forward to help you balance

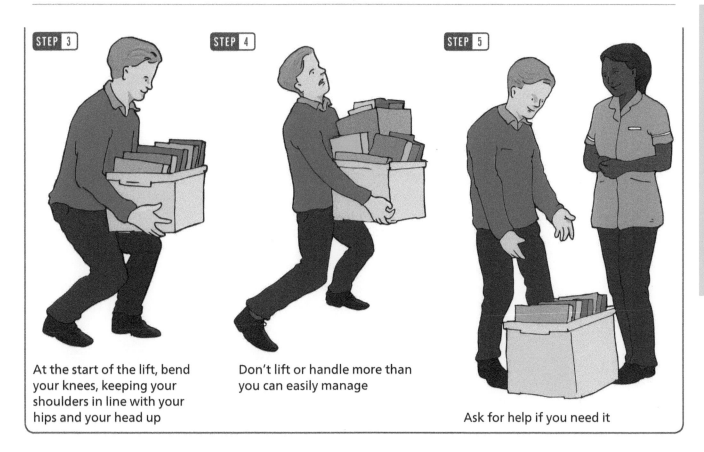

STEP 3
At the start of the lift, bend your knees, keeping your shoulders in line with your hips and your head up

STEP 4
Don't lift or handle more than you can easily manage

STEP 5
Ask for help if you need it

You should only lift children when essential to do so and if you have had appropriate training for this role.

Staff to child ratios, supervision and space requirements

The minimum staffing levels should always be maintained in your setting to make sure there are enough adults to keep the children safe. Ratios are based on the ages of the children and the qualifications of the staff in your setting. If you are concerned about understaffing in your setting, raise this with your supervisor.

The ages of the children in your setting determine how much floor space is needed. The Statutory Framework for the Early Years Foundation Stage (March 2017) gives specific measurements, with younger children being allocated more space.

Preventing accidents

Following health and safety procedures and assessments of risk helps to lower the risk of accidents. You should be **PROACTIVE** (making things happen) in this regard. If you spot a hazard, remedy it or bring it up with your supervisor before it leads to an accident. In B3 of this unit you can read more about why supervision is important to prevent accidents.

Assessment practice 1.7   AO2 AO3 AO4

Accidents happen, but by being aware of your setting's health and safety policies you can help to prevent them.

- Name one policy or procedure that helps to ensure the environment is safe in your early years setting.

- Give two examples of how you implement the policy in day-to-day practice.

B3 Safety in early years settings

Your role as an early years assistant is to promote and contribute to ensuring a safe environment.

Definitions

Let's look first at some of the words associated with safety.

- **HAZARD** – something that may cause harm to an individual
- **RISK** – the likelihood that something will cause harm to an individual
- **ACCIDENT** – an unexpected event, causing harm or damage to property or an individual
- **HARM** – injury.

For example, a wet floor in your setting is a hazard. Think about how likely it is that a child may slip; this is the risk. It may cause an accident and result in harm to a child or staff member.

The purpose of risk assessment

RISK ASSESSMENT is an important way of checking that your setting is safe. It is a legal requirement for settings with more than five employees to have a written risk assessment that is updated regularly and when needed, for example, if your setting buys a new climbing frame or a child with additional needs joins the setting.

A risk assessment lists the potential hazards in your setting so that measures can be put in place to lessen the risk of accidents and harm.

Hygiene and safety checks

You should regularly check that the environment is safe for children. This includes removing any broken or faulty toys or resources immediately. Spillages should be mopped up, dirty surfaces should be cleaned and trip hazards removed.

How to report concerns

If you notice faulty equipment or a hazard in your setting, you should report this to your supervisor immediately.

Safety

Use of safety equipment

Safety equipment can be used to reduce the risk of harm to children in your setting, for instance safety gates, window catches, door catches and cooker guards. Look around your setting to see which safety equipment is in use.

Animal and plant safety

Settings should not have pets that might bite or scratch. Children should be taught to wash hands after touching pets. Remember, some children have **ALLERGIES** (a medical condition that causes you to react badly or feel ill when you eat or touch a particular substance) to animals or fur.

Plants, both indoors and outside, can be hazardous if eaten (they may be poisonous, or cause choking). Some plants are prickly (hawthorn hedging); others can sting or cause a rash (stinging nettles).

Link it up

Go to Unit 4, B1 to see an example of how to carry out a risk assessment.

Water safety

Children can drown in just a few centimetres of water, and it can happen very quickly. Check for any rainwater that may have gathered outside and remove it. You must always supervise children during water play and empty the equipment when the session is over.

Safe outdoor spaces

Outside areas should always be checked before children use them to ensure there are no potential hazards. Check for:

- unwanted objects thrown or blown over the fence, for example, glass bottles, syringes, cigarettes, plastic bags
- broken fences or gates left open
- wet and slippery equipment and surfaces
- broken equipment and apparatus
- animal faeces (especially in uncovered sand pits).

Outing safety

Outings can provide exciting and enriching experiences for children. However, taking children out of the setting poses its own risks, so take time to read your setting's Outings Policy and be aware of the safety measures in place. It is good practice to:

- make a risk assessment of the venue before the outing
- make sure all parents have given written permission for their child to take part; take contact telephone numbers with you for the parents of children involved
- make sure that staff to child ratios are met and children are safely supervised at all times
- take a first-aid kit, your setting's designated mobile phone, children's medication, drinks, spare nappies/clothes
- take a register of the children and make regular headcounts
- use pushchairs and reins safely. Hold hands with children when needed, for example, when crossing roads.

What if...?

The pre-school children are on an outing to the local park. Macey falls over and badly grazes her knee. The supervisor realises she has forgotten to bring the setting's 'outings bag' with the first-aid kit in. While the staff attend to Macey, two children run off to the other side of the field.

1 Why is it important to take all necessary equipment on an outing?

2 Why should staff make regular headcounts on an outing?

Fire safety

There should be a designated fire officer or fire warden in your setting – make sure you know who this is.

The following list shows good practice to ensure fire safety, and to stop a fire from starting and spreading.

- Emergency exits in your setting should be clearly marked, never obstructed and easily opened from inside. Make sure you familiarise yourself with the fire exits in your setting.
- Fire doors should not be propped open. Those that close automatically when the fire alarm is set off should be free from obstacles that would prevent them from closing.

- Fire-risk assessments should be made and you should follow them, for example, not blocking fire exits with furniture, not covering up heaters.
- Potentially combustible material (such as paper, plastic packaging) should be stored away from potential sources of ignition.
- Smoke detectors, alarms and fire-fighting equipment should be available and serviced to meet regulations.
- Emergency evacuation procedures should be clearly displayed in your setting and explained to you – ask if you are unsure.
- Records should be kept of fire drills and the servicing of fire safety equipment in a Fire Log.

Fire evacuation

You should be aware of your own setting's Emergency Evacuation procedure and your role within it. If you detect a fire, you should immediately raise the alarm.

In the event of a fire or if the alarm sounds, you should:

- stay calm and safely evacuate the children from the setting, using the closest fire exit
- escort the children to the Fire Assembly Point
- remain at the Fire Assembly Point until told it is safe to re-enter the building.

The role of the fire officer is to:

- check the building, making sure everyone is out
- close internal doors to stop the fire from spreading
- bring out registers of children, staff and visitors present
- bring out emergency contact numbers of parents, and the setting's mobile phone
- bring out emergency resources (usually in a designated fire box), such as medication, nappies, drinks
- take a register at the Fire Assembly Point.

Fire extinguishers

Unless you have had special training, you should not be expected to use a fire extinguisher. However, it is useful for you to know the location and uses of the fire extinguishers in your setting. Table 1.2 shows the different types of extinguisher.

Table 1.2: Types of fire extinguisher and their uses

Water	Powder	Foam	CO$_2$ (carbon dioxide)
For wood, paper, textile and solid material fires	For solid materials, and liquids such as grease, fats, oil, paint, petrol	For use on solid material and liquid fires	For electrical fires

Look around your setting and see if you can identify the different types of fire extinguisher

Observation and supervision to keep children safe

Children should be supervised constantly in order to keep them safe. Some activities will require you to watch particularly carefully as you supervise children. When children are using climbing equipment they will need extra support and supervision. At mealtimes, children might choke on food. At home time, the setting door will be opened to allow adults in – make sure no children can leave unsupervised.

Age and developmentally appropriate activities and toys

Some toys in your setting, such as peg boards, may be suitable for pre-school children, but these would not be suitable for babies as they might swallow the pegs.

Practise

Look at the list of activities and resources below. Identify two from the list that may be suitable in a baby unit for babies aged 0–18 months:

- woodwork with hammers and nails
- marble run
- wooden shape sorters
- 24-piece jigsaw puzzles
- soft rattles
- cutting out pictures with scissors.

Name one more activity that would be suitable for babies.

Link it up

Go to Unit 5, B3 to learn more about suitable resources and equipment for play and learning activities.

Resources and activities should be organised so that children can play and learn safely. How does your setting make sure that children can only take part in activities that are appropriate?

Following manufacturers' recommendations

You should only use resources and equipment as guided by the manufacturer. For example, some toys are marked 'not suitable for children under 36 months due to small parts', or electric equipment, such as a laminator, may be marked that it is not to be left connected while unsupervised.

Security of the setting

A secure setting is important to ensure that no intruders can enter the premises. Your setting will have procedures for ensuring only known adults are able to collect children, and methods for identifying visitors. It is important that fences around the outside area are secure and some settings might use CCTV or cameras for extra security to monitor people's comings and goings.

Link it up

Unit 3, B2 tells you about the role of the early years assistant in keeping the setting secure, including procedures for visitors signing in and out of the setting.

If you do not recognise a visitor or they are not suitably identified in line with your setting's policy (for example, wearing a visitor's badge), it is vital that you either challenge them or raise your concern with your supervisor and challenge them together.

> ### Assessment practice 1.8   AO2 AO3 AO4
>
> Your supervisor has asked you to check the garden is safe before the children go outside to play.
>
> - List five potential hazards you might find in the garden.
> - Explain why it is important that you always check the environment before children play outside.

B4 Incidents in early years settings

If a child has a minor accident while in your care, remember to follow your setting's procedure for dealing with it – including reporting and recording procedures. Most minor incidents do not require treatment as our body has its own way of repairing itself, but they must be recorded. Inform your supervisor and seek advice about any treatment required.

Nominated first aiders

If a child does need first-aid treatment, you should immediately seek out one of your setting's **NOMINATED FIRST AIDERS**. These are staff who have a current paediatric first-aid certificate. If you are unsure whether a child needs treatment, always ask for advice and guidance.

Basic first aid

Anaphylactic shock

An **ANAPHYLACTIC SHOCK** is a severe allergic reaction in which a child's breathing may become difficult and their tongue can swell up. Call an ambulance immediately. The child may have an **EPI-PEN** (a syringe holding adrenaline to relieve symptoms). You should only administer an epi-pen if you are trained to do so.

Bleeding

If a minor cut is bleeding, use a clean bandage to apply pressure until the bleeding stops; this could take several minutes. The affected area should be lifted above the child's heart to help stop the blood flow. If the child is bleeding heavily, call an ambulance.

Breathing difficulties and unconsciousness

Children can experience breathing difficulties for a number of reasons. If a child is struggling to breathe, you should seek medical attention immediately. If a child becomes unconscious and stops breathing, you should perform **CARDIOPULMONARY RESUSCITATION (CPR)** (an emergency first aid procedure) if you are confident with this procedure – see later in B4.

Burns

If a child suffers a serious burn, call an ambulance. For minor burns, place the burn under cool running water for at least ten minutes, carefully removing any clothing that is not attached to the child's skin. Cover the burn loosely with cling film or a clean plastic bag.

Choking

If an **INFANT**, a child under 12 months old, starts coughing and is not ill, this could be a sign that they are choking on something. Older children may clasp at their throat. Table 1.3 explains the first-aid procedure for an infant or child who is choking.

Table 1.3: How to provide first aid to an infant or child who is choking

Infants	Children
1 If you can easily see and reach the object in the baby's mouth, remove it	1 If you can easily see and reach the object in the child's mouth, remove it
2 Sit down, lay the baby face down across your lap and support their head with one hand	2 Support the child to lean forward; from behind, give five sharp blows on the back
3 With the heel of your other hand, give up to five sharp back blows between the shoulder blades	3 If this does not remove the object, and the child is still conscious, give abdominal thrusts: a Kneel behind the child, put your arms under their arms and around the top of their stomach b Clench one fist and place it between their tummy button and ribcage c Clasp your clenched fist with your other hand and sharply pull it in and upwards, up to five times
4 If this does not remove the object, and the baby is still conscious, give chest thrusts: a Lay the baby across the length of your thighs, face up b Press down sharply five times on the baby's breastbone using two fingers. The chest should be compressed by about one third	
5 If the item is still lodged, and the child is still conscious, repeat the whole process	4 If the item is still lodged, and the child is still conscious, repeat the whole process

If the baby or child loses consciousness, call for an ambulance and start CPR (detailed in this unit).

Cuts and grazes

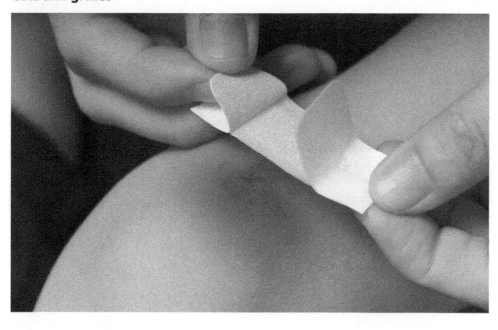

Minor cuts and grazes should be cleaned using water, patted dry with a clean towel and covered with a sterile dressing

Drowning and resuscitation

If the child is unconscious but breathing, shout for help and put them in the **RECOVERY POSITION** (the recommended body position for an unconscious but breathing casualty).

1 Place the child on their back.
2 Kneel by their side and place the arm nearest you at a right angle to their body with their hand upwards, towards their head. Tuck their other hand under the side of their head, with the back of their hand touching their opposite cheek.
3 Bend the knee furthest from you to a right angle. Gently roll the child onto their side by pulling on the bent knee; the top arm should be supporting the head and the bottom arm will stop the child rolling too far.
4 Open the child's airway by carefully tilting their head back and lifting their chin.

If a child is unconscious and not breathing, give five rescue breaths.

- Place one hand on the child's forehead and carefully tilt their head back and lift the chin.
- Pinch the child's nose.
- Place your mouth over the child's mouth and blow five times.
- For infants, place your mouth over the baby's mouth and nose and blow five times.

You may then need to give CPR. This is used when someone's heart has stopped or they stop breathing.

STEP BY STEP | **GIVING CPR**

STEP 1

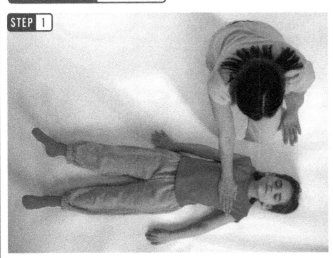

Place the heel of one hand in the middle of the child's chest, or two fingers for infants

STEP 2

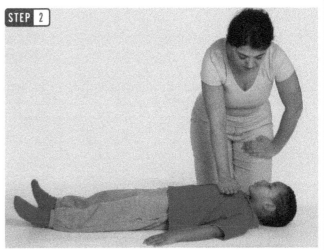

Push down 30 times by 5 cm, 4 cm for infants, at a speed of between 100 and 120 compressions per minute

STEP 3

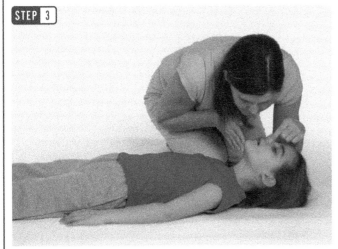

Give two rescue breaths

STEP 4

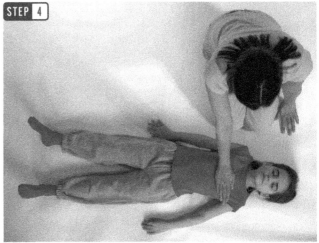

Repeat the CPR process

Practise

Visit the NHS Choices website to watch videos on how to put someone in the recovery position and how to perform CPR.

Work with a partner and practise putting each other in the recovery position.

Fractures

If you suspect a child has fractured a bone, for example their finger, keep them as still as possible and call the parents immediately. If they are in a lot of pain, or you think they have broken their leg or back, call an ambulance.

Head injuries

Minor head injuries such as a bump or bruise can be treated with a cold compress. The child may feel sick, have a mild headache or have blurred vision. Observe the child closely to look for any signs that symptoms are getting worse. Parents must always be informed if their child has had a bump to the head, even if there are no outward signs. In the event of a more serious head injury, call an ambulance immediately.

Sunburn and sunstroke

If a child's skin is burnt or they have heatstroke from being in the sun too long, you should:

- let the child rest in a cool place out of the sun
- give plenty of water to drink
- sponge their skin with cool water.

Assessment practice 1.9	AO1 AO2

During a food tasting activity, you notice that a child is having great difficulty breathing and his lips and tongue look swollen.

1 Name the type of reaction the child might be suffering from.

2 Describe what you would do next in this situation.

First-aid box

The first-aid box should be available for staff to access but kept out of the reach of children.

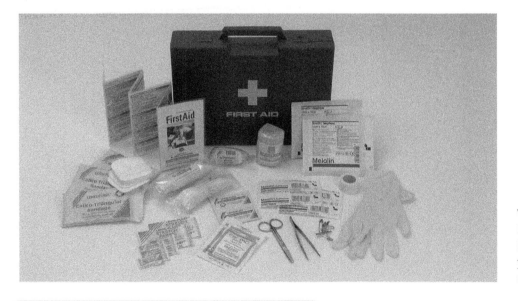

Where is the first-aid box kept in your setting? Take a look inside and make sure you know what each item is used for

How and when to call emergency services

In the event of an emergency, you should telephone 999. You will be asked which service you require: police, ambulance or fire service. You will need to know your location: the address of your setting or of the location if on an outing. There are free apps that could be installed on the setting's designated mobile phone. These provide exact grid references to help emergency services locate you.

Emergency situations

In any emergency situation, such as those in the diagram below, you should evacuate the setting.

Figure 1.4: Emergency situations that can occur

Missing children

Your setting should have a Missing or Lost Child Procedure. This procedure should be followed if a child becomes lost on an outing or manages to leave the premises unsupervised.

- Staff should look for the missing child in the immediate vicinity, while ensuring other children are still fully supervised.
- The police and the parents should be called immediately if the child cannot be found.
- The incident must be reported to Ofsted.

Link it up

Go to Unit 3, C2 to see the information that should be recorded on an accident/incident form.

Recording and reporting of accidents and incidents

If you witness an accident or incident involving a child in your setting, it is your responsibility to report this to a senior member of staff. You may be required to complete an accident or incident record of what you observed. Major accidents and incidents may also need to be reported to Ofsted and RIDDOR by your setting's management.

Skills and knowledge check

☐ I can work in a safe way, following my setting's procedures.
☐ I can supervise children during a range of different activities.
☐ I can respond appropriately if a child has an accident.
☐ I can respond appropriately if there is an emergency evacuation.

○ I can name three different pieces of health and safety legislation.
○ I understand the role of the HSE.
○ I know the difference between the terms 'hazard' and 'risk'.
○ I can list five items that should be included in a first-aid kit.

C Child health

C1 Childhood illnesses, infections and conditions

Most children at some point will become ill during their time in your setting. You need to be able to tell when a child is unwell and know how to help them.

Common childhood illnesses

Causes of infection

Different types of infections can cause illnesses.

- **BACTERIAL INFECTIONS** are caused when germs enter the body. This can happen if food is eaten that is contaminated with high levels of bacteria (**FOOD CONTAMINATION**) or if a child puts an infected toy in their mouth.
- **VIRAL INFECTIONS** can spread from person to person. Measles, chickenpox and flu are all examples of viral infection.
- **FUNGAL INFECTIONS** usually affect a child's skin, for example, ringworm.
- **AIRBORNE INFECTIONS** can be carried through the air and inhaled.
- Infections can be caused by **PARASITES** (tiny creatures that live in the child's body, making them feel ill), for example tapeworms.

Infectious illnesses

Infectious illnesses can spread easily and quickly from child to child. Here are some common conditions.

Chickenpox

Chickenpox spreads when a child comes into contact with someone who is infected. The symptoms are a **FEVER** (a temperature above 37.5 °C) and a very itchy rash with a blister-like appearance.

- Encourage the child not to scratch; calamine lotion can soothe the skin.
- Children with chickenpox should not return to the setting until all the spots have scabbed over.
- The time between catching an illness and showing the signs and symptoms of it, known as the **INCUBATION PERIOD**, is 7 to 21 days.

Meningitis

Meningitis can be a very serious illness and an infected child should be treated in hospital. The viruses and bacteria that cause meningitis can be spread through sneezing, coughing and sharing utensils. The incubation period is 2 to 10 days.

The symptoms include:

- fever
- headache
- sickness
- blotchy rash
- stiff neck
- dislike of bright lights
- drowsiness
- fits.

If you press the side of a clear glass firmly against the rash and it doesn't fade, this is a warning sign that a child has meningitis

Measles

Measles is spread when an infected person coughs or sneezes out tiny droplets that contain the virus. The symptoms include:

- runny nose, sneezing, coughing
- sore, red eyes
- dislike of bright lights
- fever
- blotchy rash.

Reducing the fever with Paracetamol/Ibuprofen, drinking lots of water, keeping away from bright light and cleansing the eyes can treat symptoms.

Measles can be unpleasant but is not usually serious unless the child develops further complications. The incubation period is 10 to 12 days.

Impetigo

Impetigo is an infection that causes red, itchy sores, usually on the face. It can spread from child to child if broken skin becomes infected with the impetigo bacteria, and it should be treated with antibiotic creams or tablets. The incubation period is 4 to 10 days.

Conjunctivitis

Conjunctivitis causes red, itchy, watering or sticky eyes that need cleansing. It can be spread easily through close contact or can be caused by an allergic reaction. The incubation period is 1 to 3 days.

Norovirus and gastroenteritis

Gastroenteritis and norovirus cause sickness, diarrhoea and dehydration so the child should drink plenty of fluids. These illnesses are spread by coming into contact with someone who is infected, by touching infected objects or eating contaminated food. The incubation period is 1 to 48 hours.

Preventative measures

A child can have a vaccine to protect them against some illnesses, such as measles and meningitis. Most illnesses can be prevented from spreading by having good hygiene practices and infection control measures in your setting.

Common childhood infestations

Head lice

Head lice are small parasites that live on the scalp, causing itching. They can transfer easily from one head to another when hair touches. It is rare for head lice to be spread from sharing towels or hairbrushes, but not unheard of. Head lice can be combed out of damp hair using a special comb, or treated by using special lotions and sprays.

Children with head lice should not be excluded from the setting, but it is advisable to tell other families that there has been an infestation and ask them to check their child for signs.

Scabies

Scabies are tiny mites that burrow into skin folds causing itching. Scabies can be transmitted through prolonged skin-to-skin contact or occasionally through sharing bedding, towels or flannels.

Scabies should be treated with cream or lotion from the doctor. To prevent the spread of infection, the child should not come back into the setting until completion of the first treatment. Your setting should wash any bedding or flannels that the child has had contact with on a hot wash above 50 °C.

Signs and symptoms that a child is unwell

You need to be able to spot the signs and symptoms (see the diagram below) that could indicate a child is ill.

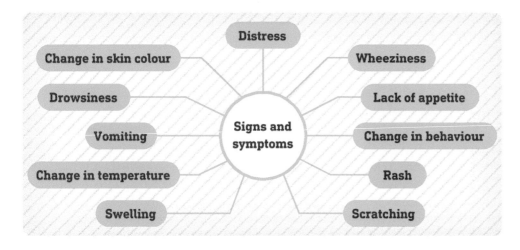

Figure 1.5: What would you do if you noticed a child showing any of these signs or symptoms?

Immunisation and vaccinations

VACCINES are the products that are introduced into your body to help develop **IMMUNITY** – protection from a disease.

Children are offered **VACCINATIONS** (injections or nasal sprays containing vaccines) at different times throughout their early years.

IMMUNISATION means that your body has learned how to protect itself, so you are now immune to a disease.

Vaccinations are given to children at different ages to protect them against preventable illnesses.

- A 5-in-1 vaccine protects against diphtheria, tetanus, whooping cough, polio and Hib.
- PCV protects against pneumococcal infections.
- Rotavirus vaccine protects against rotavirus infection.
- Men B vaccine protects against meningitis.
- Hib/Men C vaccine protects against Hib and meningitis.
- MMR vaccine protects against measles, mumps and rubella.
- Children's flu vaccine protects against flu.

NHS Choices is a useful website you can visit for more information about the ages at which different vaccines are given.

Health conditions common to children

As an early years assistant, your role may be to support children with health conditions. Unlike infections and diseases, health conditions are not contagious and can affect a child for life.

Eczema

ECZEMA is a very dry skin condition that itches intensely, causing red patches or even breaks to the skin. There are different types of eczema.

Link it up

Go to Unit 4, A1 to learn about how to support a child with eczema in the setting. You will need to know about the application of creams and the use of **PERSONAL PROTECTIVE EQUIPMENT (PPE)** (equipment and resources provided by your place of work to ensure you and others are protected from hazards and harm in the workplace).

- Atopic eczema is triggered by **ALLERGENS**, substances that the child is allergic to, such as plants, perfumes, soap, detergents and clothing. The body's immune system reacts to the allergen, causing the eczema.
- **IRRITANTS**, substances that irritate the skin, trigger contact eczema. Unlike allergens, irritants do not affect the child's immune system, but do cause damage to the skin. Examples of irritants are heat, cold wind and strong chemicals in shampoos and cleaning fluids.

Asthma

Children with asthma have inflamed airways that are sensitive to certain triggers. Symptoms of asthma include coughing, wheezing, difficulty breathing, shortness of breath and a tight chest. There are different types of asthma.

- Allergic asthma is triggered by an allergen such as pollen.
- Asthma without allergies is triggered by an irritant such as cigarette smoke or a cold or flu.
- Exercise-induced asthma is triggered by physical activities that make you out of breath.

The setting should know what to do if the child has an **ASTHMA ATTACK**. This is when asthma symptoms suddenly become much worse. The child may have a **RELIEVER INHALER**, used to relieve symptoms quickly, and a **SPACER**, a hollow container to help young children use their inhaler. It is your role to look out for any signs of an asthma attack and to tell a member of staff straight away. You should stay calm and reassure the child. If the asthma attack worsens, then call an ambulance.

Food allergies

If a child has an allergic reaction to something they eat, the symptoms can include:

- itchy skin, eczema
- swelling of the lips, tongue, face and throat
- tingling or itching in the mouth
- wheezing, difficulty breathing
- tummy ache, diarrhoea, sickness
- feeling dizzy or faint.

Link it up

Go to Unit 4, C1 to learn about how to support children with food allergies in the setting.

Type 1 diabetes

This is a condition that causes a person's blood-sugar levels to become too high. The symptoms include:

- extreme thirst or hunger
- passing lots of urine
- tiredness
- mood swings
- tummy ache
- fruity smelling breath.

The setting should be aware of what the child eats, how active they are and their stress levels, as this can affect blood-sugar levels. Senior staff may need to test blood-sugar levels if advised to by families.

Epilepsy

A child with epilepsy can experience **SEIZURES** or **CONVULSIONS**, which is when the body goes stiff and jerks. After a seizure, they may need to be put in the recovery position. If the child has a focal seizure, they may look as if they are day dreaming. Another symptom can be experiencing a strange taste in the mouth or a strange smell.

The setting should be aware of the triggers, signs and symptoms, and follow the family's guidance on what to do if a child has a seizure.

Practise

During the afternoon session at your setting, you notice that Stacey, aged four, is drinking lots of water and has asked to go to the toilet several times. She seems tired and irritable and says her tummy hurts.

1 Name the condition Stacey might be suffering from.

2 Describe what you would do next in this situation.

C2 Treatment and support for the ill child

You need to know how to respond if a child is unwell. Look at your setting's policies and procedures for supporting children who are unwell.

Use of treatments and medication

Always follow your setting's medication policies and procedures if children need to take medication, use inhalers or have creams applied. Look back at C1 for information about supporting children with different conditions. Your setting should have clear guidelines on supporting children with asthma or eczema. Familiarise yourself with your setting's procedures, including the use of personal protective equipment (PPE). For example, you may be required to wear disposable gloves if applying cream to broken skin.

Management of children with high temperatures

If a child feels hot, has flushed cheeks, feels sweaty or clammy or seems unwell, it is important to check their temperature. They may have a fever.

Taking a child's temperature and the normal range

If you notice any of the signs above, you should tell your supervisor or a senior member of staff who will use a thermometer to check the child's temperature.

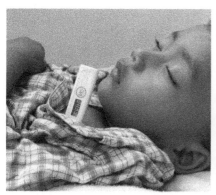
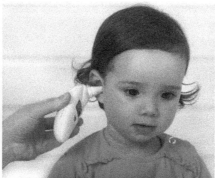
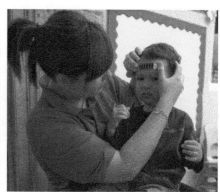

Types of thermometer: digital, ear and strip-type

Find out which type of thermometer your setting uses. The normal temperature range of a child is usually between 36.3 °C and 37.5 °C.

Reducing temperature

Ways of helping to reduce a child's temperature:

- Administer infant Paracetamol or Ibuprofen, following your setting's procedures.
- Take off extra layers of clothes.
- Offer plenty of fluids.

Febrile convulsions

If a child's temperature goes higher than 38 °C they may experience a **FEBRILE CONVULSION**, also known as a febrile seizure. This is a fit that can happen when a child has a fever. The child may:

- lose consciousness
- become stiff and their body may twitch
- wet themselves.

Witnessing a child suffering from a febrile convulsion can be very distressing, but this type of seizure is quite common and is not usually serious. If a child is having a febrile convulsion, place them on a soft surface in the recovery position.

Link it up

See B4 in this unit for details of the recovery position.

Providing support for the unwell child

If a child is unwell in the setting, there are professionals who can be contacted for advice and support, such as health visitors and specialist nurses. Public Health England is an executive agency, sponsored by the government; its role is to support health and wellbeing on a national scale. It publishes guidance on infection control in schools and early years settings.

Often if a child is feeling unwell, reassurance can be the best remedy. Make sure they are comfortable and have a quiet area to rest in. Parents should be contacted. Monitor the child, recording signs and symptoms. Regularly record their temperature if they have a fever.

If a child is extremely unwell, it is important to act quickly to ensure the child is given medical attention before the condition worsens. If in doubt, phone 999 immediately.

Assessment practice 1.10	A01 A02

Amal is 2 years old. At the snack table, he starts coughing. The cough gets worse and worse. Identify two possible reasons why Amal could be coughing. (Tick two answers.)

☐ He has eczema.   ☐ He has epilepsy.   ☐ He has norovirus.

☐ He has asthma.   ☐ He is choking.   ☐ He has scabies.

Explain what you would do next in this situation.

C3 Infection control

You need to know the importance of preventing the spread of infection to keep children well.

Cleaning procedures in the setting

How do the staff in your setting ensure that the environment is kept clean and hygienic? Find out the procedures in place to make sure that all areas, resources and equipment are kept clean.

Safe waste disposal

There are many types of waste product in early years settings, for example, food, nappies and paper. Your setting will have different methods of managing waste; ask how the various waste products are disposed of or recycled in your setting.

Use of personal protective equipment (PPE)

PPE is equipment used to keep you safe from harm or the risk of infection. The most common forms of PPE in early years settings are disposable gloves (worn when dealing with bodily fluids or changing nappies) and disposable aprons (often used when serving food, supporting toileting and changing nappies).

Sterilising of feeding equipment for babies and young children

Babies and young children are particularly vulnerable to the risk of infection from contaminated bottles, teats and other feeding implements. There are various sterilisation methods which help to prevent the risk of illness.

Personal hygiene

Good personal hygiene is key to reducing the risk of infection. You should wash your hands thoroughly when required, following your setting's procedures. It is an ideal opportunity to model good hygiene practices to children.

Link it up

Now look at Unit 4 to learn in more detail about:

- cleaning procedures in the setting
- safe waste disposal
- the use of PPE
- sterilising of feeding equipment for babies and young children
- personal hygiene, role modelling and hand-washing techniques.

Practise

Obtain a copy of your setting's Infection Control Policy.

Read the policy carefully and use a highlighter pen to identify the main points that relate to your role as an early years assistant.

Safe storage of cleaning equipment

Earlier in this chapter in B1 you learned about the Control of Substances Hazardous to Health. Your role is to ensure cleaning materials are always kept out of children's reach. You should also make sure that equipment such as mops and buckets, brooms and vacuum cleaners are stored safely, following your own setting's procedures.

Early Years Foundation Stage (EYFS) 2017 England

The EYFS Statutory Framework states that nappy-changing areas and areas for preparing meals must be hygienic. The premises must comply with health and safety legislation in terms of hygiene.

You should be aware of your role in keeping the setting clean and hygienic. Follow your setting's infection control policies and procedures and take part in training offered.

What if...?

Tim is a new member of staff at Lullaby Day Nursery. It is his first morning in the nursery and he has not yet had a Staff Induction. Tim has not had training about infection control, safe waste disposal or the use of PPE.

Tim is supervising an art activity, when a child is sick on the painting table. Tim is asked to clean up.

1 Why is it important that all staff have an induction and training about infection control?

2 What might the consequences be if Tim does not follow his setting's procedures?

Skills and knowledge check

☐ I can comfort and reassure a child who is unwell.

☐ I can help to prevent the spread of infection in my setting.

☐ I can dispose of waste safely.

☐ I can follow COSHH regulations.

○ I know at least two signs and symptoms that a child may be unwell.

○ I can list three infectious childhood illnesses.

○ I know the normal temperature range of a child.

○ I can explain good personal hygiene routines.

D Anti-discriminatory practice in the early years setting

D1 Equality, diversity and inclusion

In this section you will learn about the legislation, codes of practice and policies that help to prevent anti-discriminatory practice in early years settings. It is against the law to discriminate against others.

Later in this unit, in D2, you will learn about how British Values help support inclusion in early years settings. You will also need to understand the different terms involved in promoting INCLUSIVE (accessible to everyone) practice and the effects of discriminatory practice on children.

Equality

In your setting, children should not all be 'treated the same', but they should be treated with 'equal concern'. This is EQUALITY. All children should have the opportunity to take part fully so they feel included and valued; you should adapt activities, resources and equipment to support individual needs. If children are not treated 'fairly' this can limit their chance of reaching their full potential.

Diversity

DIVERSITY describes the visible and non-visible differences between all of us. Our society is diverse – everyone is unique. These differences can be referred to as **PROTECTED CHARACTERISTICS** and include:

- age
- disability
- sex
- **GENDER REASSIGNMENT** (changing from male to female, or vice versa, also known as a sex change)
- marriage and civil partnership
- race
- religion
- beliefs
- sexual orientation.

Discrimination

DISCRIMINATION is treating people unfairly because of their protected characteristics.

DIRECT DISCRIMINATION is when a person is treated less favourably because of their protected characteristics.

INDIRECT DISCRIMINATION is when the setting's policies treat a group of people less favourably because of a certain protected characteristic.

Discrimination can have very negative effects on children so that they:

- have reduced self-esteem and confidence
- become socially isolated
- experience verbal and physical abuse
- suffer withdrawal and depression
- have reduced choices and opportunities.

Assessment practice 1.11   AO4

Staines Pre-School has organised a Father's Day picnic – only dads and their children are invited.

Danny is 3 years old and has recently been diagnosed with autism. Danny's **KEY PERSON** (an individual who has overall responsibility for a child's daily wellbeing and acts as a point of contact for the parents) suggests to his dad that they don't come to the picnic as it might be too overwhelming for Danny with all those people there.

- How does this scenario show *indirect* discrimination?

- How does this scenario show *direct* discrimination to Danny?

- How might Danny and his dad feel?

- How might any children without fathers feel?

Stereotyping and prejudice

STEREOTYPING is when a person is defined by their characteristics, for example their gender or race. Stereotypical attitudes in early years can include, 'Only girls can play with the dolls' or 'Boys are better at football'.

Although these might be quite extreme statements, stereotyping can happen in much more subtle ways, and it is your responsibility to create an environment that avoids stereotypical views and promotes equality.

PREJUDICE is an opinion that is not based on actual experience or reason.

D2 Developing inclusive practice in early years

In this section you will learn how to develop and support inclusive practice in your early years setting.

Respecting and celebrating diversity

Wouldn't it be boring if everyone was exactly the same? It is your role to help children to learn about our diverse society and how to respect each other. You can act as a good role model by talking positively about each other's differences and similarities. This will provide a secure environment in which all children can flourish and where children's contributions are valued.

How do you make all children feel valued in your setting?

Encouraging different methods of communication

Not all children use words to communicate. Some are too young to talk; some have communication difficulties such as a hearing impairment or speech delay. Some have English as an additional language, which may mean they speak a different language from the majority of staff and children at your setting.

All children should be encouraged to communicate and should feel that their 'voice' is heard. Ways to help children communicate can include:

- signing (including baby signing and British Sign Language)
- makaton (signing used by many children with additional needs)
- braille (a tactile writing system used by people who are visually impaired)
- **VISUAL AIDS** (pictures or images to make meaning clearer, such as picture and word cue cards).

Adapting environments for children with additional needs

Children can have a range of additional needs and may benefit from small changes in the environment of the setting. Staff should work in partnership with families to find out how the environment can be adapted to support individual needs. Here are some of the changes that should be considered.

Link it up

Unit 6, B4 explores verbal and non-verbal communication strategies in more detail.

a   Space – can all children move around the setting safely?
b   Layout – are resources **ACCESSIBLE** (available to all) to all children, at the right level?
c   Lighting – is the environment too dark or too bright?
d   Quiet areas – is there a cosy area for children to rest or have time away from background noise?

Appropriate adapted resources and care facilities

Some resources and areas may need more consideration to meet children's needs, such as:

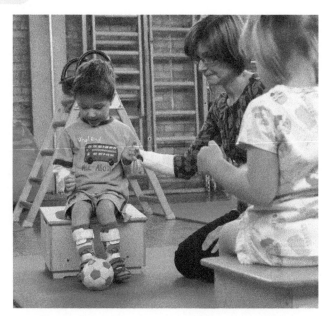

All children should be able to take part fully in the range of experiences in your setting

- ramps, wide doors, hand rails, accessible toilets and nappy-changing areas for children with limited mobility
- equipment that has been adapted for children with motor disabilities – thick brushes that are easy to grasp, chunky crayons, specialist cutlery
- earphones, so children with hearing impairments can listen to recorded stories, and music
- weighted blankets can help children with emotional difficulties to feel safe
- visual timetables – may help children cope with the change from one activity to the next
- labels on resources with large pictures and words to aid children with visual impairments.

Using positive images, resources and displays

When children see people from different cultures, backgrounds and family units, it helps break down stereotypes and develops their understanding and mutual respect for each other.

Consider:

- dual-language books, puzzles, posters
- having everyday signs and labels in English and other languages
- photographs and displays reflecting our diverse society
- varied menus to reflect food from different cultures and countries
- role-play resources reflecting different lifestyles
- small-world play resources reflecting different cultures, ethnicities, family compositions. Include small-world figures with disabilities combined with able-bodied figures so children see that differing abilities are equally valued
- displaying positive images of people in different roles (for example female doctors, male florists, a tutor in a wheelchair, a grandfather caring for a baby).

Assessment practice 1.12	AO4

Ana, age 5, has just moved to your setting from Poland. Ana has English as an additional language.

Identify and tick two resources that might support her.

☐ A standing frame   ☐ Signs with large print

☐ Dual-language books   ☐ Comfort pencil grips

☐ Low-level painting easel ☐ An interpreter

Discuss ways in which you can make Ana feel included in the setting.

Respecting beliefs and faiths

It is crucial to reflect the beliefs and faiths that children in your setting view as important. It is also helpful to give children the opportunity to share, participate in and value different religious customs.

Each festival should be explored and valued – you should show children that their faith matters.

Share books about religious festivals, provide art activities and put up displays that reflect the different beliefs of the children in your setting, and the wider society.

Promoting anti-discriminatory practice

It is everyone's role to promote anti-discriminatory practice and to follow equality and inclusion policies. As an early years assistant, you should seek advice from your supervisor about how to challenge any discrimination you come up against in your setting.

What if…?

Peter is 3 years old and goes to Rainbows Nursery. The nursery manager has employed a ballet tutor to come to the setting. Peter's father is angry that Peter has been doing ballet, saying, 'He's not a girl!' He says Peter is not allowed to take part. Peter is upset.

1 How can the manager sensitively and constructively explain the benefits of everyone being allowed to take part in ballet?

2 How do you act as a good role model in your setting to promote anti-discriminatory practice?

Children's rights to dignity and respect

At all times, you should help children to feel valued and respected. Never belittle a child's efforts or label a child. Let them know that they are a person in their own right, that what they think and say is valued, and that they are allowed to have a voice. You should encourage the children to behave similarly to each other; be prepared to step in if they are not treating another child with respect, but remember to avoid using difficult language.

Link it up

Unit 4, A3 talks about promoting children's independence during care routines.

Children's independence in personal care routines

It is your job to support children's development of independence sensitively. Your role may include helping children with hand washing or wiping their faces after lunch. Allow them the opportunity and time to have a go themselves first. Remember to praise their efforts.

Encouraging children to make choices

Children should learn that they are allowed to make choices. You should encourage children to make decisions and to learn that they are allowed to say 'no' if they do not want to do something. You should encourage children to make choices in situations that are appropriate for their age and stage of development. This can be a difficult balancing act as you also need to make sure the child's choices are in their best interest and that they remain safe.

Applying sector values in relationships with children

Your setting should provide broad and balanced experiences and activities that promote British values and ensure that inclusive practice is followed. BRITISH VALUES are the sector values that early years settings have a duty to follow. Ofsted defines them as:

- democracy
- the rule of law
- individual liberty
- mutual respect
- tolerance of those with different faiths and beliefs.

Maintaining welfare and showing children they are valued

Your role is to provide a safe and emotionally secure environment where children feel accepted and valued. You can achieve this in the following ways.

a Show children expressions of affection, care and concern.
b Encourage children to keep trying, offering activities that are challenging but achievable.
c Praise efforts and achievements, no matter how small.
d Help children build relationships with other children and adults.
e Set and enforce clear rules and boundaries.
f Treat each child fairly and with respect.

Working with other professionals and services to provide specialist support (special educational needs and disabilities context)

A range of professionals (such as those in the diagram below) can support the staff in your setting to provide specialist care for children.

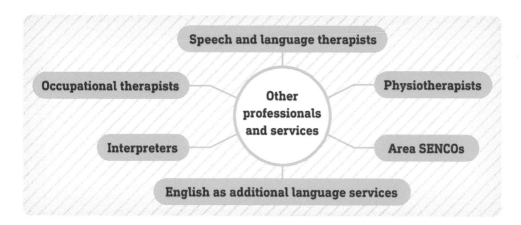

Figure 1.6: Do any of these professionals visit your setting?

D3 Equality legislation and policies

Equality laws underpin your setting's policies for inclusive practice.

Effect of equality law on your role

There are laws that support equal opportunities for children, three of which are listed below.

- Equality Act 2010 – this Act promotes anti-discriminatory practice in your setting. It ensures that everyone is treated fairly, regardless of their protected characteristics.

- UN Convention on the Rights of the Child 1989 – this Convention recognises that children worldwide have their own rights and sets out how these should be respected.
- Welfare requirements of EYFS – the statutory framework states the requirements for supporting children with special educational needs and children with English as an additional language.

Policies and procedures

Take some time to read through the policies in your setting that promote inclusive practice:

- Anti-discriminatory Practice Policies
- Inclusion Policy and Procedure
- Equality Policy and Procedure
- Diversity Policy and Procedure.

Assessment practice 1.13	AO2 AO4

- Look at your own setting's policies and procedures to promote inclusive practice.
- Discuss how they reflect and follow equality legislation.

Skills and knowledge check

- ☐ I can encourage children to use different communication methods.
- ☐ I am confident that I can report discriminatory practice to my supervisor.
- ☐ I can support children to develop independence in personal care routines.
- ☐ I can encourage children to make choices.

- ○ I know why it is important to challenge discrimination and stereotypes in my setting.
- ○ I can list three examples of how to celebrate diversity in my setting.
- ○ I can identify the professionals who might offer specialist support to children with additional needs.
- ○ I can describe two ways of adapting the environment for a child in a wheelchair.

WORK FOCUS

HANDS ON

Imagine you are working as an early years assistant in a busy pre-school.

Alice is 4 years old. Today she looks flushed, seems lethargic and feels extremely hot to the touch.

Your supervisor has called Alice's grandmother to collect her.

- Role play with a partner what you would say to Alice's grandmother when she arrives.

- Were you able to:
  - ☐ talk confidently face to face
  - ☐ use effective body language
  - ☐ give accurate information?

Alice's condition suddenly becomes much worse and she starts to have a febrile convulsion. She loses consciousness.

Your supervisor asks you to telephone for an ambulance immediately.

- Role play with a partner what you would say when you call the emergency services.

- Were you able to:
  - ☐ talk confidently on the telephone
  - ☐ listen to and answer questions accurately
  - ☐ talk clearly?

Reflect honestly on the role-play activity. Did you tick all the boxes? You may need to revisit the 'Child health' section of this chapter to improve your knowledge and skills.

Ready for work?

There are some important work-related skills and behaviours that you will need to demonstrate, which relate to this unit. Developing these could help you to gain employment as an early years assistant.

Task: Find out who the designated safeguarding lead is in your setting and arrange to interview them about their role.

- Liaise with the designated safeguarding lead and arrange a convenient time and place for the interview.·

- Prepare for the interview by writing down four questions you would like to ask them about their role.

- You may want to ask about what training they needed to undergo to secure the role, how confidentiality is maintained, their main responsibilities or how they work in partnership with other professionals.

- Conduct your interview and carefully record the answers that the designated safeguarding lead gives you. You may wish to type up the interview in a report.

This task will help build on your communication skills, your ability to work with others, your recording skills and your ability to manage information.

Getting ready for assessment

This section has been written to help you do your best when you sit the assessment test for this unit. Read through it carefully and ask your tutor if there is anything you are still not sure about.

About the test

This unit is assessed using an onscreen test, set and marked by Pearson. There will be different types of question, including multiple-choice selection questions as well as questions where you need to write in your own answer. You must answer all of them.

The number of marks for each question is shown in brackets.

There will be an onscreen notepad which you can use to make notes during the test. These notes will not be marked.

There will be an accessibility panel provided on every screen to allow you to magnify your screen and apply a range of colour filters.

An onscreen calculator is provided for questions that require calculations.

Understanding the questions

It is important that you understand what each question is asking you to do. Most questions contain 'command words' such as 'describe' or 'explain'. These words give you a hint about how to answer the question.

The table below shows some of the command words that could be used in this assessment. (This list is not exhaustive. It contains the key command words but not all of them will necessarily be used in each test. Ask your tutor for the full list as it appears in the unit specification.)

Command word	Definition
Analyse	Use ideas or concepts to explore something carefully, breaking it down into factors and commenting on which are most important or relevant.
Describe	Give an account of something, such as steps in a process or characteristics. The response should be developed but does not require justification or reasoning.
Discuss	Consider different aspects of a topic, how they interrelate and the extent to which they are important.
Explain	Provide reasoning to justify or exemplify a point. The answer should respond to the question and provide reasons.
Give	State an example or name something.
Identify	Provide or select an answer from a number of alternatives.
List	List a number of features or points without further elaboration.
Name	Give the correct term for something.
State	Write clearly, listing the facts.

Sample questions and answers

Question 1

This question tests your understanding of:

- indicators of abuse
- child protection policy and procedure
- multi-agency working.

Remember to provide reasons for your answers and consider different aspects of the scenario.

Also, you should read each question carefully; if the question requires you to state *two* reasons, make sure you do so.

Jack and Jill Day Nursery cares for children aged 6 weeks to 5 years of age.

Robbie is 4 years old and is small for his age.

He often comes to nursery without a coat, with dirty clothes and seems tired and withdrawn.

Robbie's key person is Lilly. She is concerned for his wellbeing.

1. State *two* reasons why Lilly is concerned. (2 marks)
2. Explain the procedure that Lilly should follow. (2 marks)
3. List *two* other agencies that may be able to support the nursery to help Robbie. (2 marks)

Sample answers

1. Lilly has concerns because she thinks Robbie might be suffering abuse.
2. She should report her concerns.
3. Health visitors and other professionals.

Verdict

1. This answer only gives one very general reason, instead of two. It could be improved by specifying that Robbie might be being neglected, applying the understanding that a failure to thrive, inappropriate and unwashed clothes, tiredness and being withdrawn can be indicators of neglect.

2. This would have been a better answer if the learner had said that Lilly should report her concerns to the designated safeguarding lead, following the Child Protection Policy. She should not discuss this with anyone else to keep in line with her setting's Confidentiality Policy.

3. Again, the answer only gives one type of agency, but the question asked for two. 'Other professionals' is not specific enough. The learner could have given the example of social workers who could offer support if Robbie is identified as being in need. It is a legal requirement that social workers ensure Robbie is cared for and that parenting skills are supported.

Question 2

This question assesses your knowledge of:

- how to set up safe environments for children
- how to supervise children safely
- how to embed inclusive values in your setting
- health and safety policies
- anti-discriminatory practice.

Remember to take time to consider the questions and relate the information you put in your answers to the different aspects of the scenario.

Look carefully at the command words to make sure you are putting enough detail in your answer. For example, if the command word is 'discuss', you will need to present the key points and consider the different parts of the topic.

The early years assistant, Jenny, has been asked to help set up a new role play 'hospital' for the children in Wishing Well Nursery.

The nursery has bought new equipment, including a new heavy table, stethoscopes, bandages and doctor and nurse outfits.

Jenny has been asked to display photographs and words in the 'hospital'.

1 Explain how Jenny can help to set up and supervise the role-play 'hospital' safely. (2 marks)

2 Discuss how Jenny can use the role-play 'hospital' to promote inclusive practice. (6 marks)

Sample answers

1 Make sure there is no broken equipment. Keep the area clean and hygienic. Watch the area.

2 Display photographs in the area of children in wheelchairs.

Verdict

1 This question uses the command word 'explain', so the answer needs to include reasons why something needs to be done. A fuller answer could include the following points:

- Jenny should make a risk assessment of the area before allowing children to use it, to identify any hazards.

- Jenny should follow manual handling and lifting guidelines if moving the table, so she does not hurt herself or others.

- Jenny should ensure that all the equipment provided is suitable for the ages and developmental stages of the children using the area. She should also consider the layout of the area so that children can move around safely.

- Jenny should supervise fully as children play, making sure adult to child ratios are maintained.

② The learner hasn't considered different aspects and how each would be important. They could have expanded on their answer by saying:

- In line with the Inclusion Policy, Jenny could display photographs in the hospital of female doctors, male nurses, people from different racial and cultural backgrounds, and people with dissabilities, in order to counteract stereotypes and reflect our diverse society.

Jenny could display key words in the home languages of the children in the setting so as to give children a sense of belonging and make them feel valued.

Jenny could encourage all children to take part fully, making positive comments about their responses to support choice, independence and involvement, which is important to the development of each child.

2 Child Development from Birth up to 5 Years

Have you noticed through your own experience and by looking around your work placement setting that all children learn and develop at different speeds?

Some may start to learn to walk very early for their age while others are still crawling; some children may be able to share and think of others while their friends find it more difficult.

This unit is about how babies and children grow and develop across different areas. It will help you to look out for usual patterns of growth and development so that you can help them to make progress towards the next stage.

How will I be assessed?

This unit is assessed externally. You will need to complete a realistic work-based task, which will be set and marked by Pearson. You will be given a task booklet, an information booklet to refer to and an answer booklet. The task must be completed under supervision.

You will be given a scenario and will answer a series of questions that could include:

- comparing a child's progress in a particular area of development with the expected milestones for the age group
- identifying and explaining factors that may affect the child's development
- planning an activity to support the child's development. This may include the resources you need, the timescale, any health and safety issues, and factors that could affect the implementation of your plan.

Assessment outcomes

AO1	Demonstrate knowledge and understanding of the developmental milestones and the factors affecting them.
AO2	Apply knowledge and understanding of the age-related milestones and factors to support progress across areas of development.
AO3	Analyse and evaluate information about a child in context, demonstrating the ability to interpret the impact of given factors on a child's development.
AO4	Be able to recommend an activity to support a child's development in context with appropriate justification.

What you will learn in this unit:

A   Investigate children's growth and development from birth up to 5 years

B   Factors that may impact on children's growth and development

C   Review best practice in supporting children's growth and development

A Investigate children's growth and development from birth up to 5 years

A1 Basic knowledge of the definitions of growth and development

Although children usually pass through stages of growth and development in the same order, each child is an individual and will develop at their own rate. As an early years assistant, you need a good understanding of the usual patterns of development. You also need to be able to recognise when children are not meeting expected developmental MILESTONES (points in the recognised pattern of development that children are expected to reach at particular times).

For this unit, you will need to know and understand some basic information about how children grow and develop. GROWTH is the increase in a child's physical size. Development is how children progress in different ways. This can include many different things:

- Learning and refining of skills and abilities, for example learning to throw and catch a ball and improving on this.
- Head to toe – in the first 12 months, babies' development moves from their head downwards. Starting with their head, their neck muscles will become stronger and they will be able to hold their head up and look around. They will then start to co-ordinate their arms so that they can try to hold things. Moving downwards, they will become able to hold themselves up and eventually to crawl as they begin to move arms and legs together. Finally, they will start to walk.
- Inner to outer – starting with larger, simple movements with action nearer the body and moving on to more complex ones further from the body. For example, babies start by being able to move arms and legs and progress to being able to pick things up with their hands.
- Following the same pattern of development (in the same order) but at individual rates. For example, some children may start to walk at 10 months of age whereas others may not be mobile until 14 months. Some may say their first word at 12 months and others later.

You should also know that children's development is HOLISTIC (treated as a whole thing). This means that if a child is developing in one area, it will impact on other areas. For example, as a child develops language skills they will also start to develop socially. The development of fine motor skills (see A2) means that children are more likely to be able to write and record their own ideas and develop their cognitive skills.

Link it up

See Unit 5, A3 on the importance of play that supports and promotes development.

Practise

Look at some children in your setting who are the same age. Are they the same size? Using the development charts in A2, see whether they have reached the same level of development in different areas.

A2 Areas of development

The five areas of development help us when looking at the way in which children change and grow over time. These are broken into ages or stages, known as milestones, so that you can measure progress.

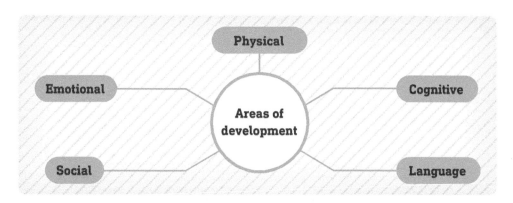

Figure 2.1: The five areas of development

The five areas of development (see Figure 2.1) are:

1 **PHYSICAL DEVELOPMENT** – development of the body. There are two different types of physical skill that children need to develop:
   - **GROSS MOTOR SKILLS**, or large muscle movement. 'Gross' in this context means 'large' and 'motor' means 'movement'. For example, to move the muscles in our legs and arms that we use for running or throwing requires gross motor skills
   - **FINE MOTOR SKILLS**, or small muscle movement. To use objects such as a knife and fork or to hold a pencil for writing we use fine motor skills
2 **COGNITIVE DEVELOPMENT** – development of the mind for thinking, using our memory and working things out
3 **LANGUAGE DEVELOPMENT** – development of speech and communication skills
4 **SOCIAL DEVELOPMENT** – development of friendships and learning social skills such as taking turns when playing with toys
5 **EMOTIONAL DEVELOPMENT** – this involves the way in which children learn to express and deal with their feelings.

For the purpose of this unit, you will be looking at milestones. Children in the above areas of development are split into the following age ranges:

- birth up to 12 months
- 12 months up to 2 years
- 2 years up to 3 years
- 3 years up to 4 years
- 4 years up to 5 years.

Birth up to 12 months

The following pictures and tables give a summary of the expected milestones in the five areas of development for babies from birth up to 12 months.

Physical development

Newborn babies are born with **REFLEXES** that help them to survive. Reflexes are automatic movements that they cannot control. They usually disappear by the time the baby is 3 or 4 months old.

The sucking reflex: babies are born with the ability to suck and swallow

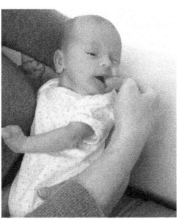

The rooting reflex: when you touch a newborn baby's cheek or mouth, the baby turns its head and purses its mouth, as if looking for the mother's nipple

The startle reflex: when startled by a loud noise or if they feel they are falling, babies fling their arms outwards, open up their fists and draw up their knees. Then they close their fists and bring the arms back close to the body, as if catching or holding onto something

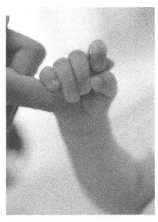

The grasping reflex: new babies will automatically grip your finger if you put it into their open hand. If you try to pull it away, their grip will get stronger

The stepping reflex: babies make small stepping movements if they are held upright and with their feet on a firm surface

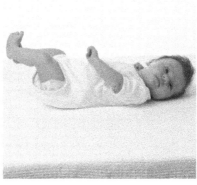

1 month: babies can turn over from their side to their back

3 months: babies can sit with a straight back, supported by an adult

6 months: babies can support themselves using their hands and arms

9 months: babies can grasp objects using a pincer grasp

12 months: babies can stand alone, unsupported

Table 2.1 shows the physical development milestones for the first 12 months.

Table 2.1: Key milestones for physical development, birth to 12 months

Age	Gross motor skills	Fine motor skills
Newborn	• Sucking, rooting, startle, grasping, stepping reflexes • Movements are uncontrolled and unco-ordinated	• No co-ordinated movement but will grasp things put into their hands as a reflex action
1 month	• Can turn from their side to their back and lift their head briefly	• Can open their hands to grasp a finger
3 months	• Can lift up head and chest when on their stomach and bring hands together over body • Can sit with their back straight when held • Can wave, bringing hands together over body	• Can watch their hands and hold a rattle for a moment
6 months	• Can roll over from back to front • Can lift head and chest while supporting themselves on their arms	• Can reach for a toy and move a toy from one hand to the other
9 months	• Can sit unsupported • Usually mobile by crawling or rolling, may pull up to stand alone • May walk by holding on to furniture	• Can use a **PINCER GRASP** (index finger and thumb) to grasp objects • Can deliberately release objects by dropping them
12 months	• Can pull up to stand, stand alone • Can walk while holding on to furniture	• Can use pincer grasp to pick up small objects • Can point using index finger

Cognitive development

Newborn: babies will gaze at a human face – in this case, the face of his mother

1 month: babies enjoy repeating soothing movements such as thumb-sucking

3 months: babies can focus on close objects and follow them with their eyes

6 months: babies can explore objects by putting them in their mouth

9 months: babies can look for hidden objects and 'find' them again

12 months: babies enjoy throwing things and watching them drop to the ground

Table 2.2 shows the cognitive development milestones for the first 12 months.

Age	Cognitive development
Newborn	• Will turn their head towards light • Will gaze at human faces • Are startled by sudden noises
1 month	• Repeat movements such as sucking their thumb • May 'freeze' for a moment if they hear a particular sound, noticing when it starts and stops, for example a vacuum cleaner or a telephone
3 months	• Can recognise familiar routines • Are alert and can follow movement with their eyes if objects are close
6 months	• Can explore objects by putting them in their mouth • Recognise voices
8–9 months	• Can look for dropped objects and objects that they see being hidden
12 months	• Enjoy throwing things to the ground and watching them drop • Learn by trying things out and repeating if successful. This approach to learning is called 'trial and error'

From birth to 12 months, babies' cognitive development takes place through their senses. They will start to recognise different faces and speech sounds, and will be beginning to link these together. As the year progresses, they start to develop memory and will know that objects are hidden when they are not in view. They will recognise routines and begin to anticipate what will happen next, for example a sleep after a feed.

Language development

Table 2.3 shows the language development milestones for the first 12 months.

Age	Language development
Newborn	• Respond to high-pitched tones by moving their limbs • May be able to copy simple actions, for example opening the mouth wide or sticking out the tongue
1 month	• Can turn their head towards an adult voice • Begin to coo at 6 weeks
3 months	• Smile when they hear a familiar voice • Cry loudly to express their needs
6 months	• Make short babbling sounds, such as 'da' and 'ba' • Squeal with delight
9 months	• Understand 'no' • VOCALISE in long strings of babbling (using the voice without saying words)
12 months	• Know their own name • Understand simple instructions

For the first few months, babies will be listening and tuning into different voices and starting to respond to these by cooing and babbling. They will cry when tired or hungry and be comforted by familiar voices. Towards the end of their first year, they will be beginning to understand words such as 'up' and 'drink', and will be starting to communicate more through babbling and simple words such as 'dadda' or 'mumma'.

Emotional and social development

Within the first 6 weeks, babies will recognise the voice of their carer. Over the next few weeks, they will develop an ATTACHMENT (close relationship) to their main caregiver and enjoy being close when feeding. They will start to show trust to those adults that they know and will show signs of being anxious when separated from them at around the age of 6 months; this is known as SEPARATION ANXIETY. They will continue to like to be near a familiar adult throughout this first year.

By 6 months, babies are likely to be wary of people they don't know

Table 2.4 shows the emotional and social development milestones for the first 12 months.

Table 2.4: Key milestones for emotional and social development, birth to 12 months

Age	Emotional and social development
Newborn	• Imitate facial expressions
1 month	• Can focus with interest on human faces • At 6 weeks babies can smile
3 months	• Enjoy being held and are happy to form attachments with different people • Will smile at strangers as well as familiar people
6 months	• Can recognise and respond to emotions in others • Will start to show wariness of strangers
7–8 months	• Can start to form specific attachments with people
From 8 months	• Will develop specific attachments • Will imitate actions of others, such as clapping • Will experience anxiety when separated from their primary carer(s)

12 months up to 2 years

During their second year, children will be starting to develop both their fine and gross motor skills. They will hold a crayon with a palmar grip and will be starting to use a pincer grip to pick up smaller objects. They will also be starting to stand and gradually learning to walk during this year.

Physical development

There are two types of grasp seen in young children:

• Pincer grasp – picking objects up by closing thumb and finger together
• **PALMAR GRASP** – holding an object such as a crayon in the palm of the hand by gripping it.

By 15 months, children can hold a crayon using a palmar grasp

At about 18 months, most toddlers can walk steadily without help, even when carrying a toy

53

Table 2.5 shows the physical development milestones between 12 months and 2 years.

Table 2.5: Key milestones for physical development, 12 months to 2 years

Age	Gross motor skills	Fine motor skills
15 months	• Can crawl upstairs • May walk hesitantly • Can kneel without support	• Pincer grasp is precise • Use palmar grasp to hold crayons
18 months	• Can walk unaided • Can walk upstairs with help • Can squat to pick up toys • Can run but unable to avoid obstacles	• Can build a tower of three or more bricks • Can feed themselves with a spoon • Can scribble using a crayon in palmar grasp

Cognitive development

Between the ages of 12 months and 2 years, children are starting to become more independent and enjoy exploring the world around them. Table 2.6 shows the cognitive development milestones between 12 months and 2 years.

Table 2.6: Key milestones for cognitive development, 12 months to 2 years

Age	Cognitive development
15 months	• Explore objects by using sight and sound, through looking and listening carefully. They will be starting to understand the names of different items
18 months	• Are curious to explore their environment • Remember where things belong

Language development

Children of this age begin to develop speech and show that they can understand some words. Table 2.7 shows the language development milestones between 12 months and 2 years.

Table 2.7: Key milestones for language development, 12 months to 2 years

Age	Language development
15 months	• Communicate by pointing and vocalising • Know up to six words
18 months	• Can communicate wishes • Can understand simple requests • Know about 10–40 words

Emotional and social development

From the age of 12 months to 2 years, children start to become a little more independent but they can still be shy and clingy. Table 2.8 shows the emotional and social development milestones between 12 months and 2 years.

Table 2.8: Key milestones for emotional and social development, 12 months to 2 years

Age	Emotional and social development
18 months	• Are emotionally dependent on parents and **KEY PERSONS** • Play alone but enjoy being near adults and siblings (brothers or sisters) • Insist on immediate attention • Can copy adult actions • Alternate between being clingy with their parents/key persons and resisting them

2 years up to 5 years

Physical development

Between 2 and 5 years, children will be developing their strength and co-ordination in both fine and gross motor skills. They will need plenty of opportunities to run around, jump and climb and throw and kick, so that by the time they are 5 they will have developed good balance and strength in these areas. From being able to pick things up and build small towers with a preferred hand at the age of 2, they will have developed their skills to be able to use scissors to cut paper, and will be starting to use a tripod grip when holding a crayon or pencil. Table 2.9 shows the physical development milestones between 2 and 5 years.

Table 2.9: Key milestones for physical development, 2 to 5 years

Age	Gross motor skills	Fine motor skills
2 years	• Can run • Can climb onto furniture • Can use sit-and-ride toys, and push-and-pull wheeled toys	• Can draw dots and circles • Can put on shoes and fasten with Velcro (but not buckles or laces) • Can pick up small objects using pincer grasp • Can build a tower of six or more bricks • Can drink from a cup • Can use a spoon to feed themselves
2 years 6 months	• Can kick a large ball • Can jump with two feet together from a low step	• Start to show a hand preference • Can pull down items of clothing • Start to develop a primitive **TRIPOD GRIP** (holding objects between the thumb, index and middle fingers)
3 years	• Can run forwards and backwards • Can steer a tricycle • Can walk upstairs with alternate feet • Can throw and catch a large ball	• Can use tripod grip • Can draw a circle • Have established hand preference for most tasks
3–4 years	• Can hop on one foot • Can walk along a line • Can aim and throw a ball and kick it with force • Can ride a tricycle using pedals	• Can button and unbutton clothes • Can use scissors to cut out simple shapes • Can draw a person with a head, trunk and legs • Can eat with a knife and fork • Can thread beads to make a necklace
4–5 years	• Can run and avoid obstacles • Can skip with a rope • Can throw a large ball to partner and catch it • Have good balance and co-ordination • Can go up and down stairs one foot at a time • Start to ride a bike	• Can form letters • Can write own name • Can colour in pictures • Can thread small beads

By 3 years old, most children can use a tripod grip to draw with a crayon

Cognitive development

By the age of 2 years, children will be developing their memory skills and will be starting to understand cause and effect. For example, if I tip my cup over, my drink will spill. As a result of their developing memory skills, children will also start to be able to 'conserve' ideas, for example, realising that if something is moved, its properties are not affected. As they get older and their vocabulary develops, they may start to talk to themselves as they are playing and be able to identify more abstract ideas such as colours. By 5 years, a child should be able to make comparisons such as heavier and lighter, or more and less, and be able to tell if two sets of objects are the same.

This 3-year-old can do simple puzzles on her own

Table 2.10 shows the cognitive development milestones between 2 and 5 years.

Table 2.10: Key milestones for cognitive development, 2 to 5 years

Age	Cognitive development
2 years	• Can recognise themselves in mirrors • Can remember past experiences
2 years 6 months	• Can recognise themselves in photographs • Can complete simple puzzles with help
3 years	• Understand the difference between past and present • Can complete simple puzzles alone
3–4 years	• Can recognise and name primary colours • Understand what is meant by 'more' • Can tell whether an object is heavy or light • Can arrange objects into categories • Can make connections between people and events
4–5 years	• Can count accurately up to 10 • Can add two sets of objects together, for example, know if I add two apples and two apples I will have four apples • Can match equal sets, for example, they can identify if sets contain the same number of items • Can understand the need for rules • Can name the time of day associated with activities • Can give reasons to solve problems

Language development

Between the ages of 2 and 5 years, children's vocabulary will develop rapidly. It will expand from around 200 to 2,000 words, although this will depend on how much others interact with them. Most children of 2 will be eager to communicate and will enjoy starting to name different objects as their vocabulary develops. At around 3 years, their speech will still be immature and their grammar may not be correct (for example, 'I bringed it'), but they will be trying to apply the rules that they know. From this age they will also be asking more and more questions as they will want to know why things happen. Between 4 and 5 years, children will be using more complex sentences and developing their fluency.

By the age of 4, children are enjoying sharing books and stories

Table 2.11 shows the language development milestones between 2 and 5 years.

Age	Language development
2 years	• Know 50–199 words • Able to join words together • Enjoy looking at books
2 years 6 months	• Know around 200 words • Start to use simple sentences • Ask questions • Use personal pronouns, such as 'me', 'you' • Use negatives and plurals
3 years	• Speech is clear to anyone unfamiliar with the child • Enjoy books and turn pages • Sing songs and rhymes
3–4 years	• Child's speech can be easily understood, although some words may be incorrect • Use questions • Language is usually fluent by 4 years (with some speech immaturities)
4–5 years	• Can count aloud accurately up to 10 • Use complex sentences with words such as 'because' • Talk about what has happened and what might happen • Use language to argue and answer back • Able to tell stories • Enjoy jokes

Table 2.11: Key milestones for language development, 2 to 5 years

Link it up

Go to Unit 6 to find out more about supporting children's communication and language development.

Emotional and social development

A child of 2 to 3 years will be starting to assert themselves as they learn that they are separate from other people. This can be frustrating if they cannot express what they want and will often lead to tantrums. They will be aware of their gender and play with their peers, starting to make friends and learning social skills such as sharing. They will start to develop empathy around the age of 3 or 4 and understand how others are affected by their actions and the actions of those around them. As they reach the age of 5, they will begin to show a sense of humour and will enjoy doing more things independently such as dressing and washing their hands.

As children get older they learn to play with others and understand the concept of taking turns

Table 2.12 shows the emotional and social development milestones between 2 and 5 years.

Table 2.12: Key milestones for emotional and social development, 2 to 5 years

Age	Emotional and social development
2 years	• Unable to wait for needs to be met • May be distracted from tantrums • Play in parallel with other children but are unable to share toys
2 years 6 months	• Play alongside other children and engage in **ONLOOKER PLAY** (watching other children as they play but not joining in) • Very dependent on adults • Jealous of other children getting attention • Respond well to adult attention and praise • Have tantrums when frustrated
3 years	• Find it easier to wait • Start to take turns and share • Enjoy being with other children • Will comfort another child • Will help adults
3–4 years	• Can cope with separation from primary carer if with someone they know • Begin to play co-operatively • Show clear preferences with friendships • Play with others
4–5 years	• Can work out what other people may be thinking (which helps them negotiate with others) • Able to understand the need for rules • Can develop close friendships • Behaviour is mostly co-operative • Able to separate from parents more easily

Assessment practice 2.1   AO1 AO2 AO3

Over a period of a few weeks, observe a child, looking in particular at one area of their development. What do you notice? Are there any changes in what they can do? What are they?

A3 Atypical development

As well as knowing about expected stages of development, which you have seen are also called milestones, you should be aware that in some cases children do not follow this expected pattern. They may become 'stuck' without progressing, or pass their developmental milestones a long way ahead of other children. This is called 'atypical' development.

- **ATYPICAL DEVELOPMENT** – the child's development in one or more areas of development is not following the normal milestones at expected times: this may mean that they are ahead or behind.
- **GLOBAL DEVELOPMENTAL DELAY** – the child is not meeting expected milestones across all of the areas of development.

In some cases the atypical development may affect one area, for example speech, and the child may be at the same stage as their friends in the other areas, such as physical development. It may also mean that a child is ahead of their friends in one area and that this stands out. However, it may be the case that they are not making expected progress in any of the five areas. This is known as global developmental delay.

Recognising atypical development

It is important that atypical development is recognised and that action is taken as soon as possible so that help and support can be given to the child if needed. If you think you notice something atypical when you are working with a child, it is important to let someone at your workplace setting know. If the child is not given help and support towards reaching their milestones, this may have a long-lasting effect on their development, not only in the affected area but also in others.

What if...?

You are working as an early years assistant in a nursery and notice that one of the older children is very clumsy when running around and playing with the other children. She has an 'awkward' walk and regularly knocks things over or bumps into them. You decide not to say anything as you have only recently started to work there and think that it is up to other members of staff to take responsibility.

Sometime later, the child is about to transfer to the local primary school. You realise that nothing has been said to the school about the child's awkward physical skills and wonder if you should have said something.

1 Why is it important that you mention anything you think may be atypical, even if it might turn out not to be significant?

2 How might it have helped the child if you had spoken to another member of staff?

3 Why is it important for the school to know about the child's physical development?

Observing children

Observing children and what they do is an important part of the adult role in the EYFS (EARLY YEARS FOUNDATION STAGE).

Observations help us to:

a assess or look at children's level of development and whether they are following expected patterns

b find out about children's interests and the way in which they learn

c build up a picture of each child over time as well as compare them with other children of the same age.

Between the ages of 2 and 3, every child will have a Progress Check. This is carried out by the early years practitioner in the child's setting and gives parents and carers a summary of their child's learning and development. It also provides information about actions planned to address any developmental concerns.

Figure 2.2 shows how practitioners work with parents and other professionals, such as a health visitor or a SENCO (SPECIAL EDUCATIONAL NEEDS CO-ORDINATOR) to support the child's development. SENCOs work in several early years settings and will support the staff in looking at ways to help children who have a special educational need or disability.

Link it up

For more on observing children and also on the EYFS, see C1 in this unit.

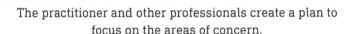

An early years practitioner summarises the child's strengths and areas where progress is not as expected.

The practitioner shares and reviews their observations with parents/carers.

The practitioner and other professionals create a plan to focus on the areas of concern.

Figure 2.2: Professionals will work together to support each aspect of a child's development

What if...?

Amal is 4 years old and is working above the expected milestones in all areas except for social and emotional development. He knows that he is able and regularly tells other children that they are 'silly' if they do not know things that are obvious to him. As a result, Amal does not have many friends because the other children are upset when he speaks to them in this way. He is about to leave the setting to go to school.

1 Explain how Amal's social and emotional development have been affected by his abilities in other areas.

2 Conclude what the setting could do to help prepare Amal for school.

Assessment practice 2.2   AO1 AO3

Carry out an observation of a child alongside a more experienced member of staff and compare your findings. You might think afterwards about:

- how long the child was focused on the activity

- any areas of concern or particular achievement

- whether you interacted with the child during the observation

- if the child was working alone or with others, and if with others, the amount they interacted with them.

Skills and knowledge check

☐ I can contribute to monitoring children's development through observation.

☐ I can track a child's development based on the established milestones.

☐ I can look out for atypical development and understand its possible impact if not identified.

○ I can name the five areas of development.

○ I know the impact of a 2-year-old's emotional development and why this means that they may have tantrums.

○ I can name three things that are developmentally 'normal' for a 4- to 5-year-old.

○ I know that children's development is holistic and what this means.

B Factors that may impact on children's growth and development

B1 Individual factors

Although children follow the same sequence of development, they may not always pass through the stages at the same age. There are a number of issues that may have an effect on a child's growth and development (see Figure 2.3) and these effects can be positive or negative. Individual factors such as the child's own personality and abilities are important, as are the life events they experience. Environmental factors, such as the amount of support that adults are able to give a child, also have a significant effect on growth and development.

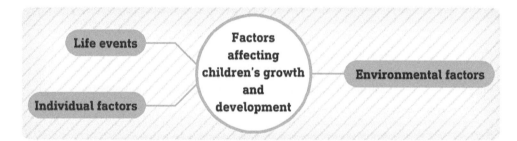

Figure 2.3: Factors affecting children's growth and development

Each child is an individual and has their own personality so will learn and develop in their own way. However, it is important to look out for differences that might mean a child has atypical development. In some cases a child's specific needs, such as a hearing impairment, may go unnoticed by adults and this may have a long-lasting effect on a child's development.

You should also remember that sometimes if children have been born prematurely it may take time for them to 'catch up' in one or more areas of development. Children who are from multiple births (twins, triplets and so on) can often be born prematurely, which may affect their development.

In other cases, children may be coached in a specific talent such as a sport or dance, which means they are focusing on a particular area and developing it more than others.

Long-term health conditions

There are a number of health conditions that can limit one or more areas of development. For example, a long-term illness such as Duchenne muscular dystrophy (a genetic condition that causes cells in the muscles to break down gradually and be lost over time) will affect a child's physical development. It may also impact on their social and emotional development, as they may be in pain or frustrated by their condition.

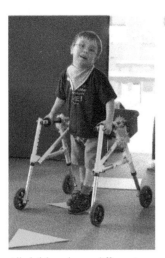

All children have different needs. Sometimes they need support to be able to join in with activities

Disability

Disabilities may be visible, but you should also remember that some children will have a disability or learning difficulty that you are not able to see. You need to know about three different types of disability:

1 **PHYSICAL DISABILITY**, which you can see and involves limited movement of one or more limbs
2 **SENSORY DISABILITY**, meaning impairment of the senses such as hearing, sight or touch
3 **LEARNING DISABILITY**, which is a disability that affects a child's ability to learn.

Table 2.13 shows the effects on development of different types of disability.

Disability	Effect on development
Physical	• The child has limited movement, so it will be hard for them to strengthen and develop their muscle control • Usually a child who has a physical disability will be given physiotherapy exercises to help them develop strength and control • They may need support to move around and access the curriculum in different ways
Sensory	• Some children may have mild hearing or visual loss, or be very sensitive to touching some materials • If undetected, a sensory impairment such as hearing loss will affect the child's ability to recognise and understand language, as well as limiting their social interactions • Sensory impairment can cause emotional distress if the child is not able to see/hear what other children or adults are doing or saying
Learning	• Children may take longer to learn and understand new things and become independent • A learning disability may vary from mild to severe; in severe cases a child is likely to need full-time care and support • Sometimes a learning disability may be due to a health condition or a specific condition such as Down syndrome • A learning disability may affect a child's ability to communicate and their language development

Table 2.13: Types of disability and their effect on development

Speech and language abilities

Speech and language ability will vary from child to child. Some children may pick up new **VOCABULARY** (words) more easily than others, or be sociable and confident and therefore practise their language skills more.

However, if you notice a child who is slow to speak, there may be an underlying issue such as a speech and language disorder or delay, which means that the child has difficulty in processing language. In this situation you should speak to others in the setting as the child will need to be assessed by a speech and language therapist.

Children who learn more than one language

If a child is learning more than one language, their speech and language development may take longer than that of other children because:

• they will be learning more vocabulary
• they need to 'tune in' to two or more different ways of speaking.

Learning two or more languages is a very positive skill for a child and has many advantages. However, it may also mask a speech and language delay and make it harder to detect.

Assessment practice 2.3 **A01 A03 A04**

Emma is 2 years old and is learning two languages as her mother is Spanish and her father English. She is not speaking at all in either language. You are working alongside her key worker and are drawing up a plan to support her language development. Looking at the expected speech and language milestones for her age, outline how you would do the following.

1 Identify Emma's language development against where she should be for her age.

2 Suggest two activities you could do with Emma to support her English language development.

3 Explain why these activities would help Emma.

B2 Environmental factors

In the same way that each child is an individual and has their own abilities and personalities, they will also each be a product of their different homes, families and environments. Environmental factors have a direct impact on the child – for example, the negative effects of being cold, tired or hungry or the positive effects of coming from a happy and settled home. You may not be aware of children's individual backgrounds but you should be aware that environmental factors may affect a child's growth and development.

Housing conditions

Housing conditions may make a big difference to a young child. Some children may have plenty of space and comfort as well as a garden or other outdoor space; for others, conditions may not be ideal. Housing conditions that could affect a child's physical, social or emotional development include:

- having to share a bedroom with other children
- limited indoor or outdoor space
- lack of heating
- lack of cleanliness
- stressful relationships within the household.

Lifestyle

Positive lifestyle factors include:

- a healthy balanced diet
- regular exercise
- enough sleep
- unconditional love from adults.

These will help children to grow and develop in the best way. However, for a number of reasons children may be denied some or all of them. A poor diet or lack of sleep or exercise will make a difference to a child's physical and emotional development and will influence the way in which they develop over time.

Impact of technology

The impact of technology on children's development may be positive or negative. Children should be exposed to technology and given opportunities to use and understand it. However, too much time spent

looking at computers or tablets may mean that children are not having enough opportunities to initiate play and to investigate their environment for themselves. There may also be other negative effects, such as staying indoors most of the time and fewer opportunities for social interaction with others. These may affect children's language and communication skills.

All children should be given the opportunity to attend an early years setting to support their learning and development

Opportunities to attend an early years setting

Where children attend an early years setting such as a pre-school, nursery or childminder, they have the chance to socialise and meet other children, as well as take advantage of learning opportunities. In almost all cases, this experience strengthens children's development.

Poverty

Children who are brought up in poverty are more likely to struggle in each area of development, although this may not always be the case. Being poor does not automatically mean that children are deprived, but, it is likely to have some negative effect. Table 2.14 sums up some of the ways that poverty may affect children's development.

Table 2.14: The effects of poverty on children's development

Area of development	Possible effects of poverty
Physical	• Lack of heat or food may deprive children of sleep or important nutrients that their body needs in order to grow and develop
Cognitive	• Parents or carers may not be able to afford to give children the experience of different activities such as cooking or visiting other places/environments • There may be few toys or activities at home to support children's development
Language	• Children may have little access to resources such as books • They may have limited opportunities to take part in different social activities • The lack of resources and opportunities may mean that their vocabulary and language take longer to develop
Social	• Children may not be able to attend early years settings because of cost or lack of transport • If parents' level of education or the amount of time they spend talking with children is low, children may have limited social stimulation from adults
Emotional	• Children may need emotional support if they are aware of the situation and find it stressful and if the adults around them are not coping well with poverty

Assessment practice 2.4   **AO3**

Sami, aged 2, has recently started at nursery. He has not attended an early years setting before and you notice that he regularly arrives hungry and in dirty clothes. His mother has told the nursery manager that they cannot afford many things although she tries her best.

1 Should staff be concerned about Sami?

2 What could you do on an individual level?

Opportunities for outdoor play

Research has shown that there are many benefits to outdoor play (see Table 2.15) and these will affect all areas of a young child's development. Here you will focus on the effects on their physical and emotional development.

Area of development	Benefits of outdoor play
Physical	• Children who have opportunities for outdoor play will be able to develop and strengthen their physical skills through running around and playing with others • Being outside is also healthy and stimulating and exposes children to sunlight and vitamin D • Children who play outdoors are more active and so will be tired at the end of the day and will sleep better
Emotional	• Children are often more independent when they play outdoors and will learn to take more **RISKS** away from direct adult supervision • Taking risks will encourage them to develop their confidence and try new activities • In a large outdoor space, children may be less influenced by adults and be able to interact with their friends in a more creative way as they are stimulated by the freedom of their surroundings • Playing outdoors gives children opportunities to observe and interact with wildlife and learn to respect and care for insects and plants

Table 2.15: The benefits of outdoor play for children's physical and emotional development

Link it up

Although children benefit from being outdoors, you will also need to be aware of the dangers to young and sensitive skin, in particular when the sun is strong. Go to Unit 1, B4 for more on action to take in case of sunburn.

Family structure

A secure family structure and a loving home create the best environment for children to learn and develop. There are many different types of family, including:

• a **NUCLEAR FAMILY** (with two parents, usually a father and mother, and their children)
• a single-parent family (one parent and his or her children)
• an extended family, which may include grandparents or aunts and uncles.

Regardless of the family type, children who have a secure family life and feel loved are more confident and therefore more willing to try new activities.

Looked-after children

LOOKED-AFTER CHILDREN (sometimes known as LAC) are children who are under the care of the local authority. Looked-after children are most likely to be cared for within the community by foster parents. But some may be at home with their parents, supported by a local team of social workers, or they may be in a residential children's home or secure unit.

Being a looked-after child may affect the child's social or emotional development. For example, looked-after children may have had a number of different homes in their lives. They may not have had a secure family life and may be less confident and less trusting of adults.

What if...?

Marietta is volunteering in a pre-school as an early years assistant. She shadows Duane, a member of staff, and has been asked to help him with his key children (the children he has main responsibility for) by observing them and telling him about anything she notices. One morning, Marietta is stopped on the way in to the pre-school by the carer of Alysha, who is a looked-after child. The carer is in a hurry but tells Marietta that there will be a meeting the following week about Alysha, as there are some concerns about her settling in. She gives Marietta an envelope to pass on to Duane but Marietta puts it in her bag and then forgets about it.

1 Why is it important that Marietta remembers to give Duane the envelope about the meeting?

2 What could happen if staff and other professionals working with Alysha do not communicate with one another?

B3 Life events

Any change can be difficult for a very young child as they will be happiest when they feel settled and in a familiar routine. Sometimes adults can prepare them for change if they know it is going to happen. For example, if they know that they will be moving house, parents or carers may talk about the move in advance so that the child knows what to expect.

However, some life events are unpredictable and children will need support and reassurance from those around them. Bereavement (death), for example, may be unexpected and will need to be handled sensitively. Early years settings may also be supporting children who are refugees and have suffered some form of traumatic life event as well as having been forced to leave their home country.

Being able to deal with change is an important part of learning and development and can help children to be more resilient, both in the short term and as they grow up. However, at the time it can be difficult for them to cope with.

In this section you will look at the effects of various life events on children's development. Some events can have a positive effect while others may be negative.

Starting a new setting

When children start at or move to a new setting, they may feel unsettled, which is likely to affect their social and emotional development. This can be helped by parents and early years workers talking to them as much as possible about what is happening and giving them opportunities to ask questions.

New sibling

A **SIBLING** is a brother or sister. A child who has a new brother or sister may be feeling more 'clingy' or in need of attention, so their short-term emotional development is likely to be affected. Older siblings may also regress, or go backwards, in their development when a baby arrives, in an attempt to gain more attention.

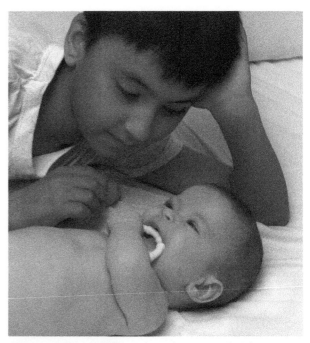

Children will react differently to changes in their lives

What if...?

Doug, aged 3, has started to wet himself on a regular basis while in the setting. He had previously been dry and there had been no problems at all with his bladder control. You know that he has a new baby sister and that there are no other siblings in the family.

1 What do you think might have caused Doug to regress in this way?

2 How could you support Doug and his family?

Similarly, when a younger sibling starts at the setting, a child who is already there may be affected in a positive or a negative way. Some children will not like it, while others might enjoy showing a younger brother or sister around. It can be helpful to encourage the older child to take on responsibility and show their sibling what to do, as older children tend to like doing this.

Moving house

Moving house can be an exciting time and children will usually enjoy it. Adults can make it into an experience for children, particularly if they have a nice new bedroom or are moving to a property with a feature that excites them such as a garden. However, moving may also unsettle a child, and initial excitement can fade when the child realises that they will not be moving back. If the child has moved some distance and is new to the early years setting, their social and emotional development may be affected as they will have to make friends again and spend time with unfamiliar adults.

Loss of key attachment

You saw earlier in the unit that attachment is when a child has a special close relationship with a key person in their life. This could be a parent or other carer such as a foster parent or grandparent. A loss of their key attachment for whatever reason is likely to be very distressing for a young child. It may happen because of bereavement or because their parents have separated. Children will need plenty of reassurance from other adults around them as well as time to cope with this loss.

Change to family situation

Changes occur in family situations for different reasons. Figure 2.4 gives some examples.

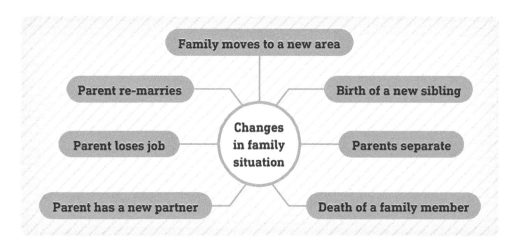

Figure 2.4: Children may be affected by changes to their family situation

In cases where children are severely affected by one of these changes, they may lose their confidence or have difficulty sleeping, which will affect their emotional development. They may also lose their appetite, which will affect their physical development as well as making it difficult for them to learn.

Assessment practice 2.5	AO1 AO2

Create a booklet for new early years assistants that outlines the kinds of factor that will affect a child's development.

Whatever a child's situation, learning and development take place most effectively if they are happy and settled. If they are stressed because they are hungry, neglected or needing love, or if they are upset by a bereavement or parental separation, you will need to reassure them and try to develop their confidence.

Skills and knowledge check

☐ I can outline what a learning disability will mean for a child.
☐ I can recognise a sensory disability, and am aware of guidance on how to support children.
☐ I can spot the effects of environmental factors on children's development.
☐ I can respond to a child who is suffering the loss of a key attachment.

○ I know about the common life events and how they might affect a child's development.
○ I know how a physical disability may affect other areas of a child's development.
○ I can explain why environmental factors might make a difference to a child's physical development.
○ I know why it is important that young children have access to outdoor play.

C Review best practice in supporting children's growth and development

C1 Supporting development of children

You will need to know about your role as an early years assistant in the workplace and how what you do relates to the EYFS. You will also need to think about how activities are planned within the nursery, and the kinds of resources that are used, so that you can see how they support children's learning and development.

The role of the key person

Each child in the early years setting will be allocated a **KEY PERSON** from among the staff. This is a requirement of the EYFS Statutory Framework 2017. This person will get to know the child and their parents or carers and make sure that their needs are met within the nursery.

Although all adults in the setting may know the children and a little about them, the role of the key person is to support all areas of the key child's development. They do this by knowing more about their background and communicating regularly with parents and carers. They also pass on any information that is important for other staff to know in order to support the child's development. The chart below shows the different aspects of the key person's role.

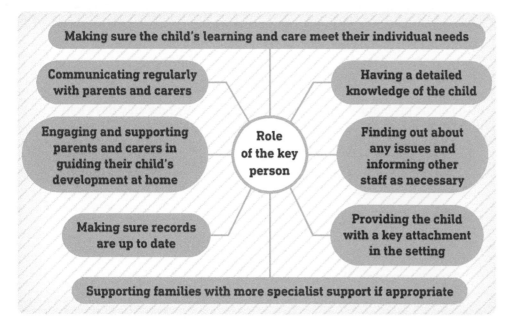

Figure 2.5: Role of the key person

A key person supports both the child and their family

The role of the early years assistant

Your role as an early years assistant is to support children in the setting so that they are able to develop and progress towards their next milestone. You will need to do this by encouraging them with play activities, using questioning and exploration to help them find things out for themselves.

Try not to be tempted to do things for the child, as this will not help them to learn and develop. If an activity is too challenging for a child, you will be able to tell very quickly and the child will lose interest. In this situation you should praise them for what they have done so far and either simplify the activity or let them move on to something else.

What if...?

You have been asked to work with two of the more able children on a problem-solving activity. Their key person has said that the activity may be hard for them but that it has been designed to help extend their learning.

They have been asked to build a bridge to cross a painted river using large building blocks. They manage to do this successfully after discussing and thinking about it and enjoying the process. However, there is another stage of the problem, which is to tell them that they now only have half the number of bricks to build the bridge and ask what they would do next. After some time and further questioning, it becomes clear that the children are finding the activity too difficult. You decide to show them how to build the bridge but the children aren't really listening. They then start to go off to choose another activity.

1 Is this the best outcome for the activity?

2 What might you say to the children when you see that they are unable to do it?

3 Why is it important that you do not let them struggle for too long over the activity?

4 Looking back, what would you have done differently?

How observation is used to assess and track progress

Adults will use observation throughout the EYFS to track and support children's progress across all areas of learning and development. Different settings may decide to carry out observations in different ways, which may include:

- using a tablet or other technology that lists EYFS stages of learning and development
- using notepads or stickers to record what children have said or done, which are then placed in a folder for each child
- using printed photographs and examples of children's work as a visual record
- using evidence from parents and carers such as notes from home that outline children's achievements, such as learning to ride a bike or swimming a width unaided. Information from parents and carers is an important part of the process of observation and must be included.

In all cases, the observations that are gathered help to build up a picture of each individual child. This means that staff have an understanding of what stage they have reached and what they need to do to meet the next milestones. In this way, the practitioners will be able to plan to support individual children's learning with activities that are appropriate for the child's stage of development.

Observing a child discreetly as they play helps us to understand their developmental progress

Assessment practice 2.6   AO3

Find out how your setting records observations of children and, if possible, look at some of the records to see this in practice. Talk to staff in the setting about what they find most useful when recording observations.

The role of planning

You need to understand the role of planning in an early years setting and how this supports children's learning. It may seem that children are 'just playing', but it is through playing and exploring that children learn and develop.

The role of careful planning is to ensure that a range of activities are covered so that children explore and develop their skills across all areas of learning and development. Remember, all areas of development are connected, and each learning activity should have an objective or purpose to support a child's learning.

Under the Statutory Framework for the EYFS (2017), the areas of learning are divided as follows.

- Three prime areas: these are considered particularly important key skills and they form the basis for the other four areas of development. They should be the focus for early years practitioners who work with the youngest children.
- Four specific areas: these strengthen and develop the three prime areas.

The EYFS describes the requirements for each area of learning. These are summarised in Table 2.16.

Table 2.16: The EYFS areas of learning

Three prime areas	
Area	**Requirements**
Communication and language development	• Children should have the opportunity to speak and listen in a range of situations • Children should be able to develop their confidence when expressing themselves
Physical development	• Children need to have a range of opportunities to develop their co-ordination, control and movement • Children should understand the importance of physical activity
Personal, social and emotional development	• Practitioners should support children in helping them to form positive relationships, develop respect for others and learn to manage their feelings • Children also need to learn how to behave when in a group and to become confident in themselves

Four specific areas	
Area	**Requirements**
Literacy	• Literacy involves supporting children as they learn their sounds so that they can start to link them and learn to read and write • Children should have the opportunity to read and listen to a wide range of materials
Mathematics	• Children should be given a chance to count regularly, to learn to understand and use numbers and move towards simple addition and subtraction • Children should be able to use mathematical language to describe shapes, spaces and measures
Understanding the world	• This area of learning is about encouraging children to explore their world, starting with their immediate community • Children should have the chance to look at and talk about people, places, technology and the environment
Expressive arts and design	• This area should give children the opportunity to explore a range of media and materials, and to express themselves through activities including art, dance, role play, music, and design and technology

The EYFS guidance also states that children should be exposed to a range of activities that are a mixture of **CHILD-INITIATED** (chosen by the child) and **ADULT-LED** (guided by an adult). The plans should reflect this so that the balance is clear.

As children move towards the end of the foundation stage at the end of their reception year, there will gradually be more adult-led activities so that they are ready for Year 1.

The four principles of the EYFS

All practice in early years settings should be shaped by the four principles of the EYFS, as shown in Figure 2.6.

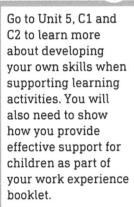

Link it up

Go to Unit 5, C1 and C2 to learn more about developing your own skills when supporting learning activities. You will also need to show how you provide effective support for children as part of your work experience booklet.

See also C2 planning activities in this unit.

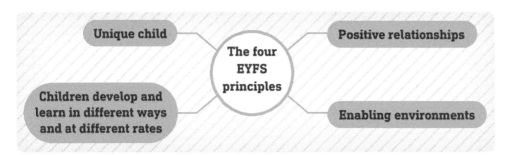

Figure 2.6: The four EYFS principles

The four EYFS principles are as follows:

1   Every child is a *unique child*, who is constantly learning and can be resilient, capable, confident and self-assured.
2   Children learn to be strong and independent through *positive relationships.*
3   Children learn and develop well in *enabling environments* in which their experiences respond to their individual needs and there is a strong partnership between practitioners and parents and/or carers.
4   *Children develop and learn in different ways and at different rates.* The framework covers the education and care of all children in early years provision, including children with special educational needs and disabilities.

(Statutory Framework for the Early Years Foundation Stage, 2017)

These principles should help early years practitioners to think about the way in which children learn so that they consider other things as well as what they need to learn. They show the importance of a positive learning environment and how relationships with others will help children to thrive.

Early years statutory guidance

The EYFS guidance is **STATUTORY**. This means that by law it has to be followed by all registered early years settings in England. It covers all of the learning and development requirements as well as the way in which children should be assessed.

C2 Planning activities

All those involved in planning for early years activities will carry out planning using a cycle as shown in Figure 2.7. In other words, they will first plan and carry out the activities with the children. Then afterwards they will look at the plan again, think about how well the activities went and decide whether they should be improved or changed.

Planning cycle and use of SMART targets

The whole team should carry out the planning cycle. You will then be able to look carefully at activities for all children across each area of learning and development and make sure that they are all covered. Team members not immediately involved in an activity may be able to give good feedback, having observed the activity from the outside.

Link it up

The guidance is updated from time to time and it is important that you are familiar with the latest information. Download and look through the Statutory Guidance for the EYFS. This is available at www.foundationyears.org.uk but check you are using the most recent version (the 2014 version was revised in April 2017). See also Unit 1, A1.

Figure 2.7: How do you plan in your setting?

What if...?

You are working in a setting where the planning is done as a team on a weekly basis but there does not seem to be any review or opportunity to look at how the activities went or how the children have responded to them.

1　Why might this be a problem and how could the provision be affected?

2　What could your role be here?

The EYFS also states that early years practitioners should plan for individual children, which means including activities that have a particular interest for them. For example, there may be a child or group of children who have a particular interest in trains and this could be incorporated as part of a 'Transport' topic.

After planning for a whole topic and age group, practitioners will look at the plans to see how targets should be included for individual children. Targets should be 'SMART'.

S – Specific – targets should be clear: for example 'be able to write their name'.

M – Measurable – it should be clear how the target will be measured: for example, 'all letters should be correctly formed'.

A – Achievable – the target needs to be something the child can achieve over time: for example, 'form a different letter correctly week by week'.

R – Realistic – the target needs to be realistic – do not set targets that are beyond the child's capability in the timescale allocated.

T – Time-bound – you should set a time limit to carry out the target: for example, 'by the end of March'.

The planning cycle is usually broken down into three different time frames:
- long (whole year)
- medium (termly)
- short-term or weekly.

It contains plans and activities covering each period for the whole setting. These are usually topic based. For example, a topic may be based on 'Transport', 'Growing' or 'Myself'. Adults in the setting will then work together to develop a plan that incorporates all areas of learning and development.

Using observations to inform choices

As you will be observing to see how children choose and carry out their activities, you will be able to make a note of how the children do them. Some activities will always be more popular than others and you should be able to get an idea about those that children would like to have more often.

Your observations and knowledge about child development should help you support children in getting to the next stage or milestone. This may also help you think about whether specific areas of their development are atypical.

Link it up

Go to Unit 5, C2 to find out more about the role of observations in supporting children's learning and development.

Identifying children's interests

The EYFS statutory guidance states that you should look at individual children's interests so that you can plan activities to provide for them. Because you will be observing children regularly as part of your role, you should look at the kinds of activity that capture their interest and are popular. For example, if adults regularly put out puzzles but the children do not use them, you should remove them and find others that are more appealing, or consider changing the activity.

You may notice that some activities are not used as you had planned or that they are less popular than you had hoped. If so, you should look at whether your planning has been appropriate for their age and stage of development and revise your plans if necessary.

You should also ask the children themselves, and their parents and carers, about their interests and talk to them about the kinds of activity they would like to have available.

You will need to use observations to identify children's interests so that you can plan suitable activities for them

Consulting with other members of staff

Usually, planning for the setting takes place as part of a team and early years staff will sit down together to discuss how to approach it and to share ideas. This is helpful, as people will often have different thoughts about how to manage practical issues as well as the kinds of activity that will benefit the children. It also enables staff to share information about individual children so that plans can be adapted to incorporate their particular needs and interests.

Link it up

Unit 7, A1 has more on how you will need to be able to reflect on work practices in your setting.

Practise

Ask your supervisor for a copy of long-, medium- and short-term plans that have been used and reviewed. Look at the way they are **ANNOTATED** (notes or comments added) and any changes or adaptations that have been made. See whether you can have a copy of current plans so that you can start to annotate them for yourself.

Selecting appropriate resources

Always make sure you think about whether the resources and materials you are using are appropriate for the children's age and stage of development. It is important that the children are supported towards the next stage of learning and it is also vital for safety reasons. An example might be ensuring that babies are not put within reach of anything that presents a choking HAZARD. Toys and resources available for babies and toddlers also need to be kept clean as they will tend to put things in their mouths.

Providing a variety of activities

When you are planning, it is important to provide children with a variety of activities that cover all areas of development. These should also be changed and updated regularly so they are kept fresh and appealing to children. In this way you will meet the needs of the children and the activities available are more likely to be interesting for them.

There should be a variety of activities available for all areas of development at any one time, for example:

- physical – ride-on toys, balls and hoops, skipping ropes, cones, bats and balls; cutting activities, opportunities for mark-making, modelling clay (for developing muscle strength)
- communication and language – story books and CDs, role play, simple games, singing and action rhymes, describing features of shapes or objects
- social – role play, board games, taking turns, having 'helpers' for the room or area
- emotional – providing a familiar environment by establishing set areas for activities so that children feel secure, which will encourage them to 'have a go'
- cognitive – counting and looking for numbers in the local area, developing phonic skills through simple reading and writing activities, looking for and creating patterns, talking about features of different environments.

Health and safety

Link it up

Go to Unit 1, Section B to find out more about health and safety policies.

When you are planning activities in the setting, you will always need to think about health and safety issues. Young children will often not be aware of or notice things that could be hazardous. Adults must always think through risks so that they can be minimised.

The EYFS document gives specific guidelines for adult to child ratios, storage of medicines and how to respond to ACCIDENTS or injuries, all of which are designed to help keep children safe. The setting should have a policy that outlines general safety procedures which you should follow.

When planning learning activities, you should look carefully at a range of issues related to health and safety. See Figure 2.8.

Resources and equipment
a Are they clean and in good condition?
b Are there any sharp edges or broken pieces?
c Do you have enough for the number of children?
d Have electrical items been tested? (You should not bring anything electrical from home to be used in the setting unless it has been tested by a qualified electrician.)

The learning environment
a Will any fire exits be blocked during the activity?
b Will the activity be indoors or outdoors?
c If indoors, is there sufficient space to carry out the activity?
d If outdoors, can the children run off?
e Are there any dangers from plants or animal faeces?

Individual needs

a Will the activity be **ACCESSIBLE** for all children, including those who have special educational needs and disabilities?

b Will everyone be able to carry out the activity safely?

c Do any of the children have **ALLERGIES** that might make the activity unsuitable for them?

Figure 2.8: What hazards can you identify in this picture?

Adapting activities where needed

You should keep an eye on the children to make sure that activities are accessible. You may need to adapt them if they are too difficult or too easy. If so, adults will need to change or modify the activity based on their own observations, or question the children carefully so as to understand what they need to do to improve the activity. Activities may also need to be adapted to help children achieve their targets.

In other cases, children may not understand how to carry out an activity and need adult support to start them off; they may then be able to continue as expected.

Assessment practice 2.7 AO4

Plan and carry out an activity for a group of three children that you know, taking into account:

- the current plans of the setting
- the age and stage of the children
- their developmental needs and interests.

Make sure you list the resources you will need.

Afterwards, make notes on your plan showing what went well and what you think you could have done to improve it. If possible, discuss this activity with your **MENTOR** (someone, ideally an experienced practitioner, who can guide and advise you).

C3 Different types of activities

Each setting will have areas set aside for different types of activity to help the children find them more easily. The layout of the setting may dictate how activities are set out, for example the sink is likely to be near the creative or messy area. The role-play area should not be too close to the area set aside for quiet reading.

Link it up

For Unit 7, B1 you will also need to reflect on what you know about child development to help support children's play and communication activities.

Link it up

Unit 7, B1 requires you to reflect on how you support and maintain the physical environment to help stimulate learning through play.

You will need to know how to plan play and learning activities that support children's progress in all areas of development. Your planning should reflect this by showing how it covers all the areas of learning and development (see Figure 2.9). Young children will need to experience and practise activities regularly to support their development, so planning does not always need to include details about how progress will take place.

Remember that any of the following activities can take place indoors or outdoors.

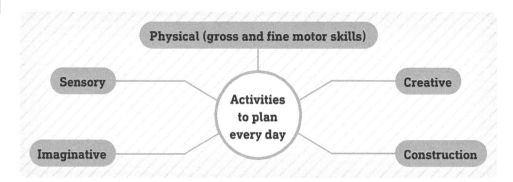

Figure 2.9: Activities to plan every day

Table 2.17 shows the range of activities that you should plan to include in the setting on any one day. Most of these activities can and should be carried out both indoors and outdoors.

Table 2.17: Range of daily activities

Activity type	Examples	How the activity supports development
Creative	• Cutting and sticking • Painting and drawing • Making things with junk materials	Allows children to develop their creativity and represent their own ideas through using their imagination
Construction	• Anything children can build with, such as blocks that link together • Large and small bricks or boxes	Supports the development of fine motor skills by linking and separating smaller items; encourages creativity and social skills through working together
Imaginative	• Role-play or home-corner activities • Small-world play • Play with small toy animals or puppets	Supports communication and language and co-operation as well as developing imagination
Sensory	• These should include 'messy' play so that children can get their hands dirty • Activities that involve exploring different textures and materials	Encourages children to talk about the sensations they are experiencing – which helps develop their language and communication skills
Physical (gross motor skills)	• Running around • Ride-on bikes and toys • Skipping and jumping • Throwing and catching	Running, skipping and jumping support the development of muscular control, balance and co-ordination Throwing and catching develop strength in the upper arm and shoulder, which will also help with children's pencil control when learning to write
Physical (fine motor skills)	• Modelling clay • Building bricks • Drawing and mark-making • Colouring • Using scissors	These activities will strengthen the development of muscles in children's hands, which will also help them when learning to write

Assessment practice 2.8   A01 A02

Take a walk around your setting and look at the variety of activities that are available to children at any one time. Do the activities cover each area of learning and development or are any missing? Is this a typical example of what is available in any given week?

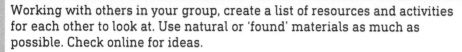

C4 Resources that support development

Your setting will have a wide range of resources available to support children's development. As an early years worker you should always be on the lookout for different items that can be used in your setting. Items from each of the following headings should always be available for children to use when they are choosing their own activity. Charity shops often have useful resources and children can also adapt everyday items for a different purpose.

Practise

Working with others in your group, create a list of resources and activities for each other to look at. Use natural or 'found' materials as much as possible. Check online for ideas.

- Bring your list to your class and ask the others to work out what age these activities or resources may be suitable for and say why. Be ready with your own answer too.

The section below gives examples of different types of resources that support children's development.

Sensory materials

These include resources that stimulate the senses – items that children will enjoy touching, smelling, looking at or listening to. This may include activities in sand and water. Using these resources will encourage discussion about what the materials feel like. If children are looking at the topic of growing, you might fill a builder's tray with soil and old flowerpots, and add laminated flowers and labels so they can create their own planters. Be prepared for this kind of activity to be messy.

Children should have opportunities to explore sensory activities, such as playing with sand, to stimulate their senses as well as developing communication and language skills

Natural materials

Settings are encouraged to use natural materials where possible as these will stimulate children's senses. **HEURISTIC PLAY** (in other words, where children explore and discover for themselves) is often used with babies from 12 months onwards.

A treasure basket can be used for this. It can be filled with natural materials and day-to-day items for the children to look at. It is ideal for developing concentration in younger children. It puts the child in control of the activity, with the freedom to choose items that interest them so there is no right or wrong way of using the materials – the results are therefore always successful. This is not always the case with shop-bought toys, where the result of their use will usually be known. With older children, natural materials to play with and explore can be more popular than traditional 'toys' and encourage them to use their imagination.

If you use a treasure basket, make sure that all the items are clean and safe for babies to use and explore, and add to and remove items from it on a regular basis to ensure they continue to engage the children's interest. The kinds of item you might use include: corks, tins, cardboard tubes, wooden spoons and pans, sponges, large chestnuts, shells, pine cones, ribbons, wooden off-cuts.

Objects made of natural materials can be used in a treasure basket to stimulate the child's imagination and senses

Drawing, painting and writing materials

These will include any object that can be used for drawing, painting or writing. Variety can be provided by encouraging children to use the same actions but with different resources. Instead of just a pencil or paintbrush, children might use a stick in a tray of sand, for example, or water on an area of dry paving. Look out for the different items your setting uses to encourage children to draw and write.

Small-world toys

These include toys that depict an everyday situation, for example, using small play people and building or interlocking bricks. These will support the child's imagination as well as their communication and language skills, and allow them to act out different aspects of their own experience.

Books and written materials

Books and written materials should always be available and on view to children. These can include common printed materials in the learning environment, as well as items in the role-play area such as price lists, menus or opening and closing times. Remember that written materials can be outdoors as well as indoors.

Link it up

Go to Unit 4, B3 for more about safely setting up resources and equipment for different activities.

Resources and equipment for outdoor play

These large items will usually be stored outside in a shed or cupboard so that adults and children can get them out when needed. They do not need to be expensive and can be sourced from a variety of places.

Look out for resources from builders' yards, such as large blocks of wood, making sure they are safe for children, and ask for offcuts of carpet from carpet stores. Children can then sit down and create a quiet area. You could use old tyres and sawdust for small-world play with animals or a mini-beast garden and so on. They may also be left outside on a permanent basis.

Children should be encouraged to use different objects to make marks

Adults can work with children to create cheap resources that are fun to use

Resources for role play and imaginative play

These resources should be changed regularly and can be related to the topic the children are exploring. For example, if they are looking at pets, you may decide to make the home corner into a vet's surgery; if they are exploring growing, it may be a garden centre.

Playing shops is a popular role-play activity

Assessment practice 2.9   AO4

Carry out an indoor and outdoor resources check in your setting. Look at what is available for different age groups. How are resources stored and labelled so that they are easy for children and adults to find? Are there any health and safety issues related to the storage of resources and equipment?

Specific resources to meet individual needs

If you have a child who has specific needs within your setting, they may have their own resources. These may have been suggested by other professionals who work with them, or may have been provided within the setting to support them with their learning. Depending on the needs of the child, resources may include items such as a visual timetable for a child who has social and communication needs, or large print for a visually impaired child.

What if...?

You have been asked to work with Sonya, a 4-year-old autistic child who has a visual timetable. Although her key person is supposed to change it each day, she regularly forgets because she has so much to do, and Sonya can easily become distressed when she doesn't know what is happening.

1 What could you do in this situation?

2 How might this also support Sonya's key person?

Skills and knowledge check

☐ I can support children's development through play activities.

☐ I can plan activities to support children's developmental progress.

☐ I can adapt activities to meet individual needs.

☐ I can use SMART targets.

○ I can name three health and safety issues that should be considered when planning activities.

○ I can name two activities that support children's fine motor skills and two that support their gross motor skills.

○ I can name the four principles of the EYFS.

○ I know how the planning cycle works.

WORK FOCUS

HANDS ON

Working as an early years assistant involves a particular range of skills, many of which relate to this unit. Follow these tips to help you practise!

1 Work as part of a team

- You need to be able to work with others when planning to support children's growth, learning and development. Make sure you use any opportunity you can to work with colleagues in your work placement setting, and keep notes of how you have done this.

- Think about your communication skills and how you interact with others. Remember to be positive, polite and professional by smiling, following instructions and responding to advice and guidance from others in the team.

2 Observe children during learning activities

- Use observations to assess a child's stage of development and plan for follow-up activities. Remember, an observation does not need to be long. One or two minutes may be enough for you to gain the information you need.

- Look at the suggested observation write-up in your work placement booklet to guide you through the process and complete an observation.

3 Be able to work with parents

- You should build good relationships with parents so that you can support children's development more effectively. Make a note of the ways in which you interact with parents and how often you do this.

- Look for ways in which your setting encourages parents to communicate with them and develop positive relationships.

Ready for work?

Answer the questions below to find out if you've got what it takes to be a great early years assistant. Some questions have more than one correct answer, so tick all that apply.

1 When working in an early years setting, which of the following should you do?

☐ A Always work closely with others and share information.

☐ B Talk to parents as much as possible.

☐ C Do your own thing.

☐ D Keep out of others' way.

2 Which of the following should you do when planning activities?

☐ A Plan the kinds of things you enjoy.

☐ B Plan the kinds of things the children enjoy.

☐ C Change the activities when you feel like it.

☐ D Make sure all areas of learning and development are included.

3 When you are preparing learning activities, which of these will support children's development?

☐ A Most activities will be okay.

☐ B A mixture of creative, imaginative, physical, sensory and construction activities would be ideal.

☐ C Choose activities that the children enjoy and use.

☐ D Focus on allowing the children to use their imagination.

4 How would you support a child who has atypical development and is not reaching their developmental milestones?

☐ A Talk to their key person and find out more about them.

☐ B Observe them over time and gather information about different areas of their development.

☐ C Make sure they are okay by having a chat with them.

☐ D Speak to others in the setting about putting a plan together.

If you have scored 12 or less, you need to go over the requirements for this unit. Make sure you have understood each of the areas of development and how they relate to the areas of learning in the EYFS.

Answers: 1 A/B=5, C/D=2; 2 A/C=2, B/D=5; 3 A/ D=2, B/C=5; 4 A/B/D=5, C=2

Getting ready for assessment

For this unit you will need to complete a test to show that you can apply the knowledge you have gained about child development to a scenario about a child.

About the test

You will have a task booklet, an answer booklet in which to write your responses to the test activities and an information booklet containing a Development Chart. You will answer the questions in supervised exam conditions. The task will have an 'Instructions for learners' section at the beginning which you should read through carefully as it contains all the information you will need to complete each activity.

Planning your time

Give yourself time to read through the questions slowly and think about what you need to say. Look at the marks that have been allocated to each section as a guide to how much you time you should spend on each.

How much you should write

The answer booklet should guide you as to how much to write as well as the marks that are available for each answer. If the question asks for two points of information, make sure you give two.

Do not try to fill every line if you have written all you need to say, but make sure you have covered everything that has been asked. Try not to write long sentences, which can sound muddled to someone reading your work.

Reading and checking your answers

Always read through and check your answers when you have finished. Ensure they make sense and relate directly to the questions you have been asked. Ensure you have covered every part of the question with your answer.

Understanding the questions

You will have several questions to answer about one workplace scenario. There will be a main paragraph that introduces the scenario.

You should look at key words in the questions to help you answer them. You may find some of the words below. It's important to be clear exactly what they mean, so try to memorise them before the test.

- **ACTIVITY PLAN** – a structured breakdown of the planned activity.
- **AREAS OF DEVELOPMENT** – physical, cognitive, language, emotional and social.
- **FACTORS** – things that influence development.
- **GOALS** – the developmental milestones that children are working towards.
- **RESOURCES** – materials, equipment or persons that support play and learning activities.

Sample questions and answers

This section gives you the set task information followed by a series of questions. It includes sample answers.

Set task information

You are an early years assistant working at Little Fishes Nursery. The manager of the setting has asked you to work with the key person to support Oliver's progress. Oliver is 3 years old and has attended Little Fishes for four months.

The key person has completed a Key Person Assessment to help adults in the setting support Oliver's development.

Child: Oliver Mackenzie	Age: 3 years 2 months
Family	**Skills and abilities**
• Oliver lives with his parents. He has no brothers or sisters • His father works as an IT consultant for a small firm in a nearby town • His mother is a receptionist at the local doctor's surgery	• Oliver was a very premature baby and this has affected some areas of his development. He has a hearing impairment and wears a hearing aid in one ear • He likes to play with the small-world toys and prefers to stay indoors. He is not confident when running and prefers to be near an adult when on bikes and scooters – he needs encouragement to use them • Oliver also plays with construction toys but has trouble with fixing them together as his fine motor skills are poor • Oliver is happy and confident in himself and enjoys interacting with other children verbally. His speech is clear although he can be very loud and interrupt others, especially if his hearing aid is not at the correct setting • He likes playing with and alongside other children and has lots of friends in the nursery • Oliver has difficulty using a spoon to feed himself and holding a pencil because of his poor fine motor skills
Home environment	**Other information**
• The family lives close to the nursery and Oliver walks there each day • They live in a ground-floor flat which has a large shared garden	• When Oliver was born he was eight weeks premature and had to spend a month in hospital • Oliver's mum has some health issues which mean that she sometimes struggles to be at the setting on time and is often late to collect him. He does not find separation from his mother difficult • Oliver has support from a physiotherapist and has exercises to do at home

Question 1

This type of question is to assess your understanding of the stage of development that is expected at Oliver's age and to think about whether he has reached the expected milestones. Remember to look carefully at the Key Person Assessment and at the Development Chart provided in the booklet.

Oliver's key person has asked you to look at his physical development against the expected milestones for his age. Use the Development Chart and Oliver's Key Person Assessment.

Your response should:

- identify the physical milestones for a child aged 3 years 2 months
- identify Oliver's current stage of physical development
- explain whether Oliver's physical development is normal and what factors if any may have impacted on it. (6 marks)

Sample answer

I think that Oliver is not at the expected physical milestones for his age. Children who are his age will usually be able to feed themselves with a spoon and also be able to run and ride a tricycle with confidence.

I think that Oliver's current stage of physical development is around 18 months to 2 years.

This is not normal for his age and I think that his development may have been affected because he was born early. Also he does not like to run around and this might stop his muscles from getting stronger.

Verdict

The first paragraph could be improved by identifying further physical milestones in relation to Oliver's development. The second paragraph could have been improved if the learner had gone on to say why they think Oliver's current stage of development is 18 months to 2 years.

Question 2

The key person has asked you to investigate the factors that may impact on Oliver's physical and social development in a positive or negative way.

Your investigation should:

- identify the factors from the Key Person Assessment report
- explain how these factors may affect Oliver's physical and social development
- suggest some targets to support Oliver's physical and social development. (14 marks)

Sample answer 1

Oliver was premature and only lives with his mum and dad and this will affect his development because he will be slower to develop than other children in all areas. He will need to work on his physical skills by practising them outside every day and his social skills by making sure he doesn't interrupt others.

Sample answer 2

Factors which may impact on Oliver's physical and social development:

- At Oliver's age of 3 years 2 months, he should be beyond the physical and social development stages which are outlined in the Key Person Assessment report.

- Physical: According to the Key Person Assessment, Oliver is 'not confident when running and prefers to be near an adult when on bikes and scooters and he needs encouragement to use them'. This shows that he lacks confidence, possibly due to immaturity and lack of strength in his muscles due to his premature birth. He also has difficulty feeding himself with a spoon and holding a pencil as well as using construction toys as his 'fine motor skills are poor'.

- Social: Oliver enjoys mixing with other children and has lots of friends in the nursery. This is consistent with a child of his age. However, his speech can be very loud and he has a tendency to interrupt other children and finds it hard to wait. This may be because he cannot always hear them or because his hearing aid is not set correctly. Although at the moment this is not too much of a problem, it may well impact on his social circle as he grows older.

To support Oliver's physical and social development:

- Liaise with physiotherapist and Oliver's parents to create a manageable programme which will improve his physical strength.

- Talk to others in the setting about how to help him to learn to wait and start to take turns.

Suggested targets:

- To be able to use a scooter confidently. Strategy – practise using a scooter for two minutes each day with early years assistant at nursery and Mum or Dad at home or on the way to nursery. Gradually build up distance from adult.

- To be able to build a tower of ten building blocks. Strategy – use play-dough and finger exercises to strengthen hand muscles each day.

- To be able to play a game without interrupting others. Strategy – to work with early years assistant and one other child on a simple game when time allows, and ensure that Oliver's hearing aid is set correctly.

Targets to be reviewed after six weeks.

Verdict 1

This answer should be more detailed. The learner needs to look carefully at the question and the marks that go towards it; they want as many marks as possible. It will help the learner to go through each point on the Key Person Assessment and look at it against child development expected milestones and factors that affect development. The learner should make sure that any targets included are SMART.

Verdict 2

This answer is better. The learner has included how different factors may have impacted on Oliver's physical and social development, although they have only mentioned the negative effects, not any positive ones. However, the learner has shown that they can use the information in the Key Person Assessment to develop targets for Oliver. These are SMART, include strategies that might be used to achieve them and provide a date for review.

3 Developing Professional Practice Skills for Work in Early Years Settings

How do you feel when you meet someone in a work situation who doesn't act or present themselves well? Does it give you confidence that they can do their job properly?

In this unit, you will learn about the importance of behaving professionally, being organised and having good timekeeping skills. As an early years assistant, you also need to show effective communication and personal skills when interacting with colleagues and visitors in a range of different situations.

Being able to provide a consistently high standard of support to your team during daily routines is an essential skill that you will need to develop in your role as an early years assistant.

How will I be assessed?

This is an internally assessed unit, which means that you will need to carry out a series of tasks, some of which will be assessed in the workplace. You should record your work-based activities in your Placement Experience Assessment Portfolio of Evidence. This will also help you to gather evidence for Unit 7.

For this unit you will be required to submit evidence of your understanding of:

- professional behaviours in an early years setting, including standards of conduct and positive organisation and timekeeping skills
- effective communication in an early years setting, including communicating with colleagues and visitors
- support for daily practices in an early years setting, including supporting colleagues to meet the needs of children and contributing to record keeping.

You will need to provide evidence that you have completed the activities successfully, which might include:

- records of your timekeeping and organisation skills, including signed timesheets, witness statements, training certificates, and reflective accounts of IT and administration skills
- records of activities completed to support other colleagues (diary accounts or work schedules), as well as witness statements from qualified practitioners about your practice when supporting daily routines
- observation records, signed by your manager/supervisor of your communication with adults working in the setting and with visitors.

Assessment criteria

Pass	Merit	Distinction
Learning aim A: Demonstrate the professional behaviours required in an early years setting		
A.P1 Demonstrate professional conduct, organisation and timekeeping skills that meet needs in an early years setting.	**A.M1** Demonstrate a consistently good standard of professional conduct, organisation and timekeeping skills that meet needs in an early years setting.	**A.D1** Demonstrate a consistently high standard of professional conduct, organisation and timekeeping skills that meet a range of needs in an early years setting.
Learning aim B: Communicate effectively with colleagues and visitors in early years settings		
B.P2 Apply appropriate communication skills when working with practitioners in an early years setting.	**B.M2** Apply a range of appropriate communication and interpersonal skills when working with practitioners and different types of visitors accessing an early years setting.	**B.D2** Apply a range of effective communication and interpersonal skills consistently in different contexts when working with practitioners and different types of visitors accessing an early years setting.
B.P3 Apply appropriate interpersonal skills when interacting with visitors accessing an early years setting.		
Learning aim C: Support daily practice in early years settings		
C.P4 Provide a standard of support to a practitioner performing daily routines in an early years setting.	**C.M3** Provide a consistently good standard of support to practitioners during daily routines in an early years setting.	**C.D3** Provide a consistently high standard of support to practitioners during daily routines in an early years setting.

A Demonstrate the professional behaviours required in an early years setting

A1 Developing professional standards of conduct

It is important that you present yourself and act in a professional manner when working in early years settings.

How does the way you present yourself reflect a professional image?

Young children love to explore our faces. They may pull on nose rings, lip piercings, necklaces and hooped earrings, so you should avoid wearing these

Personal presentation

Parents are leaving children in your care; first impressions count. If you look untidy or have poor personal hygiene, this does not show you or your setting in a good light.

Be aware of and follow your setting's dress code. Some settings do not allow facial piercings, visible tattoos, brightly coloured hair, trainers or jeans. Other settings have a more relaxed approach. Check with your supervisor if you are unsure.

Clothing

You should choose clothes that follow your setting's dress code. Bear in mind the following points.

- Your clothes should be clean and in a good condition.
- Your clothes should be comfortable; tight clothing may restrict you.
- You should wear flat shoes suitable for indoors and outdoors; some settings may require two pairs, one for indoors and one for outdoors.
- Remember to dress modestly; choose clothing that looks professional yet is practical.
- If you are provided with a uniform, make sure it is clean every day for work.
- If you are given a name badge or lanyard, make sure you wear it.

Safety

You should also consider safety when dressing for work.

- Do not wear jewellery that could scratch a child, or any jewellery that could fall off – a child might pick it up. Imagine having to explain to your supervisor that a baby has just swallowed your earring!
- Tie back long hair for hygiene purposes, particularly when handling food.
- Keep nails clean and short (no false nails) so you do not accidentally scratch a child. You cannot perform emergency first aid effectively with long nails.

Adopting a positive approach to work

It is not just your appearance that reflects professionalism, it is also the way you behave at work. Table 3.1 offers some ways you can show a positive approach.

Approach	Examples of behaviour
Have a professional attitude	Have a positive outlook and follow your setting's **CODE OF CONDUCT**, which sets out the way you should behave
Be enthusiastic	Be eager to join in at all times and show passion for your work. Don't sit around looking bored; be **PROACTIVE** and show you are interested in your role
Be trustworthy	Being reliable, dependable and honest will show that you can be trusted. Respect **CONFIDENTIALITY** (only sharing personal information you learn about children in your setting with other professionals)
Be diplomatic	Handle any difficult situations with tact and discretion, following your setting's policies. Be polite and think before you speak. Remember to seek advice in challenging circumstances
Show your caring nature	Treat others in your setting with kindness and concern. Respect and value their opinions and suggestions
Show commitment	Show you are keen to help and be part of the team by fulfilling all tasks to the best of your ability
Be flexible/adaptable	Be able to adapt yourself to changing situations and environments. Children are unpredictable, so early years assistants need to be able to think on their feet and work flexibly when things don't go as planned You should also welcome new and diverse tasks. Accepting and accomplishing out-of-the-ordinary jobs will broaden your experience, and your supervisors will recognise that you are a person to whom they can turn for support

Table 3.1: You can show a positive approach to work through your behaviour

The benefits of a professional standard of conduct

When everyone follows the same professional standards in the workplace, the whole setting benefits, including the children and families you work with. Importantly, you will also gain as an individual. Here are some examples of the main benefits.

Good relationships

A positive approach and professional attitude to work are beneficial to everyone. They show your supervisor that you are committed to your role and they support the smooth running of the team. You will find it is easier working with positive and professional colleagues. Aim to be that person; staff members, visitors and parents will all appreciate the effort.

Opportunities for your own development

Many early years practitioners start their careers by being offered employment following a successful learner placement. If you behave professionally, this is more likely to happen. Once you are in employment, you will be able to access further training and development. Imagine you are a nursery manager. You have just enough funds to send one new assistant on an interesting course. Would you stretch the budget for an assistant who is often late and complains about doing daily routine jobs?

Positive environments

When staff work well together and have good relationships, it creates a positive atmosphere and enjoyable experience in the workplace for both children and staff. This leads to an early years environment in which children can develop and learn effectively.

The impact of inappropriate conduct

You have explored the benefits of looking the part and behaving professionally. Now consider the impact on your setting, the children and you if your conduct is poor.

What if...?

Gabby is an early years assistant on placement at Angels Nursery.

Her supervisor asks her to go out and make the daily **RISK ASSESSMENT** on the outside play area.

Gabby has a quick look around outside then hides behind the garden shed to have a cigarette. She comes back inside and tells the supervisor it is safe for the children to go out now. Gabby hasn't noticed that the sandpit lid was left off overnight and the pit is now full of rainwater.

A parent comes to collect her child at home time and tells the supervisor she saw a member of staff smoking behind the shed.

- How has Gabby broken **STATUTORY** requirements (those that are laid down by law)?

- Why might it not be safe for the children to go outside?

- How might Gabby's conduct affect the reputation of the nursery?

- What might the parent do next?

- What do you think might happen to Gabby?

Practise

Now reflect on your own professional practice. Give an example from your own experience of when you have:

- contributed to the effectiveness of the team

- worked responsibly and reliably as a team member

- communicated effectively with the other staff members

- been respectful and considerate to colleagues

- fallen short of what is expected of you, even if it was a little thing. Did your supervisors notice it? If so, what happened? If they did not, what do you think would have happened if they had?

A2 Developing positive organisation and timekeeping skills in early years settings

Time management and organisation skills are central to succeeding in any role, but especially in a busy early years setting. Routines are important to young children and cannot be maintained without a firm grasp of these skills.

Strategies to plan time and manage workload effectively

Some people are naturally organised. Are you? Here are some strategies that will help you develop time management skills.

Create your own personal weekly schedule

Display a timetable in your bedroom or use technology such as your smartphone to record your schedule. This will help you be aware of the days and times you need to be in college or at your placement. See Figure 3.1 for an example.

Monday	Tuesday	Wednesday	Thursday	Friday
College			Placement	
9.00 Tutorial Room 601	9.00 Private Study Room 603	9.00 Childhood Studies Room 600	9.00 Baby Unit	9.00 Baby Unit
10.45 Break	10.45 Break	10.45 Break	10.40 Break	10.40 Break
11.00 Childhood Studies Room 600	11.00 Childhood Studies Room 600	11.00 Childhood Studies Room 600	11.00 Baby Unit	11.00 Baby Unit
12.30 Lunch	12.30 Lunch	12.30 Lunch	12.30 Lunch	12.30 Lunch
13.30 Childhood Studies Room 600	13.30 Paediatric First Aid Room 419	13.30 Private Study Room 603	13.15 Toddler Room	13.15 Toddler Room
15.45 Home	16.00 Home	15.45 Home	16.15 Home	16.15 Home

Figure 3.1: Example of a learner's schedule or timetable

Set SMART targets

Setting SMART targets can help you to achieve a goal. Table 3.2 shows you what the letters in SMART stand for. It suggests some questions to ask yourself when setting targets and gives an example of an early years assistant using SMART targets to help improve their timekeeping skills.

Table 3.2: SMART targets in practice

SMART	Question to ask yourself	I will improve my timekeeping skills
Specific	Are you clear what you want to achieve?	I want to arrive on time to my placement
Measurable	Can you track progress and achievement?	I can track my timekeeping on my timesheets
Appropriate	Is this a suitable target for you?	This is a suitable target as I am sometimes late and I need to be on time to work in an early years setting
Realistic	Is this target achievable for you?	It is a realistic target as I can use the alarm on my phone to wake me up and I can get the earlier bus
Time-bound	By what date would you like to achieve your target?	I would like to have been on time every day by the end of the term

Practise

Create your own SMART target for a personal goal you would like to achieve in your placement.

- Set your target now, with a definite end date (for example, the end of this month or term).
- Review your target regularly. Are you on track?
- At the end of the set time, revisit your SMART target. Did you achieve your personal goal?

If you know you struggle to get up in the morning, plan to have an early night

Set alarms

If you struggle to get up in the morning, use an alarm clock or set an alarm on your mobile phone – or both. It can be helpful to position the alarm out of reach so you have to sit up or get out of bed to turn it off. If you wear a watch, you can also make good use of an alarm on this device throughout the day to remind you to do set tasks.

Use a diary

Diaries can be used to write down appointments, such as a review with your tutor at college or a meeting with your placement supervisor. They are also useful later as a reminder of what you have done or accomplished, particularly if you use them to make little notes on your day. For example, you might record the day you first carried out a particular task on your own or the day one of the parents complimented you on the positive effect you had on their child's acceptance of new foods.

You can use a paper diary or make use of electronic diaries on your mobile phone/laptop. IT can be very useful to support effective timekeeping.

Plan for unexpected delays

Some delays are unavoidable – for example, if your car or the bus breaks down. However, you should try to allow yourself plenty of time for journeys and plan for unexpected delays. Don't cut it fine. If you catch an earlier bus, you might arrive early, but then you could enjoy a quiet moment before the busy day begins, perhaps using it to update your diary or make a round of tea.

Know your timetable

It can be hard to juggle competing demands on your time. You have to be at college some days, at your placement on other days, and in between you need to fit in reading those policies your supervisor gave you. You should familiarise yourself with your college timetable and your required work hours in placement.

Make sure you follow your timetable and check the key points the night before.

a Where do I need to be tomorrow?

b What time do I need to arrive?

c How much time do I need to allow for travelling?

d Do I have any college work deadlines to meet?

e Are there any changes to my usual day – for example a team meeting after work?

Expected conduct

CONDUCT is the way you behave. As an early years assistant, you should be clear about how to act in your setting and school or college.

You should be familiar with and follow set procedures to show you are professional and organised.

- Attend your placement consistently. If you are ill, let your setting or college know as early as possible. This is of particular importance for the setting, which may need to make arrangements to cover for you.
- Sign in and out every day in placement; make sure your supervisor signs your timesheets. Chasing people to complete paperwork is a distraction they do not need. If your position is paid, then incomplete timesheets may delay your pay or result in you getting less than you should.
- Attend registration at college. An incomplete or poor attendance record may affect the grade you achieve.
- Seek permission before using evidence from your placement. Most placements will be supportive; they will often know the requirements of your course. However, confidentiality needs to be respected and your supervisor will be responsible for ensuring this. They may ask you not to use certain things or to anonymise material.
- Follow procedures to keep the environment safe and secure.
- Follow emergency procedures.

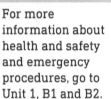

Link it up

For more information about health and safety and emergency procedures, go to Unit 1, B1 and B2.

Accessing support

If you're struggling in placement or at college, don't keep your problems to yourself – ask for help.

In your setting, your supervisor or MENTOR is there to support you. If you are worried about how to do a task or how to respond in different situations, seek advice.

Likewise, at college, if you are having difficulties understanding or completing parts of your course, then talk to a member of staff.

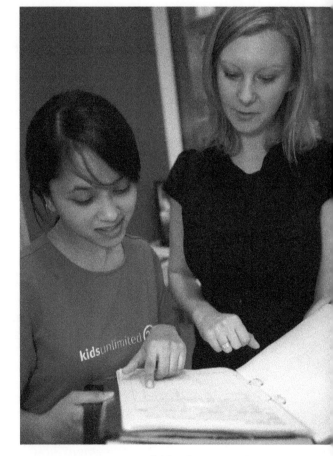

Asking for support is not a sign of weakness; it shows that you care about doing a good job

Following rules

All through life there are rules we have to follow – at home, at school, at college, in placement and at work. Familiarise yourself with your setting's policies and procedures, and follow your college's rules.

There will be clear guidelines on the use of personal items such as mobile phones and on health and safety issues such as hot drinks.

Find out about your own setting's mobile-phone policy

Mobile phones

Most settings do not allow the use of mobile phones for safeguarding reasons. Find out where you should keep your mobile if you need to take it with you.

At college, be aware that mobile phones may distract you and others while you are learning. Make sure you follow the college's policy for use of mobile phones and the internet.

Personal items

In placement, ask where you should store your belongings – for example, your bag or lunch box. It isn't safe to leave your bag lying around; it can be especially dangerous if it contains items such as painkillers or nail varnish.

Smoking

It is illegal to smoke on the premises, both at placement and in college. Do you think it is suitable to keep cigarettes in your bag while on placement? What might your supervisor say if you attend your placement smelling of cigarettes?

Hot drinks

Hot drinks are hazardous to children. Find out where you are allowed to have a hot drink while on placement, or use a special lidded cup if your setting allows.

Dietary requirements

Your placement or college may have guidelines on foods that you cannot bring onto the premises. This is to prevent the possibility of an allergic reaction, for example an allergy to peanuts.

Demonstrating additional personal organisation and timekeeping skills

You should be organised, have good timekeeping skills and show professional conduct throughout your time in the setting. Here are some tips to help you shine in the workplace and at college.

Be on time

Look back through this unit for strategies for good time management.

Make sure you let your placement and college know if you are running late or will be absent due to illness. Follow your own setting's procedures for reporting in.

Attend training

Training is a fantastic way to develop your knowledge and skills, so take advantage of all the training offered. This shows you are motivated and eager to enhance your practice.

Some training is **MANDATORY**, meaning you have to do it. Your placement induction will give you essential knowledge on issues such as safeguarding children and health and safety procedures.

Get to know your setting

Take time to familiarise yourself with the routine and layout of your setting. Make sure you know where the key areas such as fire exits, toilets and staffroom are located. Be clear about the days you should attend the placement, your hours of work, and times of lunchbreaks. Follow your setting's daily plans for play, activities and care routines.

Meet targets and deadlines

Organisation is key to meeting targets and getting things done on time. It can be useful to make a list of all the tasks you have to do and put them in order of importance or urgency.

You can write your list on a piece of paper, in a notepad, on a spreadsheet or using an app on your phone. Your list will help you to prioritise things that need to be done to meet a given deadline.

Practise

It is the last week of term. The party on Friday will be the last day for 16 children leaving to go to school.

You have been asked by different members of staff to complete certain jobs over the week:

- to wrap a present for each child to take home on Friday
- to sort through the jigsaw puzzles, ready for the new children starting next term
- to help paint a banner to display at the party.

Put the jobs in the order you think they should be done to meet the deadlines.

Demonstrating care of children

Caring for children involves more than just supervising and ensuring safety. An attentive early years assistant will be organised and put careful thought into the way they care for children.

Make sure you follow instructions from other staff members. You should show you are thorough by following your setting's procedures and taking direction from your colleagues.

Show a flexible approach

A day in an early years setting can be busy and chaotic, and things do not always go as expected. You need to be flexible and be able to adapt the way you work when the need arises. Do not be afraid to be creative and suggest your own ideas. Life can be boring when we do the same things the same way, day in, day out. Keep an open mind and be open to change.

What if...?

Jacob is an early years assistant on placement at Watford Day Nursery. His supervisor has told him it is his job to go into the kitchen at 9.20 a.m. every day to wash the fruit, ready for snack time. The setting offers fruit every day to promote healthy eating.

Jacob is very thorough and knows it is important to follow his supervisor's instructions.

Think about the following scenarios.

- It has started to snow. A member of staff asks Jacob to leave the fruit and come and help the children get their wellies on for outside play.

- The children are celebrating the Muslim festival of Eid. A staff member has made some traditional food for the children to share at snack time, and tells Jacob not to bother with the fruit.

- It is 9.20 a.m. and Jacob is sharing a story with a child who is just settling in. Jacob gets up to go to the kitchen, and the child starts to cry.

Will Jacob be in trouble for not following his usual routine in each of these scenarios?

How can having a flexible approach support the team and enhance the children's experiences?

Using your initiative

Using your **INITIATIVE** means doing things without waiting to be asked and helping with things that are within your role. Being proactive can be extremely helpful to the team, taking the pressure off your colleagues in busy situations.

Remember to offer to help whenever you can. Check either that it is within your role to take on certain tasks or that your supervisor is happy for you to step beyond your normal responsibilities.

Practise

Look at the following examples of Syma, an early years assistant, using her initiative.

- A child spills their drink so Syma gets the mop to dry the floor.
- At circle time, one child is running around the setting. Syma leaves the display she is putting up and encourages the child to sit down next to her with the group.
- Syma notices that a child's name is spelt wrongly on their drawer; she points this out to a colleague and offers to make a new label.

List three examples of times when you have used your initiative to support your team.

Supporting colleagues to promote positive teamwork

By using your initiative and showing positive organisation skills, you are helping to promote positive teamwork. Further on in this unit there are lots of examples about contributing to the smooth running of the team.

Recognising the impact of poor attendance, timekeeping and organisation

When a member of the team is regularly off work, late or disorganised, this can have a negative impact in many ways, as shown in Figure 3.2.

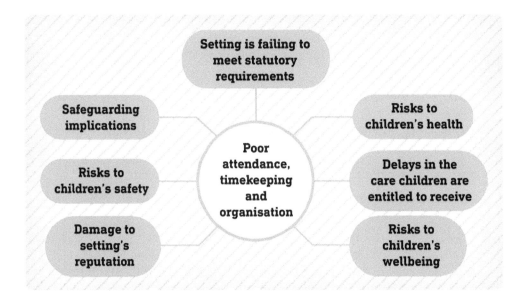

Figure 3.2: The negative impact of poor attendance, timekeeping and organisation

What if...?

Liza is an experienced nursery assistant at Meadows Nursery. She is studying hard outside her nursery shifts to gain a higher childcare qualification. Recently, Liza has been arriving late for work and seems tired and disorganised.

On Friday, Liza was 20 minutes late for her shift, which left the nursery short-staffed.

The children were learning about Diwali and were looking forward to a cookery session making Diwali sweets. Liza had volunteered to collect the ingredients for the cookery activity on her way to work, but she forgot.

At home time, Liza heard one parent commenting that the nursery did not always meet staff to child ratios, and about how disorganised things were lately.

- What impact did Liza's lateness have on the setting's statutory requirement to meet staff to child ratios?
- What are the risks to children's health, safety and wellbeing if ratios are not correct?
- How do you think the children felt when Liza forgot the cookery ingredients?
- What impact could Liza's conduct have on the nursery's reputation?
- What do you think might happen to Liza?

Skills and knowledge check

☐ I can set SMART targets.

☐ I am confident enough to ask for help if I am having difficulties completing a task.

☐ I can work flexibly, adapting my behaviour to meet the needs of the setting.

☐ I am a positive and proactive member of the team.

○ I know the importance of dressing appropriately for work.

○ I understand the benefits of being professional.

○ I know the rules for conduct in my setting and at college.

○ I understand why it is important to be organised and on time.

B Communicate effectively with colleagues and visitors in early years settings

B1 Communicating with colleagues working in early years settings

Throughout your placement, you will need to show that you can communicate appropriately and effectively with your colleagues. You should understand why this is important in early years settings.

Who will you be working with?

Most early years settings have a staff team that includes people with different roles and responsibilities. Every person is a valued member of the staff team. Look at Table 3.3 and think about how many people work or volunteer at your setting and the different roles they play.

Table 3.3: The different roles of the staff team in an early years setting

Job title	Role
Early years assistants	Supporting the team and children while undertaking a childcare qualification
Early years educators	Staff with **KEY PERSON** responsibilities who plan and carry out activities in line with the **EARLY YEARS FOUNDATION STAGE (EYFS)**
Advanced practitioners	Highly qualified staff who may have additional leadership responsibilities
Managers/ supervisors	The people 'in charge', who supervise and support the smooth running of the setting
Other learners on placement	Contributing to the setting while on placement, usually not counted in ratios
Support staff	Additional staff to support the smooth running of the setting

Communicating effectively with your supervisor

If you have a meeting or review with your supervisor or mentor, preparation is key. Try:

- making notes of any key points you want to discuss
- writing down a list of questions beforehand to focus the discussion
- listing specific issues that you need to discuss, such as any concerns or questions relating to the children
- thinking carefully about your role and responsibilities and clarifying any queries.

Communicating effectively with colleagues

Successful communication is essential to supporting teamwork, sharing information effectively and preventing misunderstandings.

You can show that you are a good communicator by:

- responding positively to requests from others
- listening and paying attention
- following instructions carefully
- clarifying points if you do not understand
- having a polite approach.

Adapting communication skills

Along with demonstrating effective communication skills, you should be able to adapt the way you interact in different work situations. This promotes good teamwork and positive relationships.

Communication falls broadly into verbal and non-verbal communication.

Your facial expressions and body language can say a thousand words

- **VERBAL COMMUNICATION** – communicating using words. Always speak positively and avoid slang words, swear words and discriminatory or offensive comments. Use language and conversation appropriate to the situation, or use written words via memos or sticky notes if needed. Do not raise your voice, but always talk calmly.
- **NON-VERBAL COMMUNICATION** – your facial expressions, gestures and body language. You should make eye contact with people to show you are listening. Be careful not to roll your eyes or drop your shoulders if asked to complete a boring task.

Consider the following aspects of communication.

- Written communication. It can be useful to write down or email information to someone in your team if you are not able to speak to them immediately, face to face. But be careful not to forget to speak to them too.
- Good listening skills. Listen carefully to others, repeating back key facts to be sure you have understood fully. Listening is not just 'hearing' but taking information on board and responding to it.
- Use of formal (professional) and informal (casual) language. Consider the type of words you use when communicating. You might talk naturally with a fellow learner on placement as you wash the paint pots together, but you will need to talk more professionally to your supervisor.
- Tone of voice. Be conscious that what you say can be interpreted in many ways depending on your tone of voice. Avoid sounding condescending or sarcastic.
- Pace of speech. Be aware that you may need to adapt the speed at which you talk in different situations. Don't talk too quickly as information may be missed, especially if your team member has English as an additional language or a hearing impairment. Also, be conscious that talking too slowly can come across as patronising.

Respecting confidentiality

As an early years assistant you need to be able to keep things confidential in order to work effectively. Your setting will have clear guidelines on confidentiality and information sharing. Information should only be shared on a **NEED-TO-KNOW BASIS**. If you have any concerns about your role, talk to your supervisor.

Link it up

Unit 1, A4 covers maintaining confidentiality to protect children and families, sharing information when required, and the occasions when sharing confidential information is in a child's best interests.

Communicating a child's needs

Your role as an early years assistant is to listen to children and respond to their needs. A child may indicate they need help or support with something that is not within your role. You should pass on this information promptly, clearly and accurately to a member of staff so that the child's needs can be addressed.

Demonstrating a good standard of English

Link it up

Unit 6, B1 covers modelling clear speech and language when communicating with children of different ages.

You should be able to show you can both speak and write using a good standard of English. That way you are acting as a good role model to young children. This is also important to ensure messages are given clearly and to prevent information from being misunderstood.

* When speaking, avoid using slang words that may not be understood.
* When writing, make sure words are spelt correctly, use punctuation as required and ensure that your writing is neat and legible.
* Remember that you can seek help and advice from your college or setting if you need extra support with your own literacy skills.

IT skills

Early years settings make use of IT, including computers and computer programs to record and display many types of information. Your college may be able to offer extra support to help you develop your IT skills. Possessing good IT skills in literacy and numeracy is key to ensuring information looks professional.

* Does your supervisor write the children's register by hand every day, or is it printed out?
* Are your setting's policies handwritten on paper or can they be accessed from a computer?
* Are there words and numbers displayed around your setting? If so, how were they produced?

Practise

Consider the following ways IT can be used in early years settings:

* registers
* policies
* data spreadsheets
* forms (e.g. medication, accident)
* health and safety checklists
* invoices
* websites.

Look around your own setting. Find ten ways IT is used to record or display information.

Why is it important that people working in early years settings have good IT skills in literacy and numeracy?

Following written instructions

Your setting's policies and procedures are written instructions about what you should do and how you should behave in different situations. Throughout this qualification, you have been advised to 'read and follow your own setting's policies and procedures'. Why is it important that you don't misinterpret information you read?

Written instructions in your early years setting could include manuals for putting together new resources, recipe cards for supporting cookery activities, or computer programs. You should:

- take time to read and re-read information
- make sure you understand it fully
- check with a colleague if you are not sure what the instruction means or what a specific word means.

There may be serious consequences if practitioners do not interpret written instructions correctly – for example, a child might be given the wrong dosage of medicine.

Positive communication

Think about the team of staff in your setting; is everyone the same? Your colleagues may have different backgrounds from you, varying levels of ability, expertise and experience, and differing beliefs and views.

It is important to make sure you communicate with everyone in your team with respect and consideration. You can achieve this by:

- being supportive to others in your team, offering help when needed
- showing empathy – trying to put yourself in others' shoes by thinking about how they might be feeling
- being non-judgemental – do not make assumptions about your team members
- respecting other people's opinions and beliefs when they differ from your own
- interacting positively, showing kindness and concern
- following your own setting's diversity and inclusion procedures.

The consequences of inappropriate communication

Think about the negative impact on your setting and the children present if you do not communicate appropriately.

- Your team members may lose respect for you if you talk negatively or communicate in an unsuitable way.
- Your supervisor may not feel you can be trusted if you fail to pass on messages or share confidential information with the wrong people.
- If you shout, swear or talk sarcastically, you are not being a good role model for the children.
- Making discriminatory comments means you are breaking statutory requirements for conduct in early years settings.
- You may face disciplinary proceedings and may even be excluded from your setting.

Practise

Here are examples of an assistant, Donna, communicating at work. For each scenario, tick the most appropriate communication method.

- Donna identifies that one of the children has a soiled nappy.

  ☐ She shouts across the room, 'What a stink! Someone's pooed!'

  ☐ She approaches her colleague, quietly saying, 'I think someone might need a fresh nappy.'

- Donna needs to book time off for a dental appointment. Her supervisor is talking with a parent.

  ☐ She writes a note requesting the time off and leaves it on the supervisor's desk.

  ☐ She interrupts and asks for time off.

B2 Communicating with visitors in early years settings

As an early years assistant you may need to interact with a range of people who visit your setting.

During your time in placement, you may start to recognise regular visitors to the setting and the family members of the children in your care. You may also meet other professionals.

Remember, you must *never* let anyone into your setting if this is not part of your role. Unknown visitors must usually show some form of identification or give a password before they enter.

Recognising and interacting with caregivers

Sometimes you may need to interact with the family members of children who attend your setting. It may be part of your role to let caregivers in or out. See Figure 3.3 for examples of caregivers.

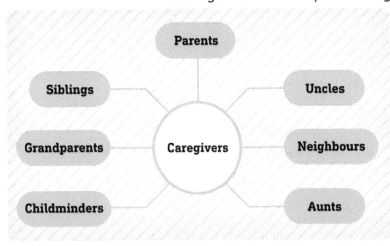

Figure 3.3: Caregivers may be parents or other family members, friends or childminders

If a person comes to the setting to collect a child and you do not know them, seek guidance immediately from a colleague. Never let unknown caregivers into your setting. Your setting may use a password system to ensure unknown caregivers are really who they say they are.

Parents and carers may often assume you are a fully fledged member of staff. Don't be afraid to refer them to another staff member if you are not able to answer a question or query.

Here are some ways you can interact positively with caregivers.

- Talk politely, using their preferred names.
- Share information accurately and positively, within your role. For example, when handing over a child's painting, tell their mother how hard they worked or how much they enjoyed the activity.

- Make time to talk to parents, giving them your full attention. Respect confidentiality; do not discuss other children or families with parents.

Recognising and interacting with professional visitors

Professional visitors may come into your setting for planned appointments, or may visit unannounced. Examples of professional visitors include:

- **OFSTED** representatives
- environmental health officers
- children's services – social workers
- early years advisory teachers
- area **SENCOS**
- other local authority workers – police officers, fire and rescue officers.

Professional visitors must always carry some form of identification – for example, an ID card with their name and organisation on it.

If it is part of your role to answer the door, always check with another staff member if you are not sure whether to let a visitor in. You will learn more about good practice when answering the door to visitors later in this unit.

You should interact with professional visitors politely, explaining that you are an early years assistant on placement. Help them if you can and refer them to appropriate staff members as needed.

Recognising and interacting with visitors offering services

Your setting may receive regular visits from people who provide services, such as:

- language tutors
- sports coaches
- music and movement teachers
- baby gym practitioners.

Interact with them in a friendly and helpful way – for example, it may be your role to help visitors bring in equipment or to sit with the children during the activities on offer. Relay any requests for information to your supervisor if it is not within your role to answer the question.

Encouraging professional partnerships

The way you communicate with visitors can influence their first impressions of you and your setting. It is important to set up and maintain professional partnerships. Consider the following points that show good practice.

Meet and greet parents/carers and visitors

Sometimes actions can speak louder than words. When you are meeting and greeting parents and visitors, think about your body language and gestures as well as what you are saying. See Figure 3.4 for tips about meeting and greeting visitors.

Show positive body language and make eye contact

Be polite and kind

Be friendly and smile

Be approachable and attentive

Meeting and greeting visitors

Be professional

Be adaptable

Listen

Figure 3.4: How to meet and greet visitors

You may need to adapt the way you communicate to meet people's individual needs.

- Make sure a person with a hearing impairment who lip-reads can always see your face when you are talking with them.
- Talk clearly and in an unhurried way to people who do not have English as their first language.
- Show concern if the person seems upset or agitated.

Respecting equality, diversity, culture and inclusion

Interacting professionally means showing respect to everyone you meet. Your setting's Inclusion Policy should give you guidance on how diversity and anti-discriminatory practice is maintained. You can demonstrate good practice by:

- showing respect to everyone, and valuing their comments, suggestions and concerns
- avoiding stereotypical or prejudiced comments
- communicating in a non-judgemental, non-discriminatory manner
- adapting your own communication style to meet individual needs
- respecting others' faith, values and beliefs
- passing any concerns to your supervisor, for example if parents or visitors make discriminatory comments.

Checking identification

Remember to ask to see the identification of all parents/carers and visitors who are unknown to your setting. Never let unknown people into the setting without checking with your supervisor or a colleague first. If you are suspicious about a visitor, even one who is seemingly accepted and already inside the setting, raise it with your supervisor.

Link it up

Take a look at Unit 1, D2 to learn more about the importance of inclusive practice.

Professional visitors carry identification, such as lanyards with an ID badge

Appropriate conversation

It is important to make time to engage in conversation with parents and visitors. You should try to get the right balance between being friendly and sociable, yet professional and formal.

Professional conduct

As well as interacting with parents on a day-to-day basis, your role may include supporting colleagues at more formal events such as parents' consultation evenings. You can be supportive by:

- being polite, approachable and professional
- finding the right time to communicate and not interrupting when other people are talking
- not making assumptions, and checking any points you are not sure about
- sharing relevant information with other staff members
- being aware of your own roles and responsibilities; it may not be appropriate for you to discuss certain issues
- ensuring confidentiality is maintained.

Demonstrating good listening skills

Positive communication should include a two-way flow of information between you and the other person. Good listening skills include:

- making eye contact and giving people your full attention
- repeating back key points to check you have understood fully
- avoiding interrupting someone in the middle of a sentence.

Recording and reporting

If parents or visitors share information or concerns with you, make sure you record this and report it immediately to your supervisor. Follow your setting's procedures and do not be tempted to try to sort out problems yourself.

Practise

Think about the way you interact with families and visitors who come to your setting.

Role play with a partner how you might respond in each of the following situations.

- During Open Evening, a parent asks you to explain why their 2-year-old child is not being taught to write their name yet.

- After a baby yoga session, the teacher complains to you that some of the parents haven't paid for their classes yet.

- At home time, a parent asks you to help find their child's book bag and wants to know if their child has any favourite books.

- During Sports Day, a childminder comments that she doesn't think it's right that your setting has employed a male early years practitioner.

Answering telephones

If answering the phone is within your role, check with your supervisor on your setting's protocol. It is important to answer in a professional manner, as directed by your supervisor or other members of staff.

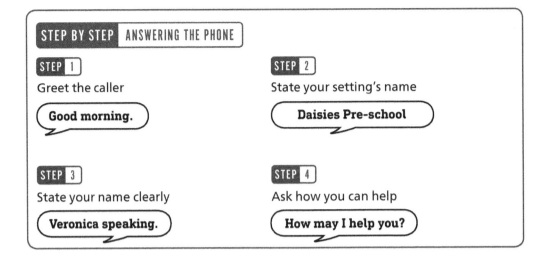

Answering the door

If it is your role to answer the door or respond to the buzzer, here are some suggestions for good practice.

- Welcome visitors in with a smile and a polite greeting.
- Address visitors by their preferred name, if known.
- Check the identity of unknown visitors before you let them in.
- Ask unexpected visitors to wait outside until you can clarify who they are. Don't worry about appearing rude; you can explain to the visitor that this is your policy to ensure safety. Any professional visitor and most caregivers will recognise the importance of security.
- Ask visitors to sign the visitor book.

Responding to parental requests

Parents may ask you for information or advice. It may be within your role to respond – for example, if a parent asks you if their child ate all their dinner that day.

Other requests should be referred to your supervisor or another responsible colleague. You should explain to the parent that you will need to pass on the request and that someone will get back to them as soon as possible.

Make sure you convey the request accurately and promptly, repeating exactly what the parent has asked. It may be useful to write down a message if you are not able to pass it on immediately.

Ensuring children are collected by 'known'/'named' persons

Occasionally, someone who is not known to the staff might come to your setting to collect a child. This might happen if unforeseen circumstances such as illness prevent the usual caregiver from coming.

Often, parents are asked to provide a list of named adults who have permission to collect their child if they themselves are held up or ill. Some settings ask parents to provide a password, and children will only be released to adults who know the password.

You should *never* release a child to an adult without checking with your supervisor first.

Practise

Ask for a copy of your setting's Child Collection Policy. List the main points that ensure safety. Is it the case that only known or named persons can collect children?

Recognising your own limitations

You should have a clear understanding of the limits of your own role and responsibilities. Common sense should tell you that it is fine if a parent asks you to help find their child's jacket, but it is most likely not your role to amend a child's invoice or discuss a complaint.

It's important to be polite, approachable and professional in your interactions with parents

Practise

With a partner, role play what you would do and say next in the following scenarios. You are the early years assistant and your partner is the visitor.

1 A woman rings the bell. You don't recognise her. She says, 'Good afternoon, I'm Tina Smith from Ofsted. I've come to inspect the setting.'

2 A man is trying to open the front door. You don't recognise him. He says through the intercom, 'Hi, I'm Jon's uncle. His dad's stuck in traffic on the motorway so I've come to get him.'

3 A man is at the door carrying a toolkit. He says, 'I got a call to fix the broken climbing frame.'

The consequences of inappropriate communication

The consequences of communicating inappropriately can be very serious.
- A parent could make a complaint against you and you could lose your job or face disciplinary action.
- A complaint could be made to Ofsted about the setting, which could trigger an Ofsted inspection.
- You could damage the reputation of the business.
- If children witness you communicating inappropriately, they may copy your behaviour. Children might be upset or frightened by your behaviour.

What if...?

Tanya is a nursery practitioner in a small village pre-school.

Luke is 4 years old and has just joined the pre-school. His family belong to a group of travellers who live on the outskirts of the village.

Tanya has been seen giving Luke's dad 'dirty looks' when he comes to the setting. She won't let her own daughter, who attends the pre-school, sit next to or play with Luke.

Tanya has been sharing her strong views about travellers on social media and has been gossiping with some of the parents about Luke's family.

- Do you think Luke will have a positive experience at pre-school?
- How might Tanya's behaviour affect the reputation of the pre-school?
- What might Luke's dad do next?
- What might Ofsted do if a complaint is made?
- What do you think will happen to Tanya?

Skills and knowledge check

☐ I have the confidence to meet and greet parents and visitors.
☐ I listen actively to my colleagues and read instructions carefully.
☐ I promote good teamwork by communicating effectively.
☐ I interact in a respectful, non-judgemental way with staff members, families and visitors.

○ I understand the importance of respecting confidentiality.
○ I recognise why it is important to have a good standard of English.
○ I know the limitations of my own role when interacting with parents and visitors.
○ I understand the consequences of inappropriate communication.

C Support daily practice in an early years setting

C1 Supporting colleagues in meeting children's needs in early years settings

Each child has diverse needs that it is the responsibility of early years workers to meet. This includes practical physical, health and care needs, as well as emotional, social and individual needs. The following section talks about your role in supporting your colleagues to give children a high standard of care.

Identifying daily routines that take place in an early years setting

There is a range of routines that take place on a daily basis in every early years setting. Routines may be based on children's care needs, such as snack and meal times, sleep times and hygiene practices. They may be based on learning opportunities such as circle time, outside play, and letters and sounds groups.

Routines are important to keep the setting welcoming, safe and hygienic, for example by changing displays, following cleaning schedules or making risk assessments.

There are also other regular activities that routinely take place for staff, such as training courses, staff meetings and designated times to observe, assess and plan opportunities to support children's development.

Practise

- Make a list of all the jobs you regularly do in your setting as part of the daily routine. The longer the list, the more you contribute to the team!

- Make a photocopy or print out your setting's daily routine. Highlight each task you support.

Working as part of a team in daily routines

As an early years assistant, you have an important role in helping the day to run smoothly. All the tasks that you are asked to do are important, whether they are big or small.

Using your initiative and being proactive

Act positively when you are asked to help, and actively look for ways to offer your assistance to support your staff team with daily routines. Remember to gain permission before undertaking new activities.

Look back through this unit for examples of being proactive and using your initiative.

Preparing and maintaining environments

Part of your role as an early years assistant is to help prepare and maintain environments for the children. This includes checking indoor and outdoor areas are safe, clean and suitable before children use them and also checking them regularly throughout the day.

Some settings use a health and safety checklist to monitor each separate area.

You should also remember to check lights, heaters and fans to ensure that there is appropriate lighting, heating and ventilation in the environment. A room may have become too cold, or hot and stuffy. An outdoor playhouse in direct sunlight might become very warm inside on a hot, sunny day.

Follow your own setting's procedures for safely preparing and maintaining environments. Remember to report any concerns to your room supervisor or a responsible member of staff.

Meeting children's hygiene needs

There will be many hygiene routines that take place during a typical day at your setting – for example, changing nappies, potty training, hand washing, wiping noses and cleaning hands and faces after lunch.

Link it up

Unit 1, B3 looks at promoting safe early years environments.

Unit 4, learning aim B talks about maintaining safe environments for carrying out physical care routines.

Remember to support hygiene needs sensitively, respecting children's privacy and promoting independence

Be clear on your role in supporting care routines, and follow your own setting's guidance. You may be able to support some hygiene routines under supervision. Think of other ways you can help the team. For example, offer to fill up the paper towel dispenser if it is empty, or hand out flannels for children to wipe their own faces.

Preparation of food to meet individual dietary needs

Some children have dietary needs due to food **ALLERGIES**, food intolerances, religious beliefs or individual preference. It is important that everyone preparing food is aware of children's specific dietary requirements.

If it is your role to prepare food for children in your setting, make sure you have up-to-date dietary information and follow your setting's procedures.

Communicating effectively with practitioners

In this unit, you have explored ways of communicating effectively with other practitioners; this is particularly important to make sure children's needs are met. Remember to interact positively in all situations, including during meetings with colleagues and when supporting them in daily practice.

Supporting colleagues in planning activities

Everyone should be involved in planning activities for children. Don't be afraid to share your ideas and be creative. If a child has shared a particular interest with you, be proactive and tell the team – the child's interest could develop into all sorts of exciting activities and experiences for both for the child and for the group.

What if...?

Dylan is a very shy and tearful little boy who always chooses to sit next to Mai, the early years assistant, as she supports snack time. Dylan hardly ever speaks. As Mai is offering him the fruit bowl, Dylan whispers, 'My mummy bought a dragon fruit. Dragons are cool!'

Mai tells Dylan's key person about his interest in dragons, and she is asked to think of some ideas for activities on that theme.

Mai looks in the book box and finds a book about dragons. Dylan and some other children gather round for a story. Dylan is very excited and points to all the colourful pictures in the book. One child asks if they can make a dragon using the junk modelling resources.

- Can you think of five more activities or experiences Mai could suggest?

- How does following Dylan's interest in dragons help to make his experience in the setting more positive?

- Do you think that using a child's individual interests as inspiration for activities for the whole group will benefit all the children? How?

Helping to set up continuous provision

CONTINUOUS PROVISION means activities and resources that are available to children all the time in an early years setting. See Figure 3.5 for some examples.

Practise

Think about your own setting and the things the children have access to all the time, both inside and outside.

Make a list of the continuous provision on offer in your setting.

Choose one area and write a reflective account of how you have helped to set it up.

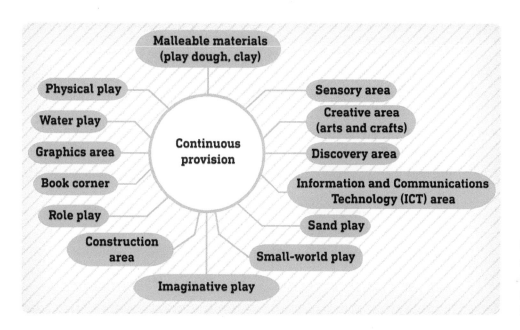

Figure 3.5: When setting up continuous provision, make sure it is appropriate for the age and developmental stage of the children present

Don't be afraid to be proactive when setting up continuous provision; your role is to make sure each area is safe, inviting and stimulating. You can also ask your supervisor if you can add to the resources. For example, you may suggest adding a 'Gruffalo' story sack to the book corner if you know a child is particularly interested in those books.

Engaging children actively in play opportunities

You can be a great help to fellow practitioners who are engaging children in play. Here are some pointers.

- Help set up resources and play activities.
- Supervise play to ensure safety.
- Follow other staff members' lead; learn from them how to engage children in meaningful play.
- Use strategies to promote play and learning through conversation. Give a commentary as children play, asking **OPEN-ENDED QUESTIONS**. This means questions that don't limit the answer to 'yes' or 'no'. For example, rather than 'Have you built a tower?' ask, 'Tell me about what you're building.'
- Be hands-on and offer to help if play is being interrupted – for example, if a child is upset, unwell or disrupting a play opportunity.

Link it up

Take a look at Unit 2, C1 and Unit 5, B1 to see examples of different activities that support development and the sort of resources you can provide.

- Follow children's play cues; if a colleague has set up a role-play café, support the children's play by pretending to drink cups of tea that they offer you.
- Offer ideas to extend play; observe children and share their interests with the team.

What if...?

You are on placement in Bradby Baby Barn and shadowing your colleague, Mandeep. Willem is 20 months old and has brittle bone disease. Mandeep supervises Willem closely; if he should trip or fall, he could suffer a fracture. Mandeep always places a special cushion on his chair to support his posture.

Willem's mother is anxious about him being in nursery. Mandeep takes time to reassure her and give feedback on his progress on a daily basis.

Today, Mandeep is not at work as she is on a training course. Think about how you might proactively support Willem's daily routine and the staff team during the following stages of the day.

- Willem and his mum arrive. She comments to you that his photo has gone missing from his peg.
- A staff member starts to sit Willem down for snack time, forgetting his special cushion.
- During free play, you see building bricks are scattered all over the Baby Unit floor.
- You sit and play with Willem; he builds a tower of three bricks. This is the first time he has done this at nursery.
- It is nearly lunchtime and the table has not been cleaned yet.
- Willem sits and enjoys his lunch, but is struggling to feed himself.
- You help settle Willem down for his sleep; you notice the Sleep Room feels very hot today.
- During outside play, Willem is having a go on the balancing beam.
- The doorbell rings; it is Willem's mother coming to collect him.

Contributing to classroom displays and noticeboards

As an early years assistant, you may be asked to help put up displays of children's work and maintain noticeboards. Your supervisor should guide you.

When displaying children's work, here are some points to consider.

- Ensure the display focuses on the children's work, not the adults' work.
- Check any words on the display are spelt correctly and can be read clearly. Think about displaying words in different languages.
- Make use of displays to promote positive images and reflect diversity.
- Think about the height of the display. Can children see their own work?
- Change displays regularly to maintain interest.

When contributing to noticeboards – for example, parent information boards – make sure that:

- information is up to date
- information is accurate
- information is displayed in the languages of the families using the setting.

Your role in working in partnership with parents

It benefits children when early years staff work together with parents. You can help to support parent partnerships in your setting by:

Link it up

Unit 5, B1 tells you more about helping to provide environments and displays that engage children and support their learning.

- being an effective communicator – passing on parents' messages, questions and complaints promptly and accurately to relevant staff members
- following your setting's codes of conduct so parents trust the setting and feel happy to communicate with the team
- sharing information with parents, within the limits of your role.

Helping parents and children through key transitions

TRANSITIONS in early years settings involve moving from one area to another. These happen on a daily basis – for example, moving from inside to outside play.

Key transitions are bigger changes that take place. As children get older, they will need to move up to the next room in the setting and will eventually leave to go to school.

Some children take these changes in their stride while other families and children find transitions much more unsettling.

Your colleagues may use a range of strategies to support key transitions. These will include:

- discussing transitions with children and families before they take place
- giving written information about the transition – the dates, timescale, the names of new people, the layout of the room
- giving simple, reassuring messages about the transitions, explaining the benefits
- introducing children and families to their new key person or teacher
- arranging settling-in sessions or visits to the new room/setting, accompanied by a familiar staff member.

As an early years assistant, you can support the process by:

- talking to children positively about upcoming changes
- sharing books and stories about starting school, and supporting role-play activities
- relaying any questions that parents have about the transition to your supervisor
- being available to reassure children who are upset or unsettled by the transition, and informing other staff members of their anxieties
- accompanying children on settling-in sessions/visits to the new room/ setting, if this is within your role.

Children can also go through personal transitions that can affect their lives – for example, the death of a family member or pet, an illness, relationship breakdowns, a new baby in the home or moving house. Reassure and take time to listen to children if they appear unsettled or troubled by the changes.

Helping on outings

Outings can be great fun but quite challenging for early years staff as there are a lot of safety issues to consider. You can be a support to colleagues by helping to keep the children safe and well supervised, following your setting's procedures.

C2 Contributing to record keeping in early years settings

Record keeping is the practice of storing and organising information, such as child and staff files, health and safety paperwork, observations of children and many other written documents. You need to be able to support your team with effective record keeping if this is part of your role.

Link it up

Unit 1, B3 looks at supporting safety on outings in more detail.

Recording different types of information

You may be required to record different types of information while at your setting. Look at the list below, showing some examples of information that often needs to be recorded in early years settings.

a Make sure you complete information accurately.

b Make sure you record information as soon as you possibly can.

> **Practise**
>
> Think about the different types of information that are recorded in your setting.
>
> Look at this list of examples of record keeping and tick the ones that are used in your setting:
>
> ☐ children's daily logs
>
> ☐ child, staff, visitor registers
>
> ☐ records/observations of experiences the children have taken part in
>
> ☐ nappy-changing charts
>
> ☐ sleep monitoring forms
>
> ☐ records of mealtimes
>
> ☐ accident/incident records (see Figure 3.6 for an example)
>
> ☐ existing injuries forms
>
> ☐ health monitoring forms
>
> ☐ medication records
>
> ☐ records of health, safety and hygiene checks.
>
> Ask your supervisor for blank copies of these or other records; practise completing them.

Accident or Incident Form

Name of child	Abi Miller
Child's date of birth	01/04/2015
Date of accident or incident	12/08/2017
Location of accident or incident	Garden
Details of accident or incident What happened?	Abi was pushing the doll's pram when she tripped over her own feet and bumped her lip on the pram.
Any injuries incurred?	Split top lip
First Aid or treatment given?	A cold compress was applied.
Follow-up observations?	Regular checks on Abi's lip to check for swelling or bleeding.
Further medical assistance needed?	No
Any witnesses?	No
Childminder's signature and date	L. Smith 12/08/2017
Parent's signature and date	M. Miller 12/08/2017

Figure 3.6: Look at this example of a completed accident form. Why is it important that all the information is completed accurately? What might happen if there is a delay in completing the form?

Information handling

INFORMATION HANDLING means managing people's personal or sensitive information. All staff in early years settings will need to have access to some degree of information. It is pointless asking parents to record children's allergies and medical conditions if no one ever refers to the record.

You should follow your own setting's policies and procedures for handling information and seek clarification from your supervisor to identify your own roles and responsibilities.

Link it up

Unit 1, A4 talks about handing information safely, giving detail about the policies and procedures that should be followed to meet legal requirements.

Being familiar with timetables and rotas

Sometimes you will need to look at your setting's written information to guide you in your role and to know the daily routine. Some examples of information you may need to refer to are listed in Table 3.4.

Type of information	Description
Setting timetable	Gives details about set activities happening every week – for example, 'Soccer Tots' every Wednesday morning
Staff rota	Gives staff their shift patterns and breaktimes for the week
Activity rota	Gives staff set duties for the week – for example, preparing a snack, laying out the sleep mats, making health and safety checks
Short-term planning	Planned children's activities for the week ahead
Medium-term planning	Planned children's activities over a longer period of time – for example, one term or half term
Long-term planning	Planned activities over the whole year, based on the seasons, religious festivals or traditions

Table 3.4: Sources of information about the daily routine

Reporting concerns to colleagues

During your time on placement, you may have concerns regarding children's behaviour, health, wellbeing or safety.

If you have any concerns, it is your role to report this to your supervisor. If you have a child protection concern, you should report to your setting's DESIGNATED SAFEGUARDING LEAD.

In some instances, you may need to provide information to support the completion of records, such as health monitoring forms, behaviour logs or existing injuries forms. Be clear about your own responsibilities and always seek clarification if unsure.

Contributing to observations of children

All early years practitioners are continually observing children; they note children's interests and assess and track development.

Each child must have a PROFILE, sometimes called a Learning Journey or Learning Story, where observations are recorded.

You can help contribute to children's profiles by sharing what you observe with other staff members. You can carry a notepad to write down what you see or hear.

It is the responsibility of senior staff members to record observations in children's profiles.

Link it up

Refer back to Unit 2, C1 and C2 for information about supporting child observations.

Recording and promptly passing on messages to colleagues

In this unit you have learned why it is important to pass on messages from parents or visitors to relevant members of staff.

These can include messages you take on the telephone, verbal messages or emails. Make sure you record messages neatly and accurately, and pass them on as soon as possible.

Filing paperwork

Think about all the different records and paperwork in your setting. Where does it all belong?

If you are asked to file paperwork, you should follow your setting's procedures.

If you are unsure of how or where to file paperwork, check with your supervisor. Some paperwork is confidential and should be kept in a locked filing cabinet. In some instances, settings also make use of electronic systems where information is filed in folders on the computer.

Recognising the impact of poor record keeping or information handling

In this unit you have looked at the many different records that are kept in an early years setting and the importance of handing information in line with your own setting's policies.

Although record keeping might not seem important, the consequences of not keeping accurate records can be very serious when things go wrong. Children's health, safety and wellbeing can be at risk – for example, if records of allergies, medical conditions or additional needs are not accurate or up to date.

Parents might be dissatisfied with the setting if messages they give verbally are not recorded and acted on.

What if...?

Phoebe is an early years assistant on placement at Humpty Dumpty Nursery.

Lottie, a baby aged 11 months, arrives at lunchtime with her grandfather. Lottie has been poorly and has medicine in her bag.

Lottie's grandfather asks Phoebe if he needs to sign a Medication Form. Phoebe shrugs and says, 'I'm late for college, I'm sure you can sign one later.'

Phoebe leaves the placement to go to college for the afternoon. Nobody else in the setting knows that Lottie has medicine in her bag.

Think about the seriousness of Phoebe's conduct.

- What might the implications be for Lottie?
- How might Lottie's grandfather feel about the situation? Would he be within his rights to complain to Ofsted?
- How could the setting's reputation be affected?
- What might happen to Phoebe?

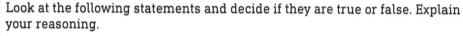

If a complaint is made to Ofsted, this can trigger an Ofsted inspection to check that the setting is meeting all statutory requirements. If Ofsted finds that the setting is not complying with requirements, the setting can be judged as 'Inadequate'. It could be prosecuted or even shut down. A negative Ofsted report, or even the public knowledge that an inspection has arisen from a complaint, can damage the reputation of a setting.

If staff members do not follow the correct record-keeping or information-handling procedures, it could damage their own professional development and they might face disciplinary action or dismissal.

Practise

Look at the following statements and decide if they are true or false. Explain your reasoning.

- It doesn't matter if I forget to sign in and out of the placement.
- I should write down messages from parents and pass these to other colleagues straight away.
- If a parent asks me how much their nursery fees are, I should log onto the setting computer and find out for them.
- If a staff member forgets to fill out a child's accident form, it does not matter as long as it is not a head injury.
- I should tell my supervisor if I notice the children's allergy list is out of date.
- I should promptly share with parents written observations I make of their children.

Skills and knowledge check

☐ I am confident in being able to help set up continuous provision and put up displays.

☐ I share my ideas and observations of children to support the planning of activities.

☐ I offer high levels of support to my team.

☐ I help support children's key transitions and help on outings.

○ I can identify the range of routines that take place in early years settings.

○ I know my own roles and responsibilities when handling information and keeping records.

○ I understand why it is important to help keep the setting safe and secure.

○ I can recognise the importance of recording and passing on messages promptly and accurately.

Ready for assessment

During your time on placement, you will need to show that you are developing professional practice skills. One way of providing evidence is to use reflective accounts, which can be written notes or a diary of your experiences. **REFLECTION** is looking back at something, in this case, yourself and your practice.

Reflect on how you have supported your team as part of the daily routine on placement.

You could talk about snack time, outside play, setting up the role-play area, sitting with the group at circle time, or any other activity that you feel confident with.

Answer the following questions, giving examples from your own experience.

- Did you work within your roles and responsibilities?
- Did you follow instructions from other members of staff?
- Did you provide a high level of support to other staff members?
- Did you communicate clearly with children, other practitioners or visitors?
- Did you share information that other staff members needed to know?
- Were you organised?
- Did you show a positive approach?
- Did you use your initiative?
- Did your actions support the children?

It's important to remind yourself of all the essential behaviours and practices in this chapter. You should also make sure you have completed Section B, Unit 3 of form CPLD 1 in your Placement Experience Assessment Portfolio of Evidence. Fill in the self-assessment form and include ideas about the different skills you have developed when completing the activities for this unit. Make a note of things you could do to keep improving these skills.

Look at Table 3.5 for an example of an early years assistant reflecting on how they supported a creative activity.

Table 3.5: Example of a reflection on support for a creative activity

Professional practice skill	An early years assistant's reflection on good practice
Working within your roles and responsibilities	I helped to set up the creative area today. This is part of my role on placement.
Following instructions from other members of staff	My supervisor asked me to provide glitter and glue for the children to make firework pictures. I checked how many glue pots to put out, and I set up the resources carefully.
Providing a high level of support to other staff members	I supported my colleague as she helped the children to make their pictures. I listened and acted quickly when she asked me to find some more glue spreaders.
Communicating clearly	I talked to the children during the activity, asking open-ended questions like, 'Can you tell me about your picture?'
Sharing information that other staff members need to know	I noticed that one child seemed anxious about getting glue on his hands, so I found his key person and told her about it.
Being organised	I asked for a list of all the children's names. I used my list so I could write their names on their pictures, making sure I spelt each name correctly.
Showing a positive approach	I showed a positive approach by following my supervisor's instructions carefully and being patient and caring towards the children taking part.
Using your initiative	I used my initiative when a child knocked a pot of glitter all over the floor. I found a brush and swept it up straight away as I was worried the floor might be slippery.
Demonstrating actions that support the children	I think I supported the children well during the activity as I gave lots of praise and made sure there were enough resources so they could all take part.

WORK FOCUS

HANDS ON

There are some important sector skills you will need to practise that relate to this unit. These include effective communication, teamwork and maintaining environments to meet children's needs.

Tick the statements that you feel you do well on placement.

Give one example from your own experience for each statement you have ticked.

☐ Sharing information and passing on messages to members of staff

☐ Communicating positively with your supervisor

☐ Being polite, respectful and interacting professionally with families and visitors

☐ Using your initiative and being proactive; offering to help

☐ Being organised and on time to your placement

☐ Following instructions

☐ Supporting daily routines in your setting

☐ Setting up continuous provision

Are there any professional practice skills you feel less confident with?

Who can you turn to for support and guidance?

Ready for work?

Developing and practising work-related skills and behaviours could help you to gain employment in an early years setting.

One important aspect of being an early years assistant is being professional.

Can you use the words below to complete the following sentences about having a professional approach?

adapting   commitment   dress   initiative

politely   positive   respect   trustworthy

1 I look professional by following my setting's _____ code.

2 I can talk _____ and show diplomacy in difficult situations.

3 I treat others with _____, valuing their views and opinions.

4 I am honest and reliable, which shows I am _____.

5 I fulfil tasks to the best of my ability and turn up on time, showing _____ to my role.

6 I can be flexible, _____ the way I work in different situations.

7 I am enthusiastic and have a _____ outlook.

8 I am proactive and use my _____ to support my team.

Write a reflective account detailing how you have shown professionalism while on placement. You can use the sentences above to support this task.

Supporting Children's Physical Care Needs in Early Years Settings

4

Have you ever thought how many care routines you are involved in for children in the setting on a daily basis? These routines ensure that children are kept safe and healthy and that their individual needs are met.

The information provided in this unit will help you in understanding and supporting these needs. You will also learn why it's important to have a high-quality environment that is kept clean and well maintained throughout the day.

On a practical note, you'll understand your role in supporting practitioners to achieve this.

How will I be assessed?

This is an internally assessed unit, which means that you will need to carry out a series of tasks, some of which will be assessed in the workplace. You should record your work-based activities in your Placement Experience Assessment Portfolio of Evidence. This will also help you to gather evidence for Unit 7.

You will be required to submit evidence of your understanding of:

- physical care routines, including procedures and guidance in an early years setting, and promoting dignity and encouraging independence
- safe environments, including safety checks, maintaining cleanliness and hygiene, and setting up and tidying away activities
- meal and snack times, including preparing food, helping to feed children, and promoting choice and independence.

You will need to provide evidence that you have completed the activities successfully, which might include:

- expert witness statements from colleagues who have observed you carrying out children's routines competently
- reflective accounts written by yourself about your role in supporting children's care routines
- a daily diary or annotated menu plans that demonstrate the knowledge and skills you have developed from your time at the setting.

Assessment criteria

Pass	Merit	Distinction
Learning aim A: Contribute to physical care routines that promote the quality of care for children		
A.P1 Show how you have appropriately supported simple physical care routines for children in an early years setting. **A.P2** Identify ways in which dignity and respect are taken into account when carrying out physical care routines.	**A.M1** Show how you have provided a consistently good quality of support for different physical care routines for children in an early years setting.	**AB.D1** Show how to provide confident and consistently good-quality support for a range of physical care routines in different environments for children in an early years setting.
Learning aim B: Maintain safe environments for carrying out physical care routines in early years settings		
B.P3 Apply basic cleanliness and hygiene standards in an environment where physical care routines take place in an early years setting.	**B.M2** Apply and promote good standards of safety and hygiene in different environments in an early years setting.	**AB.D1** Show how to provide confident and consistently good-quality support for a range of physical care routines in different environments for children in an early years setting.
Learning aim C: Support and encourage children at meal and snack times in early years settings		
C.P4 Prepare and serve a selection of snacks suitable for young children. **C.P5** Use appropriate skills to help to feed a child during a mealtime.	**C.M3** Use a range of appropriate skills to prepare, serve and provide consistent support to a child during meal and snack times in an early years setting.	**C.D2** Use a range of appropriate skills to independently prepare, serve and provide high-quality support to children during meal and snack times in an early years setting.

A Contribute to physical care routines that promote the quality of care for children

A1 Care routines – changing, cleaning and dressing, preparing for sleep

As an early years assistant you will be involved in the care of young children and may help to support many of their personal and physical care routines. You need to understand the procedures in place in early years settings for carrying out personal care.

You also need to be able to recognise and understand the needs of individual children. Parental information and requests are vital in this regard as they provide you with valuable insights that you may not otherwise be aware of or may take time to notice by yourself.

Observing nappy changing

Nappy changing is a very familiar part of an early years practitioner's daily routine. While you will not be responsible for changing nappies, it is important you know and understand the process that should be followed.

Throughout the day, staff will check a child's nappy regularly and change it as soon as any soiling is noticed. The child's **KEY PERSON** usually does this. If this is not possible, a practitioner known to the child must carry out the change as this is an intimate personal care routine.

CHECKLIST NAPPY CHANGING

☐ Clean and sanitise the changing mat before changing a nappy

☐ Wear an apron and gloves to ensure urine and faeces are not transferred to other areas of the setting

☐ Have all items to hand before lifting a child onto a changing mat or area, including nappy, gloves, bag, cream, wipes

☐ Never leave a child unsupervised on a changing mat

☐ Only use nappies, wipes and creams intended for the child being changed

☐ Dispose of soiled nappies in sealed bags and place in designated bins

---

Hand washing

Bacteria and germs are easily transferred between people through the touching of hands. Regular hand washing – for adults and children – is essential in order to minimise the spread of infection (see Figure 4.1). Effective hand washing begins with you helping children to wash their hands. Babies and younger children in particular may need you to do it for them by using individual flannels or a sink of soapy water. Around 2 years of age, children begin to develop the skills to do this for themselves but may need help from you until they have mastered hand washing for themselves.

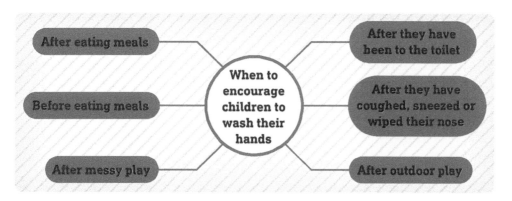

Figure 4.1: There will be many times throughout the day when children need to wash their hands

Hand washing good practice

The following strategies are important in encouraging children to wash their hands.

- Provide pump-activated soap (bar soap can harbour harmful bacteria).
- Provide individual towels, paper towels or hand dryers.
- Ensure easy access to sinks and provide step stools where necessary.
- Check the temperature of water (this is often regulated to prevent scalding).
- Remove plugs from sinks to prevent curious children from flooding bathrooms.
- Wash your hands at the same time as the children so they can see what to do.
- Put posters above hand-washing basins as a gentle reminder for everybody.

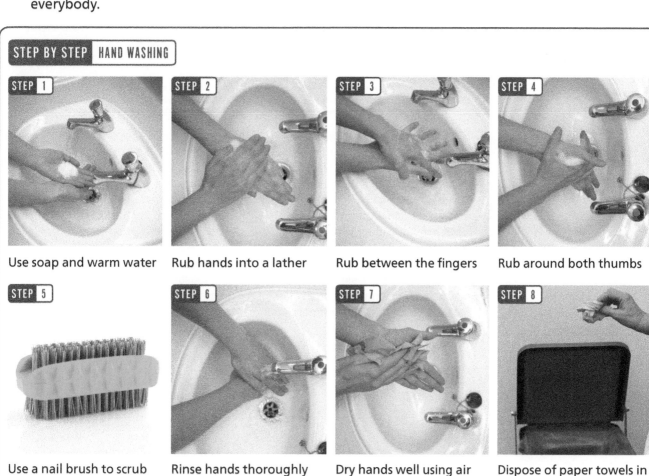

STEP BY STEP — HAND WASHING

STEP 1	STEP 2	STEP 3	STEP 4
Use soap and warm water	Rub hands into a lather	Rub between the fingers	Rub around both thumbs

STEP 5	STEP 6	STEP 7	STEP 8
Use a nail brush to scrub nails and rings	Rinse hands thoroughly with warm water	Dry hands well using air dryer or paper towels	Dispose of paper towels in appropriate waste bin

Helping with children's personal routines

Teeth brushing

Dentists recommend that you start to brush a child's teeth as soon as the teeth appear (typically around 6 months). Teeth brushing should become a regular part of a child's daily routine, usually in the morning and before bed. Some settings encourage teeth brushing during the day as well and may ask parents to provide their child with a toothbrush for use after lunch.

CHECKLIST   TEETH BRUSHING

- [ ] Always supervise children while they brush their teeth
- [ ] Use a toothbrush that is appropriate for the child's age so as not to damage the teeth or gums
- [ ] Use fluoride toothpaste
- [ ] Encourage children to brush in a circular motion and make sure they brush the gums as well as the teeth
- [ ] After brushing, spit but don't rinse as this will remove the protective fluoride in the toothpaste
- [ ] Rinse toothbrush thoroughly and store hygienically in a sealed container or sterilising solution
- [ ] Give praise and encouragement for teeth brushing

Care of skin

Looking after children's skin can involve everyday care, for example when children's nappies are changed, or it can be specific to managing a child's skin condition.

Table 4.1: Caring for children's skin

Skin care when nappy changing	Managing skin conditions
Nappy creams:	Creams and moisturisers:
• are used when a child has soreness in the nappy area	• are most commonly used in the management of **ECZEMA**.
• are usually medicated to help the healing process of sore or broken skin.	• The more oil in the cream or ointment the better it is at locking moisture into the skin and soothing symptoms. It is important to follow instructions provided exactly, in order to know how much cream to apply.
• There is no need to use these with every nappy change as they are designed for healing only.	
Barrier creams:	Sensitive skin:
• are oil-based products used to keep urine away from the skin	• For reasons unknown, some children have sensitive skin and have a bad reaction to certain products that are applied to their skin. Once identified, refrain from using again.
• are most commonly used on babies wearing towelling nappies or children who are prone to soreness.	• Wash the skin with warm water to remove product from skin and pat dry.

What if...?

Carey is 2 years old and is playing at the **SENSORY** play tray, which has foam soap and glitter. She rubs the soap on her face because she likes the feel of it. A few minutes later you notice her face and hands are red and blotchy. If you were working with Carey, this is what you would need to do.

1 Inform your supervisor about the reaction.

2 Wash Carey's face and hands using a flannel and plain water.

3 Observe Carey for any further reactions.

4 If redness doesn't disappear, contact Carey's parents as she may need an antihistamine.

5 Ensure the reaction is recorded on Carey's file so that adaptations to the activity can be made in future.

Care of hair

While it is unlikely that you will be required to wash the hair of a young child in your care, you will look after children's hair in other ways.

Brushing, combing and tying back hair

Hair clips, bobbles and bands will fall out during the course of the day. As long as a child is happy for you to do so, you can brush or comb their hair and tie it up again. You may also suggest to a child they could have their hair tied back when involved in messy play or cooking activities.

Conditioning hair

Children with afro or multi-textured hair may bring conditioning lotions with them to the setting. This is to aid brushing and styling and to protect the hair, which can become dry and brittle.

Managing scalp conditions

Scalp conditions such as **CRADLE CAP** (yellow scaly patches on a baby's scalp) do not cause any discomfort or irritation and do not need any specialist treatment during the day. Moisturising the scalp with olive oil or a similar product at bedtime can help loosen the patches of skin. Never pick at the skin as this can introduce infection.

Management of head lice

Head lice are a common childhood condition, which can be difficult to prevent but relatively easy to treat. Head lice can be easily passed from one head to another. Because close contact between young children is unavoidable, this is how head lice are spread in a setting. There is no need to send a child home if you spot head lice. However, you should inform the parents (discreetly) at the earliest opportunity so they can treat the condition.

Helping with children's physical care routines

Settling children in

When a child starts at a setting they can often be shy, anxious or upset at being separated from their parents. Before being left for the first time, children will often attend the setting for a settling-in visit. This is usually for no more than a couple of hours and helps them to become familiar with their new surroundings.

CHECKLIST | **SETTLING CHILDREN IN**

- ☐ Get down to the child's level to welcome them
- ☐ Tell them your name and give them a big smile
- ☐ Ask if they would like to join you in an activity
- ☐ Offer reassurance if they become distressed
- ☐ Provide familiar items or comforters if the child needs them
- ☐ Find out about them from their **'ALL ABOUT ME' RECORD** or personal **PROFILE** sheet so you can talk to them about things they know. An 'all about me' record has information completed by parents/carers that gives you an overview of a child's development to date and a record of discussions with parents about topics and themes that interest the child
- ☐ Provide cuddles and soothing tones for babies to help them settle

---

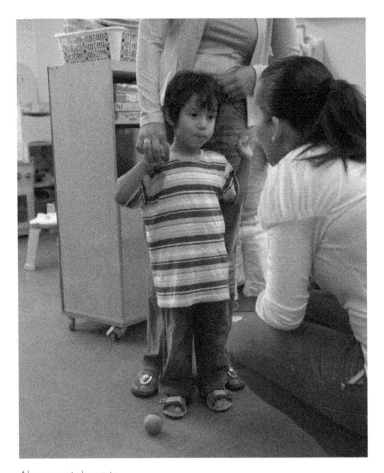

Always get down to the child's level when welcoming them into the setting. Tell them your name and give them a smile

Changing in and out of clothes

During the course of the day you may have to help to change children in and out of clothes. Reasons for this can include:

- changing following toileting accidents
- changing clothes due to drinks and meal spillages
- changing for particular activities
- changing clothing for outdoor play.

You should always explain to children why you are changing their clothes and ask their permission to do so. Informing them and involving them in what you are doing helps to promote respect and dignity.

Preparing children for indoor and outdoor play

You should always make sure children are suitably dressed for the activities they are going to take part in either indoors or outdoors. Look at the table below to find out what you should think about when getting children ready for activities.

Table 4.2: Preparing children for indoor and outdoor play activities

What activity?	What are the weather conditions?	Do the children need any particular equipment?
• Physical play – appropriate footwear to avoid slipping • Winter walk – wellies for jumping in puddles • Socks for soft play activities to avoid injuries to other children	• Coat and hat for cold weather • Waterproof gloves when making snowballs • Hats, fluids (for example, water) and sun cream on hot days	• Aprons for cooking • Old shirts for painting • Waterproof aprons for water play • Plastic gloves for sensory play for children with sensitive skin

Weather-appropriate clothing

Children need different clothing and other items depending on the season. Look at the table below to see examples of the items they should have with them in the setting during the summer and winter months.

Summer	Winter
Sun hat	Several thin layers of clothing
Sun cream	Jumper
Thin layers of clothing	Warm, waterproof coat
Spare clothing	Closed-toe footwear
Sandals or canvas shoes	Wellies
Light jacket	Woolly hat
Raincoat	Gloves

Table 4.3: Weather-appropriate clothing

Practise

You have been asked by your colleague to help prepare children for water play in the garden on a warm summer morning.

Decide how a child should be dressed for this activity. Make a list of additional equipment you may need.

Can you explain the choices you have made?

Applying sun cream

Exposing skin to the sun can result in sunburn. Even people who are not prone to burning are exposed to harmful rays, which can cause long-term damage to skin. It is important to make sure that children's skin is properly protected with a high-factor sun cream.

- Always apply cream liberally, ensuring all exposed skin is covered.
- Avoid sun cream coming in contact with the eyes and mouth.
- Make sure cream is rubbed in thoroughly and avoid sun exposure for at least 10 minutes.
- Ensure you follow the manufacturer's guidelines for time lengths between applications.
- Only apply cream approved by parents.

Changing footwear

Your setting will have its own policy on footwear, particularly in areas where babies are crawling around. Children may have to wear different indoor and outdoor footwear to stop dirt coming in from outdoors.

As children develop their physical skills, they will also learn how to put on and take off their own shoes. The easier the fastenings on shoes, the easier they will find it to do this by themselves. Wellies and slip-on shoes help children grasp the skill quickly, while shoes with buckles and laces can take more time to master.

Rest and sleep

Rest and sleep are extremely important for babies and young children because they:

- allow children to recover from physical exertion
- aid the digestion of food
- support GROWTH and development
- increase alertness
- help to maintain a healthy immune system.

Table 4.4 shows the guidelines for the amount of sleep and rest babies and children need at different ages.

Link it up

Go to Unit 2, A2 for more information about a child's physical development.

Table 4.4: Guidelines for sleep and rest – source: Professional Association for Childcare and Early Years (PACEY) website

Age	Average hours – daytime sleep	Average hours – night-time sleep
3 months	5	10
6 months	4	10
9 months	2.75	11.5
12 months	2.25	11.25
2 years	1.5	11.75
3 years	1	11
4 years	0	11.25

Settling babies

When putting a baby in a cot for a sleep, it is essential to follow these guidelines to help minimise the risk of SIDS (sudden infant death syndrome). While this syndrome is rare, it is crucial that all early years practitioners are aware of it and what they can do to minimise the risks. Look at the checklist below for best practice in putting babies for a sleep in cots.

CHECKLIST   **BABIES IN COTS**

- ☐ Ensure the cot mattress is in good condition, waterproof and firm to lie on
- ☐ Lay baby on their back to sleep
- ☐ Place baby in 'feet to foot' position, that is, with the feet touching the end of the cot
- ☐ Keep room temperature between 16 °C and 20 °C
- ☐ Use lightweight bedding tucked under arms or lightweight baby sleeping bag
- ☐ Check sleeping babies at regular intervals

Settling toddlers

Sleep rooms or quiet areas with mats and bedding should be provided for toddlers. Time to sleep is often set aside after lunch. Sleeping children should never be left unsupervised, so always make sure you can see and hear them. Be ready to help any child settle to sleep or support them as they wake.

Rest sessions

As children approach school age they are less likely to want to sleep. It is still important that they are given opportunities for rest and activities that help them to recover from the physical exertion of the morning.

Practise

Look at the list of activities below and circle the three you think are suitable for periods of quiet or rest.

- A game of hide and seek
- Jigsaws and puzzles
- Stories
- Music and movement
- Colouring

Preparing children for collection at the end of the day

End-of-the-day routines should not be rushed but should be approached in a calm manner. Many children will be tired after a busy and stimulating time at the setting. Some children will get tearful as the end of the day approaches. This can be a common reaction even if they are happy and settled in your care. In these situations, it is important to offer comfort and reassurance to the child.

> **CHECKLIST** END-OF-DAY ROUTINE
>
> ☐ Make sure all the children's belongings are ready
>
> ☐ Involve children in getting ready to go home, for example, 'Shall we go and find your lovely painting you did today to take home?'
>
> ☐ Have ready essential information for parents, including newsletters, daily diary, accident forms to sign
>
> ☐ Ensure you make enough time to hand over care of children to parents and carers

Providing good-quality support

Your role in supporting children's care routines is to help the children become independent in self-care through good-quality support and guidance, which includes the following strategies.

Showing them 'how to'

Children learn best by being shown what to do. Demonstrating care routines to children will help them understand how to accomplish tasks by themselves. The next time you are getting ready for outdoor play, put on your own shoes and coat in front of the children and explain what you are doing. You could even ask older children if they think you have put your shoes on the right feet!

Giving time

Don't hurry children to perform tasks and routines as this will hinder their success and can cause distress. Always ensure your routine allows time for shoes and coats to be put on or hands to be washed before snack time.

Allowing trial and error

It doesn't matter if shoes go on the wrong feet or a jumper goes on back to front. Never respond negatively to such situations but instead offer sensitive support to help a child swap the shoes over. With practice, they will get it right.

Giving positive feedback and praise

Children respond well to praise and encouragement so always take time to highlight their achievements and attempts. For example, say to a child who has put their wellies on by themselves, 'Wow, Johnny, aren't you clever putting your wellies on?'

Being at a child's level

When talking to and supporting a young child, always get down to their level so they can clearly see what you are saying and doing. This allows good eye contact and helps children to see a smiling face along with your encouraging words of praise.

A2 Procedures and guidance in early years settings

Your setting will have clear policies and procedures in place for all practitioners to follow when implementing children's care routines.

Following physical care procedures

Policies are written to ensure that everybody is doing things in the same way. For example, if there are no written procedures for nappy changing or administration of medication, mistakes can be made, putting the child's wellbeing at risk.

When you first join your early years setting, it may feel overwhelming to read all the policies and procedures given to you. If you are not given them, you must ask for them and it is very important that you read and understand them. Always ask for clarification if you do not understand any of the guidelines or practices detailed within them.

Being aware of staff to child ratios

Staff to child ratios refer to the number of children that can be supervised by one member of staff. These guidelines are set by OFSTED and are clearly detailed in the Welfare Requirements section of the EARLY YEARS FOUNDATION STAGE (EYFS) guidance.

Ratios will alter depending on the age of the children, the qualifications of the staff and the type of setting you are working in.

Practise

Take time to read the child to staff ratio requirements detailed in the Welfare Requirements documentation of the EYFS. You can find this document at www.gov.uk

1 Identify the ratio requirements in your setting for:

- children under 2 years
- children aged 2 years
- children aged 3 years and over.

2 Are unqualified early years assistants counted in ratios?

Health and safety guidance

Health and safety are everyone's responsibility. It is important that you know about and follow the guidance covering health and safety in early years settings. The two main pieces of guidance are:

1 the Health and Safety at Work Act 1974

2 the EYFS Welfare Requirements.

Health and Safety at Work Act 1974

The Health and Safety at Work Act of 1974 clearly details an employer's duties to its employees in keeping them safe at work, and also details the duties of employees to work safely.

The EYFS Welfare Requirements

The Welfare Requirements within the EYFS document clearly detail expectations of all early years settings in providing a safe, secure and healthy environment in which children can thrive.

The EYFS framework is a legal requirement and underpins the working practices of all settings. The policies, processes and procedures of everyday practice are based on these requirements.

Link it up

Refer back to Unit 1, Section B1 for more detailed information on health and safety guidance in the early years.

PPE (personal protective equipment)

PERSONAL PROTECTIVE EQUIPMENT ensures you and others are protected from **HAZARDS** and harm in the workplace.

Here is a reminder of the precautions to follow during physical care routines, including nappy changing and food preparation.

- Aprons – help to create a barrier against clothes that carry bacteria. Wearing disposable aprons when changing nappies or preparing food reduces **CROSS-CONTAMINATION** (spreading germs from one place to another) around the setting.
- Rubber/disposable gloves – help protect skin from chemical burns and prevent bodily fluids from entering the skin via cuts.
- Plasters – cover wounds and prevent the transfer of bacteria into food.
- Hair nets/bands – minimise the risk of hair falling into food.

Safeguarding children when providing physical care

When supporting any aspect of a child's physical care routine, you must ensure that the needs of the child come first. Your setting's safeguarding policies will give great detail about working practices that keep both you and the children safe.

Keeping appropriate records

Throughout your working day you will be asked to make notes and observations about specific aspects of children's routines. See Figure 4.2. This is to ensure that parents and carers can be given feedback about their child's day.

Link it up

Unit 1, A2 looks at safe working practices and safeguarding procedures.

What if...?

William is 6 months old and has been unsettled at nursery today. He didn't drink his milk feed at 10 a.m. and has been very tearful. When his dad collects him at lunchtime, his key person is on their break and no other practitioner passes on this information.

1 Why should this information have been passed on to William's dad?

2 How can the setting make sure important information is passed on?

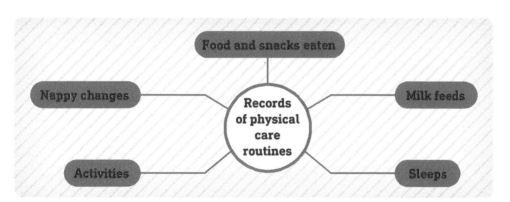

Figure 4.2: During the working day it is important to record the physical care routines of the children

This information can be given in different forms:
- a daily diary
- daily record sheets
- verbal feedback from charts and records maintained by the setting
- individual diaries, which are useful for babies as their routine needs vary greatly.

A3 Promoting dignity and respect and encouraging independence

You will need to develop the skills and understanding to promote dignity and respect and to encourage the children's independence during physical care routines.

Privacy

Nappy changing

Children should always be given privacy during nappy changing. Your setting may have a designated changing room that allows an element of privacy when changing nappies, while ensuring practitioners are working in sight and sound of colleagues. Making sure that young children are changed quickly also helps to maintain respect and privacy.

Toileting

Privacy is essential in toileting routines so that children learn from a young age that their bodies are private and belong to them. If a child is able to go to the toilet independently, encourage them to shut the door but let them know you are close by if they need you. Some children are reluctant to use the toilet and can be embarrassed or scared of their bodily functions. In these situations, it is important to reassure the child so that their fears can be overcome.

What if...?

You have been asked to accompany a colleague to the bathroom to assist the pre-school children in toileting and hand washing before lunch. One child doesn't like getting undressed and will try to avoid going to the toilet even when they really need to.

List three ways in which you can support this child.

Link it up

See Unit 1, A2 for more information about whistleblowing.

Whistleblowing

WHISTLEBLOWING is when a member of staff reports a concern about another colleague. If you witness any situation that gives you cause for concern, you must inform the designated lead for safeguarding in your setting without delay. Safeguarding is everyone's responsibility and a problem should never be ignored.

Causes for concern
- A member of staff handling a child roughly.
- A member of staff shouting at a child.
- A member of staff treating a child more or less favourably than others in the setting.

- A member of staff taking a child into a space where they cannot be seen by others.
- A member of staff using their phone during toileting/changing routines.

Developing children's skills in dressing and undressing

Always allow plenty of time for children to get dressed and undressed so they have the opportunity to practise these skills at their own pace. If you are hurrying them to dress or put on shoes and coats for outdoor play, perhaps you should consider starting preparations earlier.

Practise

When you are supporting children to dress themselves in your work setting, try following these practical tips:

- Shoes – undo buckles or laces and encourage the child to put their foot in the shoe before helping again with fastenings. Place shoes in front of the child so they know which one to put on which foot.

- Jackets – hold the jacket at the child's level and use simple instructions, for example 'Arms in, one, two, well done,' to help a child to put it on.

- Zips – put the zip into its clasp and encourage the child to pull it up for themselves.

You can support children to dress themselves by letting them have a go before helping out

Age and ability

The level of support a child will need with physical and personal care routines will be determined by their age and stage of development. As you saw in Unit 2, children develop in the same sequence but at different rates. Getting to know your children well and having a good understanding of patterns of development will help you understand how much support a child needs from you.

Link it up

Refresh your memory of children's ages and stages of development by re-reading Unit 2, A2.

Supporting personal, social and emotional development

The EYFS framework outlines the areas of learning and development for young children. Personal, social and emotional development (PSED) is one of the prime areas and is extremely relevant to physical and personal care. See the diagram below. During care routines you should be aware of how you can support children in their personal, social and emotional development. For instance, when brushing a child's hair you could compliment them on it; this will help them to develop a positive sense of themselves.

Table 4.5: How care routines benefit personal, social and emotional development

Care routine	Personal, social and emotional development
Changing a baby's nappy	Giving your full attention to the baby will help them in forming positive relationships
Dressing a child	Praising them for doing it themselves will help them to gain confidence in their own abilities

Figure 4.3: The personal, social and emotional benefits of supporting children's physical care needs

How you help and support children's physical care needs in the setting will have an impact on their development and wellbeing. The needs of the child must be central to every aspect of care you undertake.

Practise

Can you think of other ways you could support a child's personal, social or emotional development? Make a list of three things you could do next time you are involved in a child's personal care.

Link it up

Unit 2 and Unit 5 will provide you with detailed information about the prime and specific areas of the EYFS.

Encouraging participation and independence

By talking with children about aspects of their routines, you are sending a clear message that you have respect for them. For example, you might ask the child if you can change their nappy or ask if they need help when going to the toilet. Children who feel they are heard and have their wishes respected will feel a greater sense of security and wellbeing in your care. Think about how independent children feel when they discover they can drink from a cup for the first time or manage to eat their meal without the assistance of an adult. This will have a positive impact on their feelings of self-worth and self-esteem.

Encouraging children's awareness of health and wellbeing

When supporting physical care routines for children, it is important to talk to them about why you are doing things. You can explain to children even from a young age to give them a basic understanding of their own health and wellbeing. Here are some ways that this can be done.

- Nappy changing – you will notice your colleagues talking to a young child explaining that their nappy needs changing so they don't get a sore bottom.
- Hand washing – you can talk to children about germs and how they can get a poorly tummy if they don't wash their hands.
- Snack time – you can talk about foods giving us energy and muscles.

Sharing and turn-taking

Learning to share and take turns gives children the essential skills needed to develop socially and build relationships with other children. There are many ways in which sharing and turn-taking can be encouraged and practised during everyday routines, such as:

- getting children involved in taking turns to set the table at mealtimes
- encouraging children to take turns in helping prepare snacks and drinks
- developing children's ability to wait for their turn, for example washing hands or getting ready to go outside to play.

Continuity of care

CONTINUITY OF CARE means ensuring you are adopting the same approach to meeting children's physical care needs in the setting as at home. 'All about me' sheets and child information records that are completed when a child joins your setting are a useful source of information. They will provide all the details you need to make sure you follow the established routine for the child. Particular features of this may include:

- sleep times
- feed times
- methods to soothe to sleep
- favourite activities.

By making sure there is continuity between the care routine at home and in the setting, you are supporting children's sense of wellbeing and feeling of security. This will have a positive impact on how they settle in at the setting as they will feel a real sense of safety and belonging if familiar aspects of their routine are maintained.

Skills and knowledge check

- ☐ I can complete care routine records.
- ☐ I can support children to wash their hands.
- ☐ I can encourage children to be independent in dressing.

- ◯ I know how and when to use personal protective equipment.
- ◯ I understand the whistleblowing policy of my setting.
- ◯ I can list at least four strategies for settling children into the setting.
- ◯ I know what is meant by continuity of care.
- ◯ I know why rest and sleep are important for young children.

B Maintain safe environments for carrying out physical care routines in early years settings

B1 Contributing to general safety checks in the early years setting

To maintain a safe and healthy environment for children in your care, you must always follow your setting's procedures regarding daily checks, record keeping and hygiene routines.

Daily safety checks

Indoor and outdoor environments should be checked at the beginning and end of the day so that hazards, broken equipment and faults can be quickly identified and managed.

In addition, regular visual sweeps of the environment throughout the day will ensure the safety and wellbeing of children and adults.

Daily checklists should be completed for the following:
- kitchens
- toilets
- rooms and corridors used by children and adults
- outdoor spaces.

Practise

Create your own checklist for the kitchen, toilets, indoor and outdoor spaces. Now compare this with your setting's daily checklist for the same areas. How well did you do?

This will help you prepare for your end-of-unit assessment as you will need to show you have conducted safety checks when being observed supporting children's care routines.

Reporting health and safety issues

If you have any concerns about the environment, you should report them verbally immediately so that action can be taken. Concerns should also be recorded on any checklists or reporting forms your setting uses. You should tell your line manager, room supervisor or the designated health and safety officer. It is the responsibility of the designated health and safety officer of the setting to ensure that all aspects of the environment are clean, safe and managed well to minimise hazards and harm to children and adults.

Risk assessments

A **RISK ASSESSMENT** is a written document that identifies hazards for a particular activity, event or area and records how these can be minimised.

All early years settings are required to assess the risk in environments and activities for young children and demonstrate how they will manage risks on a daily basis. The table below shows an example.

Table 4.6: Example of a risk assessment

Hazard	Who might be harmed	Precautions already in place	Further action needed	Date action completed
Radiators	Children	Temperature regulators	Daily checks Regular heating service	Service completed Jan 2017
Wet floors around water-play area	Children and/or adults	Mop and dry floor regularly	Purchase 'wet floor' sign	Sept 2016
Scissors and glue on craft table	Children	Round-edge scissors used under adult supervision	Constant supervision when using scissors and glue	

It is impossible to remove all risks posed to children. Indeed, some risks in play are needed to challenge children's skills and abilities. If risks can't be removed it is important to establish how they can be managed to minimise accidents and injuries in the setting. It is your responsibility to follow any risk assessment guidance you are provided with in the setting.

Recording accidents and incidents

It is a legal requirement to record all accidents and incidents that happen in the setting and away from the setting when the child is in your care, so that clear information can be passed on to parents and to the management of the setting.

Accident and incident log books should be easily accessible so information can be recorded without delay, as soon as possible after the incident.

Practise

Find out where the accident or incident log book is kept in your setting.

When completing an accident or incident log book, it is important to include as much information as you can. This is to ensure comprehensive feedback to managers and parents, but also to help medical professionals if a child needs medical attention. Read the checklist to see what information should be included.

CHECKLIST ACCIDENT AND INCIDENT RECORDS

☐ Time, date and nature of accident or incident

☐ Name, age and DOB (date of birth) of child

☐ Where and how the accident or incident happened

☐ The type and location of any injury (a body map can be used)

☐ The action taken at the time, any action taken later and by whom

☐ The signature of the staff member who dealt with the accident or incident

☐ The signature of a senior member of staff to whom the accident or incident was reported

☐ A countersignature by the parent when the child is collected

---

Evacuation procedures

EVACUATIONS (the removal of everybody from a setting) are carried out regularly to ensure that all practitioners and children know how to leave the building in a calm and orderly manner if the need should arise in an emergency. Examples of an emergency that might require evacuation include flood, fire or an intruder.

Each setting will have a clear procedure and plan for evacuation. Make sure you are aware of what it says. The list of 'dos' and 'don'ts' below is likely to be included.

Table 4.7: Evacuation 'dos' and 'don'ts'

Do	Don't
• Stop what you are doing when the alarm sounds; gather the children and do a head count	• Panic
	• Run
• Follow instructions given by your supervisor or evacuation co-ordinator	• Stop to collect belongings
	• Ignore instructions given to you
• Make your way to the nearest available exit	
• Walk the children calmly to the designated meeting point	
• Head count again	
• Offer reassurance and praise to the children	

Link it up

Unit 1, B2 provides more information about evacuation procedures.

Fire exits

In your daily checks of the environment, you will need to make sure that fire exits are not blocked and can be opened without needing a key in an emergency. It is illegal for any premises to have blocked fire exits from either the inside or outside of the building. Exits should be easily accessible so there should not be any equipment or furniture blocking the exit route or the door. Signage should also be displayed so that the safest and quickest route can be taken to evacuate the premises.

Security measures

In addition to keeping premises safe, it is important to consider how you ensure the security and personal safety of children and adults in the setting. When you walk into the setting, it should very soon be evident that security of children is maintained.

Examples of this could include:

- keypad or card-swipe entry to the setting to prevent strangers entering unsupervised
- high-level door handles to prevent children exiting rooms unaccompanied
- visitors' signing-in book so an accurate record is maintained of people on the premises
- signing-in sheets to ensure all children are accounted for
- high, secure fences in outdoor play areas to keep children safe and secure.

Practise

How safe is your setting? Look at the following questions and identify the security features that you can see.

- How do you gain access to the setting?
- How many adults are there in the room you work in?
- How many children are in the room you work in?
- Can parents just walk into a room to collect their child?
- Can a child get out of the premises or garden unsupervised?

B2 Maintaining cleanliness and hygiene in the setting

You have a role in providing a safe environment in your setting and you should develop the skills and understanding needed to fulfil your role.

Hygiene and infection control

There are many ways in which you and your colleagues can support good hygiene practice and control infection within the setting. You will see examples of these throughout your working day, from hygiene procedures when preparing food to cleaning and maintenance of toys and equipment. See also Figure 4.4 below.

What if?

Imagine a 9-month-old baby in your care had diarrhoea this morning and has since been sick. This has been dismissed as nothing to worry about as he is teething. The baby remains in the setting for the rest of the day. The following day another baby is not in nursery as they have picked up a sickness bug.

1 Do you think the two incidents are related?

2 What should the setting have done the previous day when the 9-month-old was sick?

3 What hygiene practices should the setting follow to prevent the sickness bug spreading further?

Key hygiene and infection control points include:

- appropriate waste disposal
- hand washing
- cleaning of equipment
- good food hygiene
- cleaning and maintenance of the setting
- clear policies and procedures for illness in children.

Figure 4.4: Coughs and colds can be spread rapidly through particles in the air and poor hygiene practices. Always cover your mouth when coughing or sneezing and wash your hands afterwards

Storing food safely

All settings that provide food and drink have to ensure they meet food standards safety requirements. They must also be registered with their local environmental health department, which checks the premises to ensure food hygiene standards are maintained. Table 4.8 states how food should be stored to make sure it remains safe to eat.

Table 4.8: Safe food storage

Storing food in the fridge	Storing food in the freezer	Storing food in cupboards
<ul><li>Always ensure fridge temperature is maintained in the range 0–5 °C.</li><li>Keep raw and cooked meats separate, ensuring raw meat is stored on the lowest shelf to prevent cross-contamination of food.</li><li>Fresh fruit (except pineapples and bananas) keep for longer when stored in the fridge.</li><li>Once opened, dairy products and meat products such as cheese and ham should be resealed and kept in an airtight container.</li><li>Leftover food can be cooled, covered and kept in the fridge for 48 hours or frozen immediately.</li><li>Check use-by dates to ensure out-of-date food and perished products are not served to children.</li></ul>	<ul><li>Ensure the core temperature of the freezer remains below −18 °C.</li><li>When buying frozen foods, food should be in transit for no more than 2 hours.</li><li>Ensure leftovers you wish to freeze have been cooled before storing so the freezer temperature is not compromised.</li><li>Rotate freezer stock to ensure food with the nearest use-by date is eaten first.</li></ul>	<ul><li>Keep items such as bread, onions and potatoes in a dark and cool cupboard to prolong shelf life.</li><li>Avoid using tinned food that is rusty or badly damaged.</li><li>Regularly check dates of cupboard stock and rotate to use the oldest first.</li><li>Never store any food items directly on floor surfaces.</li></ul>

Washing up and storage of feeding utensils

When washing up cups, plates, bowls, beakers, knives, forks and spoons, adopting a 'clean as you go' approach to washing up ensures the environment is well managed and clean. It also helps to make sure you have clean equipment ready anytime you need it.

CHECKLIST   WASHING UP

- [ ] Remove loose and heavy food waste, scrape plates and rinse utensils
- [ ] Wash feeding utensils with hot water and a detergent, for example washing up liquid
- [ ] Rinse to remove any traces of detergent and food particles with clean hot water
- [ ] Leave feeding utensils to dry naturally in the air, as the use of dirty tea towels can spread bacteria
- [ ] Remember that detergent removes grease and dirt while disinfectant does the job of reducing bacteria to a safe level
- [ ] Store clean and dry feeding utensils in cupboards where dust, dirt and contamination can be kept to a minimum

Sterilisation procedures

Babies' bottles, cups, dummies and utensils should be STERILISED – a process which kills bacteria that can cause diarrhoea and vomiting. These items should continue to be sterilised until a child reaches 12 months as babies under that age are less able to fight off germs.

Table 4.9 shows the different ways of sterilising equipment.

Table 4.9: Methods of sterilising

Cold water tank	Electric steam sterilising unit	Microwave sterilising unit
• Wash equipment by hand in soapy water to remove any milk residue stuck in bottles and teats or any food residue stuck in utensils • Items should then be rinsed thoroughly of bubbles • Fill the cold water tank to the correct level, add a sterilising tablet and allow to dissolve • Submerge each item in the water, ensuring there are no trapped air bubbles • Place the cover to keep items submerged, put on the lid and leave the unit for a minimum of 30 minutes before removing any equipment for use • Shake excess water from the equipment and use • Change the tank solution every 24 hours	• Wash equipment by hand in soapy water to remove any milk residue stuck in bottles and teats or any food residue stuck in utensils • Items should then be rinsed thoroughly of bubbles • Check bottles are safe to steam • With openings facing down, place bottles and teats securely in unit • Switch on the steriliser and allow it to steam in accordance with the manufacturer's guidelines (approximately 8–12 minutes) • Bottles will remain sterile in the unit for up to 6 hours as long as it remains sealed	• Wash equipment by hand in soapy water to remove any milk residue stuck in bottles and teats or any food residue stuck in utensils • Items should then be rinsed thoroughly of bubbles • Check bottles can be put in the microwave • Place bottles and teats in the microwave • Do not seal bottles as pressure will build up in them • Microwave for 90 seconds • Use immediately

Cleaning routines

An essential part of your daily routine in an early years setting is maintaining a clean and hygienic environment. This can include:

- wiping tables before and after meals and snacks
- mopping floors following spillages and toileting accidents (settings often have colour-coded mops for use in different areas)
- cleaning highchairs before and after use
- cleaning toilets and nappy-changing facilities after use
- scheduled cleaning of toys and equipment
- cleaning at the end of the day.

Cleaning routines should always be carried out following the setting's guidelines. The manufacturer's guidelines must be followed when using any detergents or disinfectants.

Effective cleaning of materials, utensils and areas of the setting helps to:

- reduce the spread of bacteria and infections
- meet health and safety requirements
- reduce accidents, for example mopping up spillages immediately to prevent slipping
- increase hygiene standards in the setting
- discourage pests, such as flies on leftover food waste
- show the setting is committed to providing a clean and safe environment for children.

Link it up

Look back over Unit 1, B1 to find out more about legislation that covers safe storage of hazardous materials.

Personal hygiene and safe and hygienic environments

Personal hygiene plays a crucial role in providing a safe and hygienic setting – both indoors and outdoors during play activities, when supporting care routines or when preparing foods and snacks. It is important you maintain your personal hygiene as this directly contributes to or detracts from the provision of a safe and hygienic environment in your setting. See Figure 4.5 for essential personal hygiene practices.

Figure 4.5: Give careful consideration to personal hygiene practices that should be demonstrated in the setting

Being a good role model

You should follow cleaning and hygiene practices such as hand washing and good personal hygiene in the setting. You will be demonstrating to children how these can be done and done well. Developing good habits yourself helps children to develop them too.

The following are examples of modelling good hygiene practice.

- When you sneeze, use a clean tissue and dispose of it in the bin or down the toilet.
- Put litter from activities in bins as soon as you have finished the activity.
- Wash your hands alongside children.
- Use dustpans and brushes to sweep up hazards such as sand spillage, and involve children in helping.
- Have a pair of indoor and outdoor shoes to prevent muddy shoes coming into clean play areas.

Encouraging children to help

Children look up to those who care for them, and pre-school children can often be seen modelling what the adults do in their play. By involving them and giving them the role of teacher, you encourage children to feel important and should find they are more than eager to tidy up. You could challenge children to see if they can tidy away the toys before the music stops or you could have a named helper for the day who is 'in charge'. This can make a child feel very important and is lots of fun.

Using your initiative

As cleaning and hygiene routines become second nature to you, it is more than likely you will adopt a 'do it now' approach to tasks. For example, when a child spills a drink or the sand on the floor, it becomes a slip hazard; respond swiftly and don't wait around for someone else to clean it up.

Show INITIATIVE and fix the problem straight away or report it to a senior colleague. In doing so, you are not only keeping the environment clean and safe for the children, but also showing you care about the standards provided for children.

What if...?

You have been asked to collect a box of building blocks from an outdoor store cupboard for the children to play with. You notice the box is broken and the blocks are damp and covered in mould.

1   Would you give these to the children to play with?

2   What could happen if you give children dirty toys and equipment?

B3 Participating in setting up and tidying away activities throughout the day

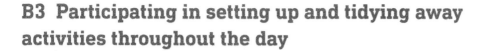

Setting up and tidying away activities throughout the day helps in maintaining a safe and hygienic environment. Imagine what impression you would give to families if all the toys and resources were tipped all over the floor and not tidied away after use.

Tidying away

Tidying away is a routine that you will take part in over and over again during the course of the day. You will tidy away toys and activities as you rotate the resources you provide for the children to play with. You will also tidy away before mealtimes, rest times and outdoor play and at the end of the day.

Tidying away ensures environments do not become cluttered or a safety hazard. Adopting a 'tidy as you go' policy makes the task of tidying up at the end of the day easier and also reduces the likelihood of toys getting lost or broken.

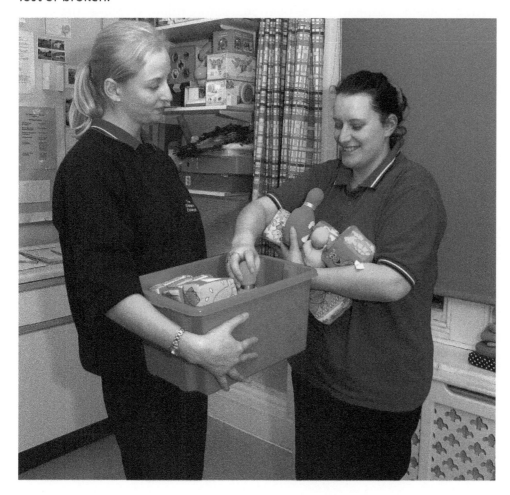

Putting toys away in their correct location allows other adults and children to find them easily

Wiping down tables

You should clean tables before and after activities, including food service, to keep them free of dirt and germs. Remember that you should always use one cloth to wipe tables before and after meals and a different cloth to wipe tables after art activities to remove paint and glue.

CHECKLIST CLEANING TABLES

☐ Select the appropriate cloth for the task

☐ Remove food or activity debris

☐ Wipe the table using the cloth and washing up liquid, which will cut through the grease

☐ Spray the table with approved anti-bacterial spray, which will disinfect the area

☐ Wipe the table again with the cloth

☐ Dry the table thoroughly using a paper towel or leave it to air dry

☐ Do not clean tables while children are still sitting at them and never use anti-bacterial sprays near to children

---

Preparing rooms for mealtimes and rest periods

Areas that are used for play are often used for mealtimes and rests too. This means you will need to adapt the environment throughout the day to accommodate the different routines. Planning ahead is important so that you have plenty of time before meals are served to get tables and chairs ready and make sure they have been cleaned for food service.

Equally, you may be using the same area or an area close by to put out beds or relaxing cushions for rest periods. Before doing so, make sure all toys and resources have been tidied away and the area is clean and fit for purpose.

Setting out rooms for different activities

If you are fortunate enough to work in a setting that has different floor surfaces within one room, you can set up activities efficiently. Hard surfaces provide the ideal location for messy activities, while carpeted areas are good for floor activities, reading books and role play.

If you have an all carpeted area, you may need to consider plastic floor coverings for messy activities and mealtimes. If the whole floor is hard, put out rugs for activities where children need to sit on the floor.

Planning is important: you must consider what activities should go where. For example, it would not be a good idea to have the book corner next to a door that is opened every five minutes. Equally, it would not be a good idea to put the water tray next to the computer.

Sweeping and mopping

Sweeping and mopping of floors is usually done after:
- food has been served
- a child has had a toileting accident
- materials have been spilled, for example sand or water tray.

A routine clean is carried out at the end of the day.

After mopping floors, including the kitchen, main rooms and toilets, it is important that the area is either shut off from public use or that clear signs and notices alert people that the floor is wet. It is best to carry out such routines when children are not present, but mopping will be unavoidable if you are cleaning up a milk spillage or responding to a wet bathroom floor after a toileting accident.

Always remember that separate mops and brushes should be used for food, materials and bodily fluids. As with cloths for tables, a colour-coded or labelled system ensures the right mops are used and avoids cross-contamination in the setting.

What if...?

You have just mopped the floor following lunchtime as drink and food were spilled. The floor is wet and is a slip hazard. You then go on your lunch break without telling anybody you have mopped the floor. Following your lunch break you are informed a child slipped and fell on the wet floor.

1 What could be the consequence of this fall?

2 What should you have done to prevent it?

Moving and handling equipment

You may be required to move and handle equipment or resources as part of your role in adapting the environment for different purposes. It's important that you protect yourself and others from any injury while doing this by:

- always seeking help if equipment is big or heavy
- following manual handling procedures when lifting and carrying objects – check with your setting to find out what these are
- making sure equipment moved is safe, stable and not causing an obstruction
- storing equipment in accordance with manufacturers' instructions
- identifying and removing equipment and resources that are faulty, damaged or broken and reporting to the relevant person in your setting.

Link it up

Procedures for manual handling are detailed in Unit 1, B2.

Taking away and disposing of food

Throughout the day you will be responsible for clearing away after snacks and meals. Disposing of food waste correctly is essential. It helps to ensure that levels of hygiene are maintained and that the risk posed by contamination from pests in the setting is kept to a minimum.

Appropriate food disposal

The strategies listed below will prove effective in maintaining a clean and safe environment and reduce the likelihood of contamination in the setting.

- Scrape food waste from plates into a designated bin.
- Store food-waste bins away from children's play areas.
- Do not mix food waste with toilet and nappy waste.
- Empty food-waste bins daily into an external bin.
- Clean food-waste bins daily to destroy bacteria and nasty smells.
- Ensure external food-waste/compost bins are sealed to deter pests.

Storing children's belongings and work products

Most settings will have designated areas where children's belongings are stored. Table 4.10 shows good practice for storing some of these items safely.

Table 4.10: Safe storage of children's belongings and work products

Coats and bags	Nappy-changing equipment	Milk feeds	Artwork or other products
• A labelled coat peg is often provided so that children can put away their belongings on arrival and access them easily when preparing to go outdoors to play • All coats, shoes and spare clothes should be labelled to avoid mix ups	• Children's changing equipment can be stored in their own bags on a coat peg, but some settings have baskets in nappy-changing rooms where children's nappies, creams and wipes are stored • These should be labelled and only used for the named child	• For young babies on milk feeds, settings will have a designated milk fridge where bottles can be stored until needed • These must be labelled so that a baby receives the correct milk	• Settings will often provide a drawer where children can store anything they make during the day • Always write the child's name on their artwork and check the spelling of the name.

Skills and knowledge check

☐ I can sterilise feeding equipment for babies.

☐ I have carried out daily health and safety checks in the setting.

☐ I have supported daily cleaning routines.

☐ I have been involved in an evacuation procedure.

○ I understand the aim of a risk assessment.

○ I can give three examples of safe food storage.

○ I know the difference between a detergent and a disinfectant.

○ I can explain how to dispose of food waste.

C Support and encourage children at meal and snack times in early years settings

C1 Preparing snacks for children

You will need to develop and show the ability to prepare meals and snacks within your setting.

Encouraging healthy eating

What is healthy eating? Healthy eating is ensuring you eat a wide range of foods that provide the nutrients the body needs for health and wellbeing. As an early years assistant, you will have a responsibility to ensure that children are aware of what healthy eating is. You will also encourage children to make healthy food choices for themselves.

The Eatwell Guide, see Figure 4.6, recommended by the government, provides information about the amount of foods that should be consumed from each essential food group to ensure a healthy balanced diet.

Providing a wide range of meals and snacks that contain all of the essential food groups gives children variety in their diet. It can encourage healthy eating.

In addition to providing balanced healthy meals and snacks, you can encourage healthy eating through activities such as making smoothies and fruit salads and playing taste-testing games with children.

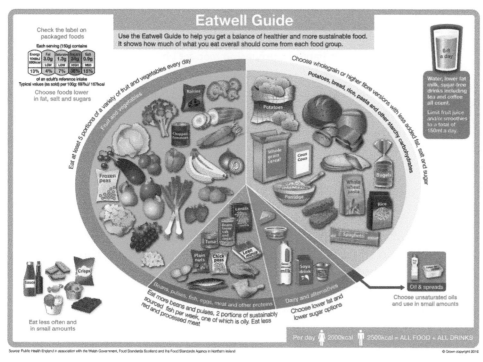

Figure 4.6 The Eatwell Guide

Food allergies

There are many food **ALLERGIES** that young children can suffer from today but it is important to understand the difference between a food allergy and a food intolerance.

Food allergies involve the response of the body's immune system to foods. Most allergic reactions are mild. However, it is possible for a child to have a serious, life-threatening response to an allergy. **FOOD INTOLERANCES** cause you to react badly or feel ill when you eat or touch a particular substance. Symptoms can be similar to those for food allergies but they are not life-threatening. Common **ALLERGENS** include: dairy, eggs, fish, milk, nuts, shellfish, soya and wheat. Posters summarising these allergens are readily available online for display in kitchens and food preparation areas.

Table 4.11: Symptoms of allergic reactions and intolerances

Symptoms of allergic reaction to food	Symptoms of food intolerance
• Vomiting	• Bloating
• Raised itchy rash on face or body	• Wind
• Swelling of the face including eyes, lips tongue and inside mouth	• Stomach cramps
• Itchy feeling in mouth or ears	• Diarrhoea
• Anaphylaxis	• Skin rashes

ANAPHYLAXIS is a response of the immune system to a substance. It results in symptoms including skin irritation, altered heart rhythm and restricted airway. This is the most serious and potentially life-threatening reaction and requires immediate medical attention.

Link it up

Look back at Unit 1, B4 to identify how to respond to anaphylaxis in young children.

CHECKLIST AVOIDING ALLERGIC REACTIONS

- ☐ Ensure you have collated information about children's dietary restrictions and update these in discussion with parents regularly. Know where this information is kept and refer to it regularly
- ☐ Check ingredients of processed food that may cause allergies
- ☐ Never assume or guess whether any freshly prepared food item does or does not contain specific ingredients
- ☐ Keep separate utensils for preparing and cooking snacks and meals for children with allergies
- ☐ Always wash your hands between preparing food for children with and without allergies
- ☐ Clearly identify which foods are to be served to children with allergies
- ☐ If in doubt, ask for help

Religions and cultural dietary considerations

Some children in your setting will be unable to eat some foods owing to religious or cultural beliefs. It is never acceptable to dismiss the family's wishes regarding these foods and you should always respect their decisions for food choices and restrictions. In addition to specific foods listed in the table, **FASTING** (going without food) is observed at particular times such as Ramadan. Children generally do not take part in fasting until puberty.

Religion/Culture	Food restrictions
Buddhism	• No meat
Hinduism	• No beef • Restrictions on other meats and fish
Islam	• No pork • Certain birds cannot be eaten
Judaism	• No pork • No shellfish • Meat and dairy cannot be eaten at the same meal
Rastafarianism	• No pork • Unlikely to eat other meat and shellfish • Will only eat fish less than 30 cm long
Seventh Day Adventist	• No pork • Avoid meat and fish
Vegetarian	• No meat • No fish
Vegan	• No meat • No fish • No dairy or animal products

Table 4.12: Foods that may be excluded on religious or cultural grounds

Supporting the intake of regular fluids

Water is essential for life. It helps to keep us hydrated and helps with our bodily functions. We would not survive without water; equally, restricted access to water can have devastating consequences for our health and wellbeing. The Welfare Requirements of the EYFS state that drinking water should be readily available to children at all times.

This can be provided in the following ways:
- a water fountain
- a jug of water and cups on a table
- individually labelled drinks bottles for children
- regular reminders throughout the day to have a drink
- offering drinks after sleep or physical exercise
- encouraging children to drink more in hot weather.

Timings of meals and snacks

Meal and snack times are planned so that food and drink are served at regular intervals throughout the day to rehydrate and refuel children.

Settings that are open all day will provide:
- breakfast
- a morning snack
- lunch
- an afternoon snack
- tea.

Your setting will have a set time when these are served but will always adapt timings of meals and snacks to a change in routine, such as a late return after an outing.

Appropriate snacks

Fresh fruit and vegetables are good choices and make up a large proportion of snacks offered to children in early years settings. But it is also essential that children have a balance of all food groups in the snacks served to ensure they have enough energy.

CHECKLIST | **APPROPRIATE SNACKS FOR CHILDREN**

- [ ] Fresh fruit, for example grapes, banana, apple
- [ ] Chopped vegetables, for example carrot sticks, cucumber
- [ ] Toasted crumpets with jam
- [ ] Breadsticks and hummus
- [ ] Cheese and crackers
- [ ] Dried fruit, for example raisins, apricots
- [ ] Yogurt
- [ ] Home-made biscuits
- [ ] Buttered toast
- [ ] Soup
- [ ] Sandwiches

Practise

Obtain a copy of your setting's menu plan and make notes on the following points.

- Does the menu provide a balanced and healthy diet for children?
- How many portions of fruit and vegetables are provided daily?
- What food types are missing from the menu? Why do you think this is?

Portion sizing

Appetites and appropriate meal portions can vary greatly from child to child. The following ideas will help to ensure children do not feel overwhelmed by the foods they are given.

- Start with small portions; too little is better than too much.
- Use child-sized plates.
- Avoid adult-sized plates as this can lead to overeating.
- Respect a child's decision about how much to eat.
- Never insist a child cleans their plate.
- Involve children in serving food so they can begin to make judgements about how much they can eat.

Some children will have a good appetite and may need or ask for more food than others. This is fine so long as a healthy balance is maintained. If you have concerns about overeating, raise these with your supervisor.

Preparation of snacks

Your setting will have its own system for preparing snacks. This may be done in the setting's kitchen by the chef or cook. Increasingly, in many settings, snacks may be prepared at the table with the children's involvement.

Involving children in preparing food and snacks has many advantages.

- Children can find out more about the foods they eat.
- Children can experiment with new tastes and textures.
- It helps control portion sizes.

- It provides a wonderful opportunity to talk to children.
- It creates a relaxing snack time.
- It helps to develop children's social and communication skills.

Involving children in the preparation of snacks can be a great way of encouraging them to try new food

Food hygiene and EYFS requirements

The Welfare Requirements of the EYFS clearly detail what your setting should be doing to maintain good hygiene standards when preparing snacks and meals.

Settings should provide:

- a suitable area for the preparation of foods, for example a designated kitchen or kitchen area
- suitable equipment for food preparation, for example chopping boards, sterilising equipment for babies' utensils
- food hygiene training for all staff members who prepare children's snacks and meals.

CHECKLIST   FOOD PREPARATION

☐ Put on an apron and tie your hair back if it is long

☐ Wash your hands thoroughly

☐ Remove any jewellery

☐ Avoid wearing nail varnish

☐ Use correct colour-coded chopping boards for dairy, fruit and vegetables, meat and fish products

☐ Wash fresh fruit and vegetables thoroughly to ensure soil and dirt are removed

☐ Cut up items that could pose a choking hazard, for example grapes

☐ Never leave food out that should be refrigerated longer than absolutely necessary

☐ Always clean food preparation surfaces before you start and 'clean as you go'

☐ Ensure snacks for children with allergies are prepared separately to avoid cross-contamination

What if...?

You have been asked by your colleague to prepare buttered toast and fresh fruit for snack time. In the kitchen you discover there is only one white chopping board and are told it is okay to use this for all food preparation.

1 Do you think the setting is following good food hygiene practices?

2 What are the dangers of using the same chopping board for all food preparation?

Setting tables appropriately

Sitting children in groups at tables provides great social opportunities and also encourages the development of skills as they watch and learn from each other. Where possible, position younger children in highchairs or booster seats close to the table so they too are engaged in the social experience of mealtimes.

Tables should be set with enough equipment for all the children eating. Equipment should be adapted to suit the individual needs of young children. For example, some children may need cups with lids and others may need an open-topped beaker.

Serving meals and snacks

Meal and snack service can vary from setting to setting. Some settings serve food to the children while others actively involve children in the process.

Involving children in the service of food helps to:

- enable children to express their wishes
- make you aware of children's likes and dislikes
- decrease food waste
- encourage children to try new foods
- allow children to learn about portion control
- encourage social skills as they learn to say 'please' and 'thank you'.

C2 Helping to feed children

Your role in helping with feeding is much wider than helping children to handle cutlery or spoon feeding very small children.

Sitting with children at mealtimes

Children should always be supervised at mealtimes. This is important to ensure they do not choke on foods, and to manage any spillages that may occur. In addition to these health and safety factors, it is important to sit with children at mealtimes so you can monitor how much they eat and offer help as and when they need it.

Sitting with children can also enhance development as you support them to use equipment independently and build **FINE MOTOR SKILLS**. Chatting to the children as you sit with them also encourages development of communication and language.

Promoting positive responses to food

Children can be reluctant to try foods they have not seen or eaten before. In these circumstances it is important to reduce any anxiety about the new experience. You will have much more success if you gently encourage children to try to eat something and children will be less likely to develop long-term issues about food.

Strategies to help children try new foods and snacks

Look at the strategies that can be used to help children try new foods; in your setting this will be part of everyday practice.

- Talk about where foods come from.
- Introduce cooking activities to children so they can experience foods first hand.
- Use activities to present food, for example a tasting game or food lotto.
- Allow children to control how much they take, for example start with a small amount.
- Allow children to touch, smell and lick foods even if they choose not to eat them.
- Listen to children regarding food preferences.
- Never force a child to eat food.
- Be a good role model and try new foods yourself in the presence of children.

Provide a relaxed and social environment

A relaxed social environment is just as important for children as it is for adults. Mealtimes should always be an unhurried occasion where children have time to eat and enjoy their food and to join in conversation. Like adults, children enjoy food more when it is part of a calm, relaxed and social event. See Figure 4.7 for ideas to support this.

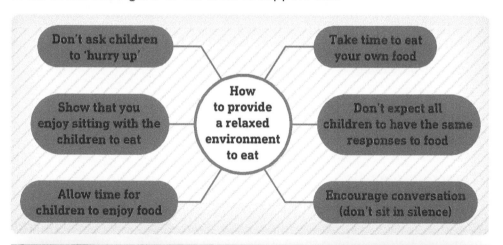

Figure 4.7: A relaxed environment to eat in

Sitting with children at mealtimes can have a positive impact on their enjoyment of food and on their social interactions

Feeding children according to their developmental needs

Babies should have an exclusive milk diet until 6 months of age. After that time, solids can be slowly introduced and milk slowly decreased. The process of starting a baby on solid food is known as WEANING.

Weaning

Solids are introduced slowly. Single items such as carrots are pureed so they are soft and can be swallowed with ease. Different purees can be gradually introduced to include a variety of fruit- and vegetable-based meals over the next few weeks. However, milk remains the primary source of nutrition as a baby becomes familiar with food. Purees can then be replaced with semi solids, which introduce small soft lumps into foods so the baby can begin to learn to chew.

Baby-led weaning

This is an alternative form of weaning. Babies are not given foods that have been pureed but are introduced to foods in the original form from the beginning of the weaning process. They are encouraged to exercise choice over what they eat and to feed themselves.

Finger foods

Finger foods must be soft or easy to break down otherwise they can be a choking hazard. Appropriate finger foods include bananas, bread and butter, avocado, cheese chunks and cooked carrots.

By the time a child is 1 year old, food should replace milk at mealtimes and babies can eat a varied diet. This should include plenty of fruit, vegetables, meat and dairy products in lumpy form or a chopped-up consistency.

Practise

Work with a colleague to research and make your own list of foods appropriate for:

1 weaning

2 baby-led weaning

3 finger foods.

Share your ideas and give reasons for your choices.

Appropriate utensils

When children are fully weaned, it is important to allow them independence during mealtimes. Always observe how a child manages for themselves before helping them. They may wish to do it for themselves. You should provide children with child-sized cutlery and encourage them to use it correctly, starting with a spoon, before moving on to handling a spoon and fork at the same time. From this stage, children eventually progress to using a knife and fork.

C3 Promoting choice and independence

You can do a lot to give children choices and to promote their independence with regard to food and snacks.

Encouraging choice

Allowing children to choose for themselves develops self-esteem and demonstrates to a child that their wishes are respected and that they are heard. Choice should be encouraged at mealtimes.

Children can be given a choice of:

- milk or water to drink
- the colour of cup they drink from
- how many pieces of fruit they have at snack time
- how much food they want at lunchtime.

Involving children in talking about healthy foods

Mealtimes and planned activities can provide opportunities to talk about healthy foods with children.

During mealtimes, talk to children about foods. For example, eating a banana can give us energy for exercise or drinking milk can help us to have strong teeth.

Get children involved in growing their own fruit and vegetables in the garden. This provides real first-hand experiences of where our foods come from and how they can make us healthy.

Pouring drinks and feeding themselves

As children begin to feed themselves, allow for trial and error as this is how children learn. Don't worry about the mess – it can easily be cleaned up.

You can support children to use cutlery and cups and to feed themselves by:

- cutting food into manageable sized pieces
- loading each spoonful ready for children to pick up
- providing child-sized cutlery
- starting by using a spoon only, before introducing a fork
- showing them how to use cutlery
- offering praise and encouragement throughout.

Children can learn to pour drinks for themselves if practitioners provide them with appropriate resources

Encourage children to pour and drink fluids by:

- providing small jugs with small amounts of water in so children can practise pouring
- helping children to progress from cups with lids by holding a cup for them to drink from
- encouraging children to hold a cup with two hands and only adding small quantities of liquid
- demonstrating to children how to hold a cup
- praising and encouraging throughout.

Encouraging children to help prepare for meals and tidy away

Children like to help. By enabling them to do so, you are providing them with skills for life. Involving them in setting the table for snack time or lunchtime can be easily achieved.

You can involve children before mealtimes by asking them to:

- wash down tables
- set tables
- collect jugs of water.

You can involve children after mealtimes by asking them to:

- clear plates and cups
- help to wash up
- put eating equipment away.

Always praise children and thank them for their help. They will experience a great sense of pride and feel important.

Joining in with mealtimes

Sitting with children to eat at snack and mealtimes can provide opportunities to:

- talk about their day
- discuss the foods they are eating
- give assistance where needed
- encourage them to try new foods
- develop social, physical and language skills.

What if...?

Karen is sitting at the lunch table in the pre-school room of Dorset Avenue Day Nursery. The children are eating vegetable lasagne. Karen does not like vegetable lasagne so she has brought in a sandwich and a packet of crisps.

1 Do you think Karen is demonstrating good practice?

2 What do you think the impact on the children could be?

Celebratory meals and festivals

As well as providing children with meals and snacks to meet their nutritional needs, early years settings also like to introduce children to foods from other cultures. This can be done as part of the daily menu or as a stand-alone activity. See Figure 4.8 for some of the main celebratory foods and festivals.

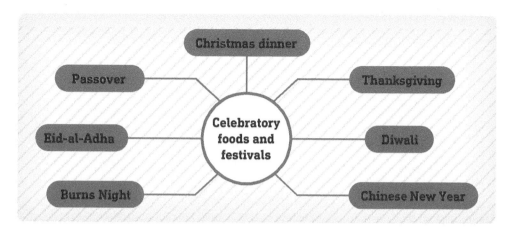

Figure 4.8: Enjoying foods from other cultures can give children experiences beyond what they already know

The benefits of celebratory meals are that they can:

- give an insight into the foods and customs of some of the children in the setting
- give children and practitioners greater understanding of the world around them
- introduce children to new tastes and textures
- involve parents and family members in the preparation of traditional foods.

Practise

Look at the celebrations identified in Figure 4.8. Challenge yourself by selecting one that you have little knowledge of. Research the food and related festivities and plan an appropriate meal for children aged 3 to 4 years in your care.

Supporting the development of social skills

Mealtimes and snack times provide an ideal opportunity for children to socialise; after all, when you go out for a meal with friends you don't sit in absolute silence until your plate is empty. Children learn from what they see so they will copy the behaviours of other children and adults. By observing how to sit and take part in conversation over meals, they will soon learn appropriate mealtime behaviours. Praise and encouragement are always the key to success and help the children to feel good about themselves and their behaviour.

Skills and knowledge check

☐ I can plan and prepare a range of healthy snacks for children of different ages.

☐ I have sat with children at mealtimes and encouraged social interactions.

☐ I can follow hygiene practices when preparing snacks.

☐ I can support the weaning process.

○ I understand why food hygiene practices must be followed.

○ I can give three examples of healthy snacks for children.

○ I can list four common food allergies.

Ready for assessment

You will be observed carrying out physical care routines and supporting meals or snack times in your setting. Start by considering which care routines and activities you can be involved in. Remember, you will need to demonstrate a consistently high standard and quality of support – not just on one occasion. As well as supporting children, you will need to demonstrate how health and safety practices are identified and followed.

So, it is important to remind yourself of all the essential behaviours and practices in this chapter. You should also make sure you have completed Section B, Unit 4 of form CPLD 1 in your Placement Experience Assessment Portfolio of Evidence. Complete the self-assessment form in your booklet and include ideas about the different skills you have developed when completing the activities for this unit. Make a note of things you could do to keep improving on these skills.

You will need to collect evidence to show how you have supported children's routines in the setting. This should include:

- daily routine logs

- witness statements from your setting supervisor or your college assessor

- menu plans and snack preparation accounts to demonstrate how you support healthy eating in the setting

- reflective summaries (these show how you have evaluated the effectiveness of the support you offer to young children during care routines).

WORK FOCUS

HANDS ON

There are some important occupational skills that you will need to practise which relate to this unit. As an early years assistant you will be responsible for basic care routines, so make sure you follow these tips.

1 Support the health and safety of yourself and individuals

- Always follow the policies and procedures of the setting when supporting children's care routines.

- Familiarise yourself with the evacuation procedures of your setting.

2 Support the care of babies and children

- Practise effective steps in hand washing so you can model good practice to children and colleagues.

- Know your role in supporting children's care routines in your setting.

3 Develop your own knowledge and practice

- Carry out your own research into a healthy diet. This knowledge will help you in the planning and preparation of food for children.

4 Maintain the environment to meet children's needs

- Carry out daily checks of the environment and report concerns to the health and safety lead practitioner.

- Complete a risk assessment for an activity to demonstrate you know how to identify and manage hazards in the setting.

Ready for work?

Imagine you have been asked by your setting to plan a fruit-salad making activity to encourage healthy eating in your pre-school room.

1 What is the most important consideration for this activity?

- [ ] A The cost of the fruit
- [ ] B The children's dietary needs, including allergies
- [ ] C When to do the activity

2 What is the best way to engage the children in the activity?

- [ ] A Make the fruit salad yourself and tell them what you are doing
- [ ] B Let them touch, taste and prepare the fruit themselves
- [ ] C Arrange for the children to go into the kitchen to watch the cook prepare the fruit salad

3 How could you encourage a reluctant child to taste the fruit?

- [ ] A Tell them they have to try it
- [ ] B Taste some yourself and allow them to explore the smell and texture for themselves
- [ ] C Remove them from the activity

4 How could you develop children's understanding of healthy eating?

- [ ] A Give them a word search
- [ ] B Talk about what fruit does for our bodies
- [ ] C Ask them to write a story.

Did you answer B for every question? If so, well done! You clearly understand how to plan and support a healthy eating activity. If not, don't worry. Take time to revisit Unit 4, Section C to improve your knowledge and skills.

5 Supporting Children's Learning through Play

Have you ever stopped to consider what play is and how it enhances children's development? In this unit you will discover what play means to children and the many benefits it has. You will find out about the wide range of play experiences available to children in early years settings. You will also learn more about the role of the practitioner in effectively supporting children's play and providing a stimulating and enabling environment where children can discover and learn.

How will I be assessed?

This is an internally assessed unit, which means that you will need to carry out a series of tasks, some of which will be assessed in the workplace. You should record your work-based activities in your Placement Experience Assessment Portfolio of Evidence. This will also help you to gather evidence for Unit 7.

For this unit you will be required to submit evidence of your understanding of:

- a range of play types
- identification of stages of play
- the benefits of each type of play for children's development
- the role of the practitioner in the activity and how they progress children's learning through play.

You will also need to demonstrate skills in:

- the preparation of play environments and providing appropriate equipment and resources for learning activities
- supporting practitioners in your setting to plan play activities and carry out some of these activities with children.

You may be asked to submit evidence in the form of:

- observations
- witness testimonies
- reflective logs
- play plans.

Assessment criteria

Pass	Merit	Distinction
Learning aim A: Explore play and learning provision for children up to five years old in an early years settings		
A.P1 Produce a brief and accurate record of the ways in which an early years setting promotes children's development through play and learning activities.	**A.M1** Produce a detailed record of ways in which an early years setting promotes children's development at different stages through different types of play and learning activities.	**A.D1** Produce a comprehensive record, assessing the ways in which an early years setting promotes different areas of children's development, for children at different stages, through different types of play and learning activities.
Learning aim B: Assist early years practitioners in preparing an enabling environment to stimulate learning through play		
B.P2 Prepare an appropriate physical environment for learning through play. **B.P3** Follow instructions accurately to prepare resources for an indoor and an outdoor play activity in an early years setting.	**B.M2** Prepare a stimulating physical environment as well as age- and stage-relevant resources that demonstrate own initiative in supporting the delivery of an early years setting's play and learning plans for indoor and outdoor play activities.	**B.D2** Prepare stimulating physical environments as well as age- and stage-appropriate resources, demonstrating independence in supporting the delivery of an early years setting's play and learning plans for indoor and outdoor play and learning activities.
Learning aim C: Support children up to five years old in planned play and learning activities in an early years setting		
C.P4 Provide appropriate support to children during planned child-initiated and planned adult-led play and learning activities. **C.P5** Produce accurate records of the impact of planned play and learning activities on an individual child's development or progress.	**C.M3** Provide effective support to children, using a range of relevant skills throughout one planned child-initiated and one adult-led planned play and learning activity.	**C.D3** Provide effective, confident and responsive support throughout planned child-initiated and adult-led play and learning activities in early years settings.

A Explore play and learning provision for children up to five years old in an early years setting

A1 Identifying types of play

As an early years assistant it is important you understand the different types of play that promote children's learning and development. During your placement you will be expected to support children during play. To do this you will need to know the different types of play (see Figure 5.1) as well as the range of play experiences and activities, and how they support the delivery of the early years framework.

Observing and categorising types of play

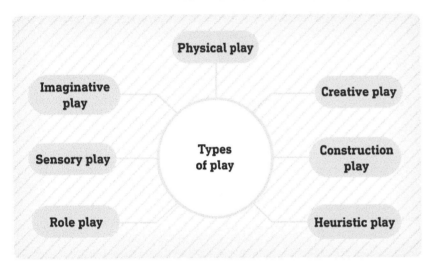

Figure 5.1: Different types of play support children's development

From the moment you step into the baby, toddler or pre-school room of your setting, you will see a wide range of play activities set up for the children. These are categorised into types of play to make it easier to understand how they support children's development. Your skills of observation will help you identify how children play so that you can plan, provide and support children's play in your setting. To observe children is to watch what they do and how they do it. Making notes of your observations will form a starting point for supporting children's ongoing learning and development.

Role play

Role play involves children acting out roles that they have directly experienced or that they have little knowledge of. Role play can involve props such as costumes and equipment. Or it can take place with just the child's imagination to support the roles being acted out.

Role play examples include:
- the home corner
- the hospital
- the café
- shops, for example hairdressers or supermarket.

Sensory play

SENSORY relates to the senses of touch, taste, smell, sight and sound. Sensory play includes very hands-on play experiences where children will use one or more of their senses as a primary source of exploration.

Activities can include:
- light boxes
- torches in tents

- food tasting
- foam, rice, gloop, pasta, popcorn play
- sand and water play
- play involving sound recording, such as talking tins.

Imaginative play

Using the imagination allows children to direct their own play using props provided. Small-world figures such as jungle animals or play people will allow children to narrate and create their own story or sequence of events. Superheroes can unleash a really imaginative world in which children become absorbed in what their heroes can do. When the imagination takes over, props are not always necessary.

Activities can include:

- a doll's house and similar playsets
- babies and pushchairs
- farm sets
- dressing-up outfits, such as superhero costumes
- small-world animal sets, such as dinosaurs or sea creatures.

Some role-play opportunities can be situations that children have experienced directly themselves

Physical play

Physical play involves children in the use of their bodies. Physical play experiences can be anything from a simple game of tag to a more complex obstacle course set up in the garden to challenge their physical skills and abilities. Physical play allows children to burn off excess energy, is essential for health and wellbeing, and develops FINE MOTOR SKILLS and GROSS MOTOR SKILLS.

Activities for gross motor skills can include:

- bikes and tricycles, slides and see-saws
- dance
- parachute games
- obstacle courses
- fixed outdoor climbing frames
- tents and tunnels.

Activities for fine motor skills include:

- threading
- painting
- play dough
- action songs and rhymes.

Creative play

In creative play there is not always an end product as the process of creativity is more important in developing children's freedom of expression than the result. Creative play allows children to experiment, explore materials and tools, and find things out for themselves.

Activities can include:

- painting
- collage and glueing
- junk-box modelling
- clay and play dough
- making own musical instruments and musical sounds.

Treasure baskets provide young children with the opportunity to investigate and learn about the world around them using their senses

Construction play

In construction play, children put things together, or build. The equipment provided often has a determined outcome or a set way in which it is put together, as with interlocking bricks. However, construction materials can be used in any way the children wish. Construction play promotes fine motor skills, imagination and the ability to solve problems.

Activities can include:

- bricks
- boxes
- interlocking straws.

Heuristic play

HEURISTIC PLAY allows children to discover for themselves. Opportunities for heuristic play include treasure baskets and **SELF-RESOURCING AREAS**. These are low-level storage boxes or shelves from which children can select objects and resources whenever they wish.

Activities can include:

- treasure baskets
- recyclable materials
- curiosity boxes, such as a box of wool and ribbon
- pots and pans and wooden spoons.

Treasure baskets contain a range of natural and manufactured materials, which may or may not have a specific theme, such as shiny or wooden. The materials allow a child to investigate properties for themselves in their own time – to touch, fill, move, stack or put together. These activities help children to make sense of the world around them.

Practise

List the types of play identified in this unit. Then look around your setting to see if you can find different play opportunities that are not listed in Learning aim A. How many different play opportunities have you identified?

Play activities that can take place indoors and outdoors

During the day, children should have access to the outdoor environment. Free-flow play between indoor and outdoor environments can encourage the children to access the outdoor spaces. Routines should be designed so that opportunities for play outdoors are maximised.

In early years settings a lot of the equipment that can be used indoors can also be provided in the outdoor environment.

Weather conditions tend to control the types of activity that can take place outdoors. For example, it is nice to have a book area in the garden, but if this is not sheltered and it rains, the books will get damaged.

Physical play equipment

Climbing frames, slides and see-saws are often a permanent fixture in the garden of an early years setting. A range of sit-and-ride toys, pushchairs, bikes and tricycles should also be available. This equipment can help build and challenge children's physical skills, including climbing, balancing and negotiating spaces.

Sand trays

Sand trays can easily be provided outdoors as long as a protective cover is in place when not being used so that the neighbourhood cats don't use it as a litter tray. Having different resources available in the outdoor and indoor sand trays will help to capture children's different interests. For example, you could offer traditional items such as buckets and spades for outside but change them for other items, such as shells or dinosaurs, when indoors.

Water play

Water trays should be filled and emptied daily in the outdoor area to minimise HAZARDS such as drowning and contaminated water. Encouraging children to choose their own resources for the water tray will make play more engaging. Add food colouring or bubbles to the water to make play more interesting.

Playhouses and dens

Increasingly, early years settings provide wooded areas or dens in their garden for children to play in. If such resources are not available, playhouses make a suitable alternative. These areas can be equipped with a wide range of resources – for example, a mud kitchen is certain to entice most children in to play. If the den or playhouse is watertight, equipment can be stored here too.

Role play

Role-play activities taken outdoors can provide a whole new meaning for children as the change in environment can steer the imagination in a different direction. Children may or may not need the support of props for role play. The dressing-up rail can provide useful props as outfits can be easily washed when they get dirty.

Plan ahead

By planning ahead, the setting can maximise the opportunity to bring other resources into outdoor play that can be brought back indoors at the end of the session. Here are some examples:

- table activities such as mark making, puzzles and games
- mats for small-world play with toys such as cars and farm animals
- trays with construction toys such as building blocks or interlocking shapes
- pop-up tents/tunnels and soft-play equipment.

A2 Recognising stages of play

To help you understand and support children's play, you will need to develop your skills of observation and to think about your role and how you may need to adapt it based on what you have seen.

Children's play at different ages and stages

Play can be self-directed or involve sensitive adult intervention. Knowing how stages of play develop in children at different ages will also help you to identify the role you have in supporting their play.

Participatory play

PARTICIPATORY PLAY means to participate or take part in play. Your interactions with children can sensitively guide the play in a given direction. Or you can enhance play as you talk to the children about what they are doing and ask them questions during play.

Questions can be direct. For example, in the home corner you might say, 'Ooh, can I have a cup of tea, please?' This type of question sets the direction of play at that moment. Or questions can be of a more open nature, such as 'What are you going to do now?' This allows a child to tell you the upcoming sequence of events and involve you in what is going to happen.

Facilitative play

FACILITATIVE means to make easier, or easy. With facilitative play, children are provided with materials and resources to enable them to access and engage fully in the play experience. This requires you to be readily available for the children should they need your help or support, but you should not need to direct their play.

Onlooker play

Your role is very passive with **ONLOOKER PLAY**. You are there to observe play and make sure the children are safe and well supervised, but not there to intervene in play or resourcing for the children. This may be hard to do, but take time to watch children engrossed in play of their own making and see how resourceful and imaginative they are when they rely on themselves and not the adult. You will only need to intervene if there is a safety issue or a dispute that children are unable to resolve for themselves.

Stages of children's play

Play is categorised into four main stages. Many early years professionals have observed children at great length to see how they play at different ages and stages, so there is general agreement about the following stages of play.

Solitary play

SOLITARY PLAY is the process of playing alone with toys. Babies and children will play alone up to around 18 months of age and will quite happily explore resources given to them using their senses of touch, taste, sight, smell and sound.

Older children revert to solitary play for specific activities when they are immersed in their own world and need no interaction from peers or adults.

Activities

The following are examples of items that can be used in solitary play activities:

- treasure baskets
- rattles
- light and sound toys
- stacking cups.

Role of the adult

The role of the adult is to:

- provide a wide range of resources for children to explore in treasure baskets
- show how things work, such as pressing a button on a toy to make a sound
- ensure toys are within easy reach for children who are not mobile
- praise and encourage children as they achieve successes in play.

Parallel play

PARALLEL PLAY simply means to play alongside another child. Around the age of 2, children will be seen playing at the same activity but are not engaged in each other's play. Equally, they are also aware of and enjoy each other's presence even though there is little or no interaction.

Activities

The following are examples of items that can be used in parallel play activities:

- sand trays
- water trays
- mats with a variety of building blocks
- a bucket of vehicles and a road mat.

Role of the adult

The role of the adult is to:

- ensure there are enough resources for the participation of all children
- supervise play to make sure resources are shared equally
- praise and encourage children as they share the play space with others.

Social play (associative and co-operative)

Around 3 years of age, children begin to play socially and engage with other children as they play. They begin with associative play, where they start to share toys and talk about their play while often still engrossed in a different activity. For example, two children may share the pile of cars between them but one may play with the garage while another is happy piling cars in a traffic jam elsewhere. From associative they move on to co-operative play, where play is fully interactive between children, follows a pattern and often has roles and rules.

Activities

Activities for social play can include:

- dressing up
- role play
- table-top games that require turn taking and have simple rules.

Role of the adult

The role of the adult is to:

- encourage conversations between children
- encourage children to share resources
- help children with attention skills to recognise when it is their turn and when it is someone else's
- praise and encourage children for sharing, taking turns and considering the needs of others.

Games that involve turn taking build social skills and help children to understand the needs of others

Practise

Observe a child in your care as they play. Note what they are playing with and with whom.

- Which stage of play can you identify from your observation?
- What evidence tells you this?
- What resources is the child using to support their stage of play?
- Think of two ways in which you as an early years assistant could support this child's learning through play.
- Put this into practice then write your own reflective log detailing how your support benefited children's play. You can use this as evidence for assessment.

A3 Benefits of play

You will need to develop the skills and understanding to recognise the importance and benefits of play and to provide informed support.

The relationship between play and learning

Professionals often define play as 'children's work'. Children learn through play and use a range of toys, resources and experiences to investigate, explore and gain a greater understanding of the world around them.

The EYFS

Link it up

For more information about the EYFS, go to Unit 1, A1 and Unit 2, C1.

The **EARLY YEARS FOUNDATION STAGE (EYFS)** is the framework that sets out standards for early years education in England. The **STATUTORY** framework document provides guidance to help you in your growing understanding of the stages of children's learning and development. It explains the broad range of development that takes place between ages 0 and 5 and the links between the areas of development. This guidance is essential for practitioners as it helps them to plan activities and experiences for children based on their current stage of development. It also helps them to consider how they can plan for and support children's progress in the early years and prepare them for school.

Prime and specific areas of learning and development

The EYFS areas of learning and development are split into two areas: the prime areas of learning and the specific areas of learning. As can be seen in Table 5.1, the prime areas of learning and development are the foundations for children's learning and they develop from birth. They are crucial in supporting the specific areas of learning and development.

Also within the EYFS are the characteristics of effective learning. These underpin the areas of learning and development.

Playing and exploring

Children learn by exploring toys and activities, starting with what is familiar to them and then finding out about things that are new by having a go for themselves. For some, this will involve watching the actions of other children first – for example, getting their hands stuck into a sensory activity such as sand play.

Active learning

Children need the opportunity to be hands-on: to get involved and concentrate on what they are doing. Active learners are happy to keep trying and gain much fulfilment from their involvement in an activity – for example, when building a tower of blocks for the first time.

Creating and thinking critically

Children learn to express their creativity using different media. They come up with ways to do things themselves and make effective links between what they say and what they do – for example, when creating a model lorry out of cereal cartons and milk-bottle tops they will talk about where the wheels will go and how they can stick them on.

Area of learning and development	Aspect
Prime areas of learning	
Communication and language	• Listening and attention • Understanding • Speaking
PHYSICAL DEVELOPMENT	• Moving and handling • Health and self-care
Personal, social and emotional development	• Making relationships • Self-confidence and self-awareness • Managing feelings and behaviour
Specific areas of learning	
Literacy	• Reading • Writing
Mathematics	• Numbers • Shape, space and measure
Understanding the world	• People and communities • The world • Technology
Expressive arts and design	• Exploring and using media and materials • Being imaginative

Table 5.1: The three prime areas of learning underpin the four specific areas of learning

How play provision supports the EYFS areas of learning and development

Table 5.2 shows how specific activities link to the EYFS and how they can link to more than one area of learning.

Table 5.2: How the different activities provided in early years settings link to the EYFS

Play provision	Links to EYFS
Tabletop games that involve turn taking	• Personal, social and emotional development (making relationships) • Communication and **LANGUAGE DEVELOPMENT** (speaking)
Sharing stories and rhymes	• Communication and language development (listening and attention) • Literacy (reading)
Outdoor play equipment such as climbing frames, balancing beams	• Physical development (moving and handling) • Personal, social and emotional development (self-confidence and self-awareness)
Mark-making activity such as paint brushes and water on concrete	• Literacy (writing) • Expressive arts and design (exploring and using media and materials)
Water play Emptying and filling containers	• Mathematics (shape, space and measure) • Physical development (moving and handling)
Dark dens Using torches and fairy lights	• Understanding the world (technology) • Expressive arts and design (exploring and using media and materials)
Role play	• Expressive arts and design (being imaginative) • Personal, social and emotional development (making relationships)

Practise

Choose an activity from your setting. Using the EYFS framework and the information in this chapter to help you, see if you can identify the areas of learning this play activity supports. Can you identify more than one area of learning within the EYFS? If you can, you are beginning to look at children's **HOLISTIC** development.

Link it up

See Unit 2, A2 for more on areas of development: physical, cognitive, emotional, social and language.

Play that supports different areas of development

It is important that you provide a wide range of opportunities for play to support different areas of learning. This will help children's holistic, all-round development.

Children's development is holistic

When you support children's development through a range of activities you will see that a given activity supports more than one aspect of their development. For example, you may set up an outdoor area with equipment to challenge children's physical skills and abilities. The activity will also support children's social skills as they learn to take turns and follow safety rules. Further, it will support language development as they tell you what they are doing or talk to their friends as they play on the equipment.

Recognising children's needs is important in helping you adapt activities to enable all to take part

Helping children to learn through play

Activities need to challenge children's skills and abilities. Children are extremely curious about the world around them and take great delight in new experiences or having resources presented in a new way. When children are stimulated and are interested in what is offered to them, they are more likely to learn from these experiences.

Different needs and abilities

An important part of your role in supporting children's play is to ensure that you recognise different needs and abilities. You will have learned about child development in Unit 2, including the sequence in which children are broadly expected to develop and the rate at which they do so. So, your first consideration is to recognise that children of the same age will not necessarily require the same level of support in play. You will need to adapt your practice accordingly. In addition, you will need to give a lot of thought to how you support children with specific needs or disabilities to ensure they have full access to the wide range of play opportunities available in your setting.

Your setting's paperwork may identify children who need additional support to learn through play and will detail how they will achieve this using members of staff and appropriate resources.

Recognising, observing and recording play information

It is best to observe children at play when the opportunity presents itself, rather than fixing a time in advance or deciding you should write a new observation every day. Observations should be about quality and not quantity.

a Try not to observe development when a child is not at their best.
b Always observe in naturally occurring situations.
c Observations should be based on your day-to-day interactions with children; take time to write a reflective account of what happened.
d Observations should not affect the quality of your work, so don't rush off to get a notebook only to miss a period of crucial focused time with a child.
e Consider carefully what you record. Ask yourself if it is significant.

What if...?

Emma is working in the toddler room of Wheatland's Day Nursery and is supporting a messy-play gloop activity. Emma observes the children at play and watches how they explore the gloop. The children squeal with delight as they bash their hands together to see what happens. Emma leaves the activity to get a pen and piece of paper to record what the children are doing, but when she returns the gloop activity has been abandoned.

Did Emma need to rush off to get a pen and piece of paper? What could she have done instead?

There will be many opportunities for you to observe the children you work with throughout the day; these can be planned or spontaneous.

Planned

It may be useful to plan what you are going to observe if you wish to find out about a specific aspect of a child's development. Planned observations provide you with a clearly defined purpose that can be easily linked to the learning and development areas of your plans.

Spontaneous

Spontaneous observations help us identify children's responses to activities, experiences and everyday happenings in the setting. Be careful not to overuse this method as you can end up with a folder full of sticky notes that tell you nothing significant about a child.

Take the opportunity to observe children throughout the day, in a range of situations

Play that promotes different areas of development

Table 5.3 shows how different types of play provision in your setting can promote children's development.

Table 5.3: The various activities provided promote different areas of children's development

Play provision	Physical development
Climbing equipment Sit-and-ride toys Milk crates, tyres and beams Playing with clay or play dough Threading cotton reels, peg boards, Using scissors to cut paper, card and textiles Painting, finger painting, hand printing	Gross motor skills Strength, stamina, balance Fine motor skills Manipulation Hand–eye co-ordination
	SOCIAL DEVELOPMENT
Team games Role play Tabletop games	Co-operative play Taking turns
	EMOTIONAL DEVELOPMENT
Stories, puppets and pictures addressing feelings Independently chosen and **ACCESSIBLE** play	Helping children to express their feelings Building confidence and self-esteem
	COGNITIVE DEVELOPMENT
Construction, inset puzzles and jigsaws Junk-box modelling and sticking items together Growing plants and food Cooking Minibeast hunt	Thinking about and solving problems Finding out why things happen
	Language development
Sharing books, stories and rhymes Using sound tins to record voices Puppet play Following instructions in games, songs and dance Going on learning walks to listen for emergency vehicles or birds singing	Encouraging speech and language Developing listening and understanding

Skills and knowledge check

- ☐ I can identify different types of play.
- ☐ I can identify activities that support holistic development.
- ☐ I can describe stages of children's play.
- ☐ I can list three activities that support children's language development.

- ◯ I know how to support stages of children's play.
- ◯ I know the prime and specific areas of learning.
- ◯ I understand what holistic development means.
- ◯ I can list three activities that support children's physical development.

B Assist early years practitioners in preparing an enabling environment to stimulate learning through play

B1 Enabling and stimulating environments

Your role as an early years assistant will require you to support the planning, creation and maintenance of a stimulating and accessible environment for children by bringing in your own ideas and using your own **INITIATIVE**.

The presentation of the play environment is crucial to stimulating and engaging the interest of children. Toys, activities, resources and equipment and the environment itself need to be given a lot of thought and consideration to ensure they meet the play needs of the children.

Stimulate learning through play indoors and outdoors

A well-organised and stimulating environment will draw in children's attention and capture their interest. This will enhance play experiences both indoors and outdoors. Children have curious minds and will seek to discover how things work or why things happen.

Indoors

There are a number of things you could do to stimulate learning through indoor play.

- Provide opportunities for children to do things for themselves, such as mixing paint for the easel.
- Provide activities that require problem-solving skills such as junk-box modelling, and working out how to fix two things together.
- Ensure **ADULT-LED** activities allow for questioning and reasoning.
- Provide cooking, making and building activities to help children understand how things work, happen and change.

Outdoors

Stimulating learning through outdoor play might include the following ideas.

- Capture children's interest in the world around them by building bird-feeding stations or habitat boxes for watching wildlife in the garden.
- Provide resources including magnifying glasses and cameras so children can look at and photograph mini beasts or worms in the grass.
- Provide a mini allotment in the garden to encourage children to grow fruit and vegetables and to understand where their food comes from.

Stimulate children's learning by providing them with resources to investigate the outdoor environment

Identifying and planning areas that stimulate play

You will be involved in planning sessions with your colleagues. The sessions will provide the opportunity to discuss and consider how play areas are planned to best effect. The ultimate aim when planning play environments is that they are stimulating and interesting to the children, drawing the children in. There are other considerations when planning play areas. For example, health and safety are crucial in providing a stimulating and interesting but also safe environment.

Health and safety issues include:

- supervision of areas
- suitability of equipment
- hazard management – for example, with water play, high climbing frames or broken equipment.

Risky play and challenging play

Managing and avoiding risks is very important, but activities should not be dismissed because they pose some form of RISK to children. As long as they have been well planned and are well supervised, with hazard management strategies in place, children will benefit greatly from risk-taking activities.

Risk and challenge activities

Challenging activities that have an element of risk include:

- climbing apparatus
- cooking that involves managing warm liquids
- using equipment such as scissors for cutting
- using tools for woodwork.

Organising and preparing play areas

Throughout the day you will be working with your colleagues to prepare the environment for routine and play needs. Organisation is extremely important as time is precious and children can miss out on vital play time if the environment is not organised well and in a timely manner.

Play areas should always look enticing and appealing to young children. If toys and resources are dumped on a mat or thrown into the middle of a table and left, there is every chance children will bypass them as they haven't been drawn in by them.

Practise

When setting up play areas ask yourself the following questions.

- Is there enough room for children to access activities fully?
- Are activities designated to appropriate areas? For example, is water play on a washable floor?
- Are the resources appropriate to the age and stage of development of the children?
- Are the resources clean and in good working order?
- Are activities set out in a way that engages children's interest?
- Are children able to play in groups, pairs and on their own?

Did you answer yes to all of these? If not, consider what you may need to do next.

In some settings, particular play equipment is set in a designated spot. This may be due to the size of the room, the flooring or the location of windows and doors. It is important to think about where activities are best placed.

Here are some examples for you to consider.

Book corners

Book corners should be situated in a quiet area. Cushions, chairs or beanbags should be provided so children can feel cosy. They should be located away from doors and windows so that they are not cold, draughty or noisy areas. Books should be displayed in a suitable bookshelf at the children's level so they can see what is available.

Role-play areas

Role-play areas should be situated where there is plenty of space so that children can use the resources and equipment without tripping over each other. Items such as dressing-up outfits should be within easy reach so children can access them for themselves.

Creative areas

Creative areas should have easy-clean floor, wall and furniture surfaces so that children can use materials such as paint, glue, sand and water freely. These surfaces also allow spillages to be mopped up quickly without creating further hazards.

Outdoor play areas

Outdoor play areas should be accessible throughout the year, so consideration should be given to the types of surface made available. Grass, concrete, barked and artificial surface areas all have many and individual benefits for outdoor play. Concrete is particularly good for bikes and tricycles whereas artificial surfaces such as rubber play areas are good for climbing and balancing apparatus.

What if...?

Jess is on the early shift at Longrood Nursery School and is setting up the toddler room ready for the children's arrival.

She has taken time to make the book corner look cosy and inviting, using several beanbags which she has spread out close to the creative area. Jess decides to move the water tray but is limited on space, so it is still quite close to the beanbags. Jess decides this is okay and prepares to welcome the children into the setting.

Do you think Jess has planned the play areas well? If not, why not?

What would you have done differently?

Skills for maintaining designated play areas

Continual observation of children at play will tell you whether they are getting the best from the areas and opportunities provided. It is not enough just to set up the areas; they need to be maintained and monitored throughout play.

CHECKLIST | ORGANISING AND MAINTAINING PLAY AREAS

☐ Do you need to bring more supplies – for example, more glue or paint?

☐ Are there any items on the floors? Does the sand-tray area need a sweep?

☐ Are any activities being avoided? Could they be presented differently?

☐ Are there any broken items that need removing?

☐ Are there enough resources for all children who wish to participate?

What if...?

Lewis has been asked by his supervisor to set up the garden ready for outdoor play on a sunny day. On his way out he gets distracted and starts talking to the cook by the kitchen door.

When he realises the time, he rushes outside and pulls some sit-and-ride toys out of the shed and wipes down the climbing frame. When the pre-school children come outside to join him, they find little to play with and begin to argue over the toys.

- Why is it important to plan ahead?

- How could Lewis have avoided this situation?

- Imagine you are Lewis. What activities would you have set up in the garden?

Keeping play areas tidy

Keeping a play environment tidy helps children to see what is available to them and also demonstrates respect for toys and equipment. It is important to strike the right balance, though, when keeping play areas tidy. You don't want to stifle children's creativity or make them feel things can't be played with. Children will often want to transport equipment in play – for example, they may want to take the cars off the mat onto the brick table where they have just made a garage. This play should be supported and encouraged as it helps in developing imagination and creativity.

Removing items that children are not using

It is important to identify and remove any equipment that you can see is not enhancing children's play or is getting in the way. An example might be an over-resourced home corner, with too many different items. Children may not get the most out of an activity if they struggle to use the cluttered play space.

Adding to resources

There are several reasons why you may need to add to existing resources.

Topping up supplies

Activities that use resources such as paint and glue will need checking regularly so that children have enough of what they need. Making sure there are enough supplies before the activity starts will ensure all children can access the activity.

Increasing the volume of resources

You can never predict how many children will want to engage in an activity at any one point in time. As long as space allows, there is no reason why several children should not be involved in the same activity. This is where your observation skills are put to good use. Recognise when numbers increase and make sure there are enough resources for all children to participate.

Responding to children's resource requests

Children's play can take many directions – for example, in the home corner they may begin by cooking dinner but play may evolve into hunting dinosaurs. In such cases, respond to children's resource requests by asking them what they may need for their dinosaur hunt. Play areas should never be restricted to the primary purpose of the resources provided. It can limit children's imagination if they are not encouraged to explore and adapt their play.

Changing resources

When children are not using an activity, change it for something else. The lack of participants around the table clearly tells you that's not what they want today. Ask the children what they would like out instead or use the space to extend an activity in which a growing number of children are engaged.

Using own initiative to maintain play areas

It is crucial that you use your own initiative while working in the setting, especially in relation to maintaining play areas. Leaving the picking up, stocking up or tidying up to someone else does not set a good example to young children. If they see you looking after resources or picking up puzzle pieces that have fallen from a table, they are more likely to develop these behaviours. Using your own initiative in this way is a skill that many employers value and shows you are a team player.

Planning and preparing room displays

If you walk into any room of your setting, you will see the walls are filled with rich and vibrant examples of children's artwork, posters and displays. These often focus on children's interests or a particular theme. As you can imagine, a lot of time and effort goes into producing these so that children's work is displayed in a way that recognises and celebrates their achievements. You need to develop these skills so that you can produce stimulating and valuable room displays.

Wall displays

Wall displays should be eye-catching, well presented and not too busy. They should be inviting for children to see and explore. You will need to make sure they don't look as if they have been thrown up in seconds and that they serve a purpose rather than just filling an empty space. Wall displays can include:

- examples of children's artwork
- photographs of children
- eye-catching posters
- well-written words or phrases in the home languages of children in the setting
- interactive information such as recorded messages on talking tins
- captions added to a wall display to explain the photographs and artwork.

Tabletop displays

Tabletop displays are very useful in allowing children to have hands-on experiences of items and objects of interest. Bear in mind that tabletop displays are designed for touching, so all objects must be accessible and the children must be allowed to explore objects as and when they wish. Tabletop displays should encourage discussion about a particular topic or experience the children have been involved in. It is important to give a lot of thought to what you put on the table.

Tabletop displays should be touchable so children are able to explore them freely

Preparing work and materials for display

The way in which you present children's work tells the observer much about the value that has been placed on children's creative efforts. Therefore take time to consider how you are going to display work and materials, following the suggestions in Table 5.4.

Table 5.4: It is worth thinking about the best way to display children's work so that it looks attractive and it is clear that the work is valued

Wall displays	Tabletop displays
• Choose a wall that is in easy view of children and adults • Display boards should be backed and framed with paper so that children's work stands out • Back children's artwork with contrasting paper to the background paper to draw the eye to it • Provide additional display materials to enhance the wall – for example, picture borders • Give the display a title and context to provide a conversation point • Clearly label children's work so that families can identify their own child's piece	• Consider where the table will be displayed; avoid putting it close to doors or windows where items can be knocked or blown off • Cover the table with a suitable fabric or paper that will show off the exhibits you are displaying • Think about the items out on the table – are they safe and suitable for the children to handle? • If the items are perishable, such as a display of fruit, consider how often they will need to be changed • Add labels – for example, a nature table collection of leaves and cones could be labelled, 'Look what we found on our welly walk today'

Labelling displays

Displays should be clearly labelled. If you have neat and legible handwriting, you can produce handwritten labels and signs. If not, find a colleague with better handwriting or use a computer to type them. Try not to 'over-label' displays as this can damage the overall effect you are trying to create. Think about why you are adding labels. Make sure they are specific to the work being displayed.

Labelling displays for adults as well as children

Your aim is to draw the attention of both children and adults to the children's creations. Older children will often be able to tell adults what they have been doing and what the display is about even if there is little labelling. However, you also want to draw in adults, including parents of younger children who may need a conversational starting point. Labels with statements and questions can really help capture the attention of adults, and encourage conversations with children about what they can see.

Plan and independently produce wall and tabletop displays

When planning a wall or tabletop display in your setting, there are several aspects you will need to consider.

Planning and organisation

a   Think about the resources you need for your display as you may have to ask for items to be bought or you may need to collect items that are not readily available.

b   Consider where your display is going to be located and make sure everyone is happy with this location.

c   Take time to plan and organise your display – a hurried display will not look as good as one that has been properly planned.

Purpose

a   Think about why you are producing a display. What do you want it to say?

b   Think about your audience – is it age appropriate?

c   Don't produce a display just to fill space; give it meaning.

Recognising children's interests

a   Have you engaged children in the planning of the display?

b   Ask children what they want on the wall.

c   Involve children in creating tabletop displays – for example, collecting autumn leaves from the garden.

B2 Play and learning curriculum plans

You will have the opportunity to contribute to the planning of play and learning in your setting. You should develop the skills and understanding to enable you to do this effectively.

The structure and purpose of play and learning plans

Purpose

Having written play and learning plans is beneficial to children, practitioners and parents. It shows the setting's approach to providing for children's individual learning and development needs. Plans should be shared with every practitioner working with the children and with parents too.

Plans should be working documents, which means they should be adapted to reflect the changing needs of the children in your care. For example, if you observe that a child has a specific interest, you can add this to the plan and consider how resources can be used to meet their individual needs.

Written plans help make outcomes clear to all practitioners. That way, you know what is expected of you when supporting children's play and can do this to the best of your ability.

Written plans show clearly that the indoor and outdoor environment has been planned and resourced to best effect and that activities cover all areas of learning. They also help to identify that a balance of **CHILD-INITIATED** play and adult-led play has been identified.

Structure

Each early years setting will have its own format for recording play and learning plans. These should be completed with the input of all colleagues who have key children so that every child's needs can be provided for. Once complete, plans are clearly displayed in the room so that everyone has a point of reference to check what should be happening on a day-to-day basis.

Play plans contain a wide range of information including:

- the weekly focus or theme (if the setting has a topic-based approach)
- **CONTINUOUS PROVISION** available – activities that children can source independently
- adult-led activities specific to the age and stage of development of individual children
- learning Intentions for adult-led activities to support children's progress
- resources needed for indoor and outdoor provision
- differentiation strategies such as changes to support or resources for children with specific needs
- an evaluation or comments box – this could include questions such as 'What worked well?' or 'Would be even better if…?' Observations of children's responses in play can also be recorded here
- what next? Practitioners can identify considerations for the following week as the planning, observation and assessment cycle continues.

Practise

Look at your setting's plan for the week ahead.

Does it contain the information identified in the list above?

What additional information is recorded on the plan?

Can you identify what your role is in supporting play from reading the plan?

Methods of recording plans for play and learning

In all early years settings there will be established methods for recording play and learning plans. There is no prescribed method but many settings will develop short-term, medium-term and long-term plans. Plans should always be a working documents and adapted to suit the ever-changing needs of the children in the setting. While adults may draw up plans, they should include play experiences based on children's interests and their level of development.

Short-term plans

Short-term plans usually cover the duration of a week and give detailed information day by day about the play activities that are to be provided for children. These will include a balance of child-led and adult-led activities and will link to specific learning outcomes from the EYFS. Practitioners are encouraged to **ANNOTATE** play plans and to 'challenge and change' to meet the ever-changing needs of the children. Where there are specific learning intentions for individual children, practitioners will add the child's initials to the document so the focus is evident. An evaluation box is included so that practitioners can reflect and feed back on the effectiveness of the play plan. This information can be used in children's learning journals and informs future planning. A **LEARNING JOURNAL** is an individual file for a child that includes photographic and written evidence showing the child's responses to activities and experiences in the setting.

Medium-term plans

Medium-term plans provide an overview of intention over a period of six weeks or more. These plans enable practitioners to bullet point general ideas and to incorporate information about occasions and festivals from children's **'ALL ABOUT ME' RECORDS**.

Long-term plans

These often take the form of a general overarching plan, giving a brief outline of provision for six months to a year. These plans help settings to identify resource and budget implications so they can be well prepared. They will not give detailed information but will inform the setting's medium and short-term planning.

How plans support areas of learning in the EYFS

With written plans, practitioners can make links between the play provision and the prime and specific areas of the EYFS. During planning meetings, practitioners will take time to think about what the children will gain from the activities they are being offered. They will also look at the issue from another angle and consider what play activities can develop a particular skill or ability for a child. Refer back to A3, Table 5.2, which gives examples of play provision and their links to the EYFS.

Clear links should be made to the prime and specific areas of the EYFS so that you and your colleagues can think about the role you have in supporting children's play and progressing development.

Practise

Get involved in a planning meeting in your setting. Note how your colleagues draw up their plans.

- Do they use the statutory EYFS guidance?
- Do they think about children's all-round development in planning activities?
- Can you see any links to the EYFS prime and specific areas?
- Are the individual learning needs of children discussed?

Recording and using observations of children to assist planning

How children respond to activities will influence the setting's future play plans. While it is important to observe children individually to plan for their play needs, it is equally important to observe groups of children at play so that you can plan appropriate group activities.

For groups

Observations of groups of children are often recorded on the setting's play plans so that practitioners can see what the children gained from a particular activity. This type of observation is useful for gathering information about the effectiveness of the resources, staff or layout of the environment and how children interact and play with each other.

For individual children

All settings will have in place a system of recording observations of individual children to help them plan for their next steps. These usually take the form of a learning journal or learning story. These observations are then used to think about what comes next for that child and help inform the setting's planning.

What if...?

Johnny is 2 years old. He has just returned to nursery following a holiday abroad. He comes in clutching a model aeroplane and informs you at every opportunity that planes go up in the sky. He finds a story book with planes in it and asks you to read it over and over again.

- How could Johnny's interest in planes be incorporated in the planning?
- Give two examples of activities you could plan to enhance Johnny's play experience.

The planning cycle

The planning cycle in Figure 5.2 shows how you should use observations to inform future provision.

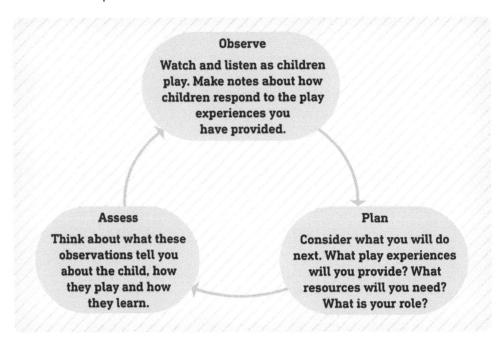

Figure 5.2: The planning cycle, showing how observation of children's responses influences the activities provided in the future

The physical environment, and delivering play and learning plans

The physical environment plays a crucial role in supporting the delivery of play plans. The EYFS includes four key themes that underpin the approach to children's learning. One of these themes is 'enabling environments'. The document 'Development Matters in the Early Years Foundation Stage' states the principles of how the physical environment or an enabling environment supports children's learning and development.

Table 5.5 lists the four key principles of the EYFS and shows how they can be used in early years settings to support children's learning, development and wellbeing.

Table 5.5: How to apply the four EYFS key principles in practice

EYFS principle	How you can apply the theme in practice
A unique child	Recognise that every child is individual and ready to learn
Positive relationships	Understand that you play a role in building positive relationships with children
Enabling environments	Provide an environment that children can access easily and that is stimulating and inviting
Learning and development	When the elements above are combined, children have the tools they need to learn and develop

B3 Resources and equipment for play and learning activities

As an early years assistant it is important that you are familiar with and can select and use appropriate equipment to support children's play.

Resources and equipment to support play and learning activities

You will see in your setting a variety of resources that are used in the indoor and outdoor environment. Throughout this unit you have had the opportunity to identify a wide range of resources and equipment to support play and learning activities.

Table 5.6 shows a few more examples.

Type of resource	Examples
Natural materials	Stepping stones, logs and tree stumps Pine cones, leaves and stones Shells and rocks Feathers
Small-world toys	Animals such as farm, jungle and sea creatures Dolls' houses People playsets – for example, a fire station Garage sets, cars and vehicles
Creative materials	Junk boxes for modelling Ribbon, tissue, fabric Paint, play dough, clay Recyclable materials Glitter, sequins, pompoms

Table 5.6: Resources and equipment to support play

Practise

Imagine you have been asked by your supervisor to plan an outdoor activity for children of 3 and 4 years old. The children are very interested in the materials they have been recycling. These include plastic bottles, cereal boxes, egg boxes, tinfoil trays, tin cans, cardboard tubes and jam jars.

Select as many items as you wish from the list above. Explain why you have chosen these resources and how you will use them.

Explain how they will support children's play and learning.

Hazards and ways to eliminate or control risks

With risk inevitably comes hazard, which needs to be identified and managed so that children can still have access to a wide range of activities. As you will have discovered in Units 1 and 4, **RISK ASSESSMENTS** provide practitioners with the opportunity to consider carefully how they can eliminate or control risks associated with the use of resources and equipment in the setting.

Children should be able to climb outdoor equipment, use scissors and take part in cooking activities. As long as these activities are age- and stage-appropriate and supervised, with hazard controls in place, there is no reason to avoid them. Table 5.7 shows a few examples of the hazards associated with resources and equipment.

Link it up

Unit 1, B3 discussed the purpose of a risk assessment and Unit 4, B1 provides an example.

Resources and equipment	Potential hazards
Using scissors	Children cutting themselves
Using outdoor climbing frame	Falling from equipment
Cooking	Burns from the oven
Woodwork	Hitting self with hammer

Table 5.7: The potential hazards of children's resources and equipment

Practise

Take time to look around your setting. Can you list any other resources or activities that have potential hazards? Consider how these hazards can be managed.

Adult supervision can help with risk management so that children are able to take part in challenging activities

Helping children to manage risk in play

Talk to children about their responsibility for their own safety; even toddlers will understand when you ask them not to run indoors. Modelling good practice to children will also help them to manage their own risks. For example, show them how to carry scissors or stand a safe distance from the cooker when opening the door. Pre-school children can take part in conversations about managing their own risks – for example, you could ask them, 'What do you think could happen if you run around with scissors in your hand?'

Preparing resources and equipment for play activities

It is important that you make time at the beginning of your working day to prepare the play environment for children. By doing this you can ensure the environment is appealing to children, everything is in good working order and there are adequate resources.

Paint
- Use pots with lids to avoid spillage.
- Provide different painting tools, such as sponges and rollers, to capture children's interest.
- Involve children in mixing paints and making new colours.
- Cover tables with newspaper or a wipe-clean tablecloth.
- If using an easel, clip paper to it ready for use.
- Make sure aprons are clean and accessible to protect children's clothing.

Play dough
- If making play dough, add food colouring, scents or glitter.
- Check playdough is fit for use; throw away any hard or mouldy dough.
- Make sure tools are clean and free of dirt.
- Make sure there are enough tools, cutters and rolling pins for a group of children to take part.

Sand and water trays

- Check sand is clean and free of dirt.
- Replace water in water trays regularly.
- Empty water trays at the end of each day.
- Cover sand trays when not in use.
- Ensure you have enough resources for the children – for example, cups, funnels, scoops and sieves.
- Provide clean and dry aprons for children using the water tray.

Creative materials

- Ensure children can access creative materials of their own choosing.
- Make sure you have enough paper, materials, glue and scissors for each session.
- Build up a wide range of stock, including ribbon, fabric offcuts, straws, pipe cleaners, lolly sticks, tissue paper and feathers.
- Ensure children can access materials for themselves so they can express themselves freely.

Treasure baskets

- Ensure materials are clean with no sharp edges.
- Ensure variety in the basket; include metal spoons, wooden egg cups, cardboard tubes, pine cones and natural sponges.
- Build up resources and change the contents regularly so as to capture interest in new items.

Ride-on toys

- Check toys are safe, clean and dry before use.
- Ensure adequate space is provided for the use of ride-on toys.

You can use your own initiative to help ensure resources and equipment are ready for use.

- Notice when stock needs replenishing, such as when the glue has run out on the craft table.
- Supervise children who are using hazardous equipment such as scissors.
- Remove items that are broken during play and report the breakage.
- Reorganise abandoned activities to make them appealing to the next child.
- Sweep and mop sand and water spillages to avoid ACCIDENTS.

Organising resources for children to access independently

Children should be provided with opportunities for free play throughout the day so they can be totally independent in their play choices. To do this well, you will need to ensure resources are easily accessible to children.

You will need to think about the following issues.

a   Are toy boxes easy for children to pull out and use?
b   Can resources be seen easily so that children can exercise choice?
c   Where space is limited, can children exercise choice using an alternative method – for example, choosing toys from pictures on a board?
d   Are resources organised effectively so children get the best from them – for example, a shelf with boxes containing a range of craft and collage materials?

Practise

Find out how accessible children's resources are in your setting. Get down on your knees and shuffle around the room. See if you can reach the toys you want to play with without standing up.

Selecting stories and rhymes

When selecting stories and rhymes, you need to be aware of the age of the children you are choosing them for. Think ahead and plan in advance, and in doing so you will avoid losing children's interest during the session.

a   How old are the children you are selecting stories and rhymes for?

b   Check the contents of stories. Is a story too long? Is the ending appropriate?

c   Are your song and rhyme choices easy for young children to join in with?

d   Think about the favourite stories and rhymes the children may have and include their selections.

Supporting children to access resources independently

The layout of the environment is important in enabling children to access resources to support their play, but you can do more to make children independent.

- Label storage units and boxes with pictures so children can spot equipment easily.
- Provide appropriate pots and baskets so children can easily transport smaller items to tabletops.
- Give children tasks – for example, setting up a collage table for them and their peers to use.
- Ask them to find things – for example, 'Do you think you could find some aprons for the water play?'

How to clean and tidy the play areas

Link it up

Look back at Unit 4, B1. You will find information here about maintaining play environments and the importance of risk assessments.

By keeping play areas tidy and clean, you are showing the children how to respect and look after toys and equipment. Activities and play experiences will also be more appealing to children if they are clean and tidy. Encourage children to tidy away after themselves by doing it yourself so they can see what to do. Consider health and safety as well when maintaining the play area. If toys are broken, remove them from play. If an activity requires a risk assessment to be completed, make sure this is done before the activity starts.

Skills and knowledge check

☐ I can plan and prepare a display of children's work.

☐ I can identify and manage hazards and risks in children's play.

☐ I can select stories and rhymes for the children in my care.

☐ I can encourage children to access resources independently.

○ I know how to prepare play areas for children.

○ I know what information should be included in a play plan.

○ I understand the difference between short, medium and long-term planning.

○ I know the three features of the planning cycle.

C Support children up to five years old in planned play and learning activities in an early years setting

C1 Ways to support children in their play

In your role as an early years assistant you will need to understand your setting's assessment and planning cycle. This will enable you to support colleagues in the delivery of play plans and use your own initiative in planning activities for the children in your care.

Differences between 'casual' play and play that is appropriate in childcare settings

Before starting your career in early years, you may have had previous experience looking after young children as a babysitter or being in charge of younger SIBLINGS. This informal relationship differs greatly from that in the early years setting as you are not ruled by policies, procedures and guidelines.

Play will be different in early years settings as it is planned in accordance with the requirements of the EYFS and the learning and development needs of the child. There is also a requirement to provide a wide range of opportunities that are balanced between child-led and adult-led play.

Casual play has no defined purpose or focus and is totally driven by what you and the child want to do. If you are babysitting a child, the parents may be happy for you to let their child watch television when they want, but this would not be appropriate in an early years setting.

Maintaining professional relationships

The relationship you have with a child in a home environment differs from that in your setting. You have a professional role when working with children and your behaviour must reflect this.

Here are some tips for good practice.

- Address children by their name and not by any pet names. Sometimes a shortened version of a child's birth name may be used if this is what a parent wishes.
- Treat all children with equal concern. Do not show favouritism to any child, even if you know them or their family.
- Remember confidentiality. It is not your place to share information with your colleagues or anyone else about the child's home life.

Enabling children's learning through play

To ensure that children are able to learn through play, it is important to provide an environment that enables INCLUSIVE access for all and meets individual needs and interests. An inclusive play environment is one that is accessible to all children in your care regardless of needs or abilities. This means that you will need to give a lot of thought to the layout of the environment and the presentation of resources so all children feel valued and have a sense of belonging. By responding to the individual needs and interests of children, you are showing them that they are valued and their views and wishes are heard.

Supporting children in their play

Your role and responsibilities reach far beyond putting a few toys out for children to play with on a daily basis. Your day-to-day practice could include:

- providing a wide range of play experiences
- ensuring frequent access to the outdoor environment
- changing play experiences to keep children interested
- responding to children's play needs, for example, with additional resources
- ensuring the play environment is clean and safe
- observing and recording children's responses to play
- planning for children's play so as to progress development
- enhancing play so as to extend and challenge skills and abilities
- supporting children in their play
- praising and encouraging children during play
- developing positive relationships with children.

Practise

When you are next at your setting, observe another early years assistant.

- Do they carry out all the roles identified in the list above?

- What other responsibilities might an early years assistant have in supporting children in their play?

Supporting play in different contexts

It is important that you know when and how children need your support in play. They do not always need you there asking them what they are doing or encouraging play to take a specific direction. Think carefully before stepping in to support, and when you do step in, think about what you should be doing. Figure 5.3 shows the different contexts for children's play.

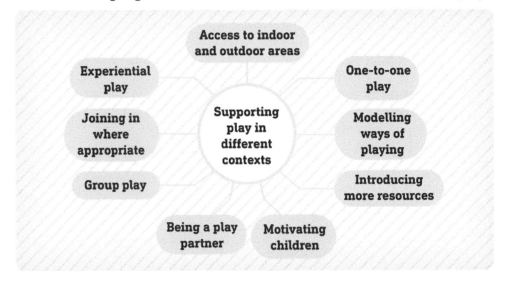

Figure 5.3: There are many ways to support children's play. The diagram shows examples of different contexts and ways that you might provide support

The list below explains how you can support children's play in different ways.

- Indoor/outdoor – managing free flow between indoors and outdoors where possible. Ensure staff to child ratios are adhered to and supervision is maintained.
- Experiential play – provide opportunities for children to explore, discover and create in play.
- Group play – ensure the needs of all children are met and that you provide balanced, focused attention.
- One-to-one play – sustain children's interest with eye contact, conversation and questioning.
- Knowing how and when to join in with play – watch for children's cues for you to join in play, such as being offered a plate of food in the home corner.
- Being a play partner – for example, you might be a patient and allow the children to wrap you in bandages and cover you in plasters.
- Motivating children – give children play cues such as asking who can build the biggest tower or the most unusual shape of building.
- Introducing more resources – help to extend play and meet individual needs (these can be individual or cultural needs), encouraging children's new ideas.
- Modelling ways of playing – if you sit at a table and play you can show a reluctant child how they can use the resources available to them.

Approaches to supporting play

Supporting child-initiated play

Child-initiated play means that children not only choose what they want to play with but also choose the direction of their play. This does not mean the adult is not responsive or supervising play. In fact, the role of the adult is to ensure the children have exactly what they need for play to occur uninterrupted. You should also recognise when they want adult involvement in their play.

Above all, a well-resourced and accessible environment will be the key to children being able to exercise choice and get toys and materials for themselves.

Supporting adult-led play

Adult-led play may be initiated by a child's interest or brought about to help enhance a particular skill in children. The EYFS guides practitioners to identify learning and development outcomes for children in their care. The practitioner will then embed these outcomes in the play experiences provided. It is important that adult-led activities have a defined outcome so you all know what you are expecting the children to gain from the play. A good example of this is establishing if children are effective in turn taking during play. You might plan to play a game where turn taking is central to the success of the game.

What if...?

Philip is supporting a group of children in the toddler room during a sound lotto game. This has been planned with colleagues to support and encourage children's listening skills as they identify different sounds. Philip sets the game up with four children at the table. He plays the CD then sits back and watches the children. It is not long before the children get up and leave the table.

Why do you think the children left?

What should Philip have done during this adult-led activity?

Supporting literacy activities

Children should be exposed to a range of communication methods, including verbal and written communication. This will help them develop language skills and early literacy.

- Model effective communication with children and encourage communication with others.
- Provide a well-resourced accessible book corner and show children how to use books.
- Provide a wide range of mark-making activities – for example, provide envelopes and paper for children to write their own letters and make their own lists.
- Use ICT such as a tablet for literacy activities and the development of hand/eye co-ordination.
- Provide a picture- and text-rich environment to enable children to understand that print has meaning – for example, label children's pegs.
- Make effective use of Makaton and picture exchange communication systems (PECS).

Link it up

Unit 6, A3 provides more information on supporting children's communication, literacy and language development, particularly relating to the use of Makaton and PECS.

Supporting mathematical activities

The environment for young children should be rich in mathematical resources so they are able to learn about the concept of number, shape and size. Having visual equipment will help children to gain a more concrete understanding of what these mathematical concepts mean.

- Put a child-friendly clock on the wall so children can see the numbers and relate them to key times in the day.
- Create number-line displays for children to count in order.
- Provide stories, songs and rhymes that involve numbers – for example, singing 'Five Little Speckled Frogs'.
- Provide sorting and classifying activities, such as pairing socks or sorting a group of objects into big and small.
- Provide a wide range of role-play activities, such as a shop, which can introduce children to the concept of money or 'how much?' 'how many?'
- Provide jigsaws and games that encourage children to fit shapes into spaces.
- Use the setting's routines to develop a knowledge of numbers through counting plates and cups at mealtimes, for example.

Sharing stories, rhymes and songs

Most early years settings will have a book area accessible at all times where children can look at and share stories with others. You will share stories, rhymes and songs with children at both planned and spontaneous opportunities. This may also be as a group activity or on a one-to-one basis with a child.

Reading stories

- Always make sure the story is age-appropriate and not too long.
- Choose stories with vibrant pictures to capture and hold interest.
- Involve children in choosing stories.
- Sit at the children's level and seat them so they can all see the book.
- Hold the book in front of you to read – you will soon develop the ability to read upside down!
- Take time to read the story at a steady pace.
- Respond to children's enquiries and observations about the story.
- Engage children in the telling of stories – for example, through letting them say the last word of a rhyming sentence.

Singing songs and rhymes

- Use props and instruments to broaden children's musical experience.
- Ask children what they would like to sing.
- Vary songs between 'sitting down' songs and 'moving around' songs.
- When introducing new songs and rhymes, repeat them several times so children become familiar with them.
- Use actions to develop number skills and fine motor development.
- If children choose songs you are unfamiliar with, ask a colleague for help.

Action rhymes can support children's mathematical and physical development

C2 The individual play and learning needs of a child

You must be able to support your colleagues in meeting individual children's play and learning needs.

Observing and assessing the play and learning needs of a child

Throughout this unit you have learned the importance of observing children at play to help you assess and provide for their play and learning needs. You can learn what a child needs by looking and asking. Settings will use a range of methods to observe children; these can be spontaneous or planned and will be driven by the individual needs of the child.

Looking on

Watching closely as children play or looking on gives you a real window into a child's world. As you watch, you will see how individual children are able to make connections, imitate real-life experiences and develop their imagination in their play. From these observations you will be able to think about what comes next for these children.

What if...?

Priya is 4 years old. She is playing in the home corner of the pre-school room. She has the teddies sat on chairs and has been busy making them their dinner. She uses the resources in the play kitchen and sets the table ready for the teddies to eat.

- What does this role play tell you about Priya?
- How can you develop this play and learning experience for Priya?

Talking to children about their play

Children will often delight in talking to you about their play. From about the age of 3, children begin to give a detailed step-by-step narrative about what they are doing or they might take you on an imaginary journey where they are invisible and are going to save the universe.

You don't have to wait for children to talk to you about their play; you can ask questions about what they are doing to encourage deeper thinking and communication skills. Try to ask **OPEN-ENDED QUESTIONS** to encourage conversation with children.

Here are some examples of open-ended questions.

- That looks interesting! What's happening?
- You're very busy – what are you doing?
- I can see that you've built a den. Can you tell me how you did it?

Asking children questions as they play can enhance learning and help them gain a deeper understanding of what they are doing

Sharing information about a child's play, learning needs and interests with colleagues and parents

When a child first joins, your setting will provide parents with information about the EYFS and how play is planned in order to meet the needs of their child. Settings will always ask parents for permission to observe their child and take photos as a record of their development. All early years settings that store records and photos of children are registered with the Information Commissioner's Office (ICO). Your setting's policies will clearly detail the procedures for sharing information and for keeping it confidential. Make sure you read these and ask your supervisor to explain anything you don't understand. It is important that you follow the setting's procedures at all times.

Sharing information with colleagues about children's play is essential for the learning and development needs of children but is also vital in helping you build your skills of communication in the workplace.

As an assistant your opportunities to share information with parents will be very limited. However, if a parent approaches you asking for or giving you information, you must always refer this to your supervisor immediately.

CHECKLIST | **GOOD PRACTICE IN SHARING INFORMATION**

- [ ] Written permission for observation and photos should be sought from parents
- [ ] Clear information on how observations and photos are stored should be given to parents
- [ ] Observations and photos should be shared on a **NEED-TO-KNOW BASIS** with parents' prior knowledge
- [ ] Written observations should be stored securely
- [ ] Photos stored on a computer should be protected by password encryption
- [ ] Photos of children should not be published on the setting's website or any other domain without the consent of parents
- [ ] Settings should check parents are happy for their children's photos to be displayed in the setting

---

Adapting support to meet individual learning needs

All children are individuals and have different learning needs. Your role is to know the children you look after and understand the support they may need from you in play.

- Children who are shy may need sensitive adult guidance for them to get involved in activities with other children.
- A child who finds it difficult to share may need your support in managing social situations and turn taking with other children.
- A child who uses a wheelchair may need activities to be moved to a table of an appropriate height so that they can access them.
- A child who has a speech and language difficulty may need to exercise their play choices through a visual timetable.

Whatever the learning need, it is important that the play environment is accessible to all the children in your care.

Recording the learning and responses of a child during a planned play activity

There are many methods of observation used by practitioners to record children's responses to planned play activities. These observations are used to build a picture of where a child is at in their development and to help practitioners think about how they can help the child progress.

When supporting children during a planned activity, you will find that the quickest methods of observation are the best as they do not take the focus away from the children.

Sticky notes

Making notes about what a child is doing or saying can be a really effective way to observe the child's responses. This is particularly true when capturing a skill or a moment in a child's development that you have not seen before. While sticky notes only contain a snapshot of information, it should still be clear what has been seen or heard.

Photographs

Photographs are a great way to capture a moment in time and can clearly show a child demonstrating a particular skill. However, they are limited in use as they are a visual record of a single point in time. For instance, photographs cannot capture children's language, which may be the focus of the planned activity. Neither can they show how a reluctant child opens up to other children or to you as an activity develops.

Checklists

Preparation is needed for the use of checklists in recording children's responses to play activities. You will need to write a list of outcomes before the activity starts so that you know in advance what you are hoping to observe. Checklists can be particularly useful for observing children's physical development – for example, during a cutting and sticking activity.

Safeguards for observing children

When observing children the priority must always be the wellbeing and safety of the child.

- Photos should be removed from devices and stored securely in a computer file at the earliest opportunity.
- Observation records should not be left lying around for anyone to see.
- If children are aware and uncomfortable about being observed or photographed, you must stop.
- Avoid observing tired, unwell or unhappy children as they need your undivided attention.

Practise

Talk to colleagues in your setting about the methods of observation they use to record children's responses to play activities. Ask what works well and why.

Planning play to support children's progress

Watch children closely as they play and you will see how they use the resources they have been given. Children use resources as they are intended to be used, but also adapt them to suit their individual play needs.

For example, you may have a table set up with bricks with which the children will make towers and buildings, as you would expect. But as play unfolds and changes direction, these bricks may come to represent something else in play – for example, children may develop their play into role play and the bricks suddenly become a plate of food.

Closely observing the direction of play helps you think about the planning of future play opportunities. You will also have the chance to spot areas where individual children may need support. A child who hoards half the bricks may need support to share and interact with others. Without even thinking about it, you have involved the children in play planning.

Extending activities to meet individual children's needs and interests

Your skills of observation will help you to identify when children's activities should be extended to meet their needs and interests. Taking time to notice how far children are engaged and absorbed in play and how they use the resources available to them will help you understand what you should do next.

Take a moment to reflect and ask the following questions.

a   Do the children need additional resources?
b   Do the children need sensitive adult intervention to keep play going?
c   Do the children need support to take play in a new direction?
d   Are the children questioning and trying to find out more about what they are doing?
e   Are the children sustaining activities for long periods of time?

What if...?

George is 3 years old. He is playing in the den in the garden and has built his own campfire using twigs he has collected. George stands over his campfire with his arm outstretched and tells Cicely, his **KEY PERSON**, that he is toasting marshmallows.

Explain how Cicely can extend the activity to meet George's individual interests.

Skills and knowledge check

☐ I can list four roles and responsibilities of the early years assistant in supporting children's play.

☐ I can select equipment to support mathematical development.

☐ I can select resources to extend children's play.

☐ I can identify potential hazards when using equipment and resources for play.

○ I know how to record observations of children's responses to play activities.

○ I understand the difference between child-initiated and adult-led play.

○ I can identify when I might need to adapt the way I support children during play.

○ I can list three safeguards when observing children.

Ready for assessment

You will be assessed on supporting the implementation of your setting's play and learning plans and maintaining a stimulating play environment for young children.

Evidence methods can include:

- observations
- reflective logs or diaries from your work placement
- witness statements from your setting supervisor or your college assessor
- play plans (annotated with your observations and evaluations of practice).

Consider observing practitioners supporting a range of play types for children of different ages in preparation for your own assessment.

Take time to note how they:

- select toys and equipment for play
- maintain the play environment
- support children during play
- observe and record children's response to planned play.

It is important to remind yourself of all the essential behaviours and practices in this chapter. You should also make sure you have completed Section B, Unit 5 of form CPLD 1 in your Placement Experience Assessment Portfolio of Evidence. Complete the self-assessment form and include evidence of skills you have developed when completing activities for this unit.

WORK FOCUS

HANDS ON

There are some important occupational skills that you will need to practise, which relate to this unit. As an early years assistant you will be responsible for supporting children's play and preparing and managing the play environment, so make sure you follow these tips.

1. Observation/recording

- Always follow the setting's procedures for recording observations of children.

2. Effective interaction with adults and children

- Get involved in planning meetings and share your thoughts and ideas with colleagues.
- Recognise children's play cues and respond when they want you to join in.

3. Reflective practice

- Consider how you can adapt your support to meet children's individual needs.
- Seek feedback from colleagues, children and parents.

4. Planning/recording

- Annotate play plans to show children's responses to adult-led play.

5. Constructive assistance to colleagues

- Use your initiative in maintaining play environments.

6. Respecting confidentiality

- Remember to ensure parents' permission has been sought before photographing or observing children.

Ready for work?

Working with a partner, look at the transferrable skills listed below. Can you link these to scenarios in the workplace?

Transferable skills

1 Communication – writing, speaking and listening to others

2 Working with others – taking on roles and responsibilities

3 Demonstrating thinking skills and showing adaptability – be prepared to use your own initiative appropriately

4 Problem solving – asking questions to clarify information

5 Managing information – presenting information in different ways

6 Self-management and development – being flexible

Scenarios

A Your supervisor has asked you to support children playing a number game to encourage understanding of numbers and turn taking. You take time to ensure the children experience the activity fully and also make sure that all the children have had the opportunity to play the game during the morning session.

B You have been invited to sit in on a planning meeting with colleagues. You listen to their ideas and feel able to suggest appropriate activities and resources needed to carry them out.

C You are supporting the creative area with a colleague. Another colleague asks for extra help in the garden, so you offer to go outside and support the children using the climbing frame.

D Returning from your break, you notice the floor space around the water tray is very wet and slippery. Without hesitation, you get a dry mop to wipe the floor and prevent any slip hazards.

E Your supervisor has asked you to observe the children in the home corner and make notes about their communication and language skills. You decide to record this information on paper but you also take a photo of what the children are doing while they are communicating.

F You have been given a copy of the week's planning, which you take time to read. The activities are linked to the learning outcomes within the EYFS. You are unsure of some of the language used and ask your colleague to explain what this means.

Discuss why you have made these links. Now look at the scenarios again – do they link to more than one transferable skill?

6 Supporting Children's Communication, Literacy and Language Development

You probably can't even remember learning to communicate with others. But what would it feel like if you were unable to communicate? COMMUNICATION is a skill that forms the basis of many other areas of a child's development and learning, particularly literacy. In this unit you will be learning about communication, literacy and LANGUAGE DEVELOPMENT for children of different ages, needs and abilities. You will need to show how you support the development of children's language and literacy in early years settings by being aware of their needs and responding to them in a positive way.

How will I be assessed?

This is an internally assessed unit, which means that you will need to carry out a series of activities, which will take place during the work placement period. You should record your work-based activities in your Placement Experience Assessment Portfolio of Evidence.

For this unit you will be required to submit evidence of your understanding of:

- the links between communication, language and literacy development, including: how children's skills develop; your role in supporting them; and approaches suited to different ages and abilities
- supporting children with different communication abilities, including: communicating with children of different ages; suitable resources to support literacy; strategies for children with special educational needs, English as a second language and English as an additional language; **VERBAL COMMUNICATION** and **NON-VERBAL COMMUNICATION**; providing clear instructions; and adapting your own behaviour to meet the needs of a child or group.

You will need to provide evidence that you have completed the activities successfully. This might include:

- records of interaction and observation from work placements
- evidence of planning
- signed observation record of learners' communication skills when supporting groups of children in different activities on work placements
- observation records, signed by the setting's assessor, of learners interacting with a child or children in a language-based activity
- a reflective log discussing approaches to communication on work placements.

Assessment criteria

Pass	Merit	Distinction
Learning aim A: Explore the links between communication, language and literacy development		
A.P1 Conduct an accurate observation of an experienced practitioner engaged in a communication, language and literacy-based activity with children in an early years setting.	**A.M1** Conduct a focused observation of an experienced practitioner engaged in communication, language and literacy-based activities with children in an early years setting.	**A.D1** Conduct an observation that analyses an experienced practitioner engaged in selected communication, language and literacy-based activities with children in an early years setting.
Learning aim B: Support children with different communication needs and abilities		
B.P2 Communicate appropriately and follow instructions and guidance accurately when interacting with children with different communication needs or abilities in a communication-focused and language-based activity in an early years setting.	**B.M2** Communicate appropriately using a range of strategies in providing support to a child, and a group of children, with different communication needs and abilities during a communication-focused and language-based planned activity in an early years setting.	**B.D2** Communicate appropriately and confidently using a wide range of strategies to provide support and develop the language skills of a child, and a group of children, with different communication needs and abilities in a planned communication-focused and language-based activity in an early years setting.

A Explore the links between communication, language and literacy development

A1 How children's communication and language skills develop

You will need to be able to use and understand the terms 'speech', 'language' and 'communication' so that you can effectively support the development of children's communication and language skills. In this section you will be looking at how a child's age and level of communication development affects their emotional, social and COGNITIVE DEVELOPMENT. You will also look at how to identify factors that affect development and the kinds of interactions that support it.

Speech, language and communication

Have you ever thought about the difference between speech, language and communication? Have you ever tried to explain them? You will need to be clear about what they mean so that you can develop your skills and understanding in this area and learn to support children more effectively. Although they are closely linked and overlap with one another, there are some differences between them:

1 SPEECH: the physical act of talking and the way in which we do this
2 LANGUAGE: the code or sounds we use to communicate to one another through speech or sign language
3 COMMUNICATION: the way in which we pass information to one another. This can be verbal or non-verbal.

Links between communication and language and other areas of development

Communication and language form one of the prime areas of the EARLY YEARS FOUNDATION STAGE (EYFS) because of their importance as a basis for other areas of learning and development. Being able to process language is the first step towards the development of reading and writing skills as it enables us to link our own thoughts together. It is also closely connected to children's age and stage of development in other areas.

- SOCIAL DEVELOPMENT: Young children will naturally want to communicate and form relationships with others. By learning to talk and developing their language skills, children start to strengthen these relationships as they begin to communicate with those around them.
- EMOTIONAL DEVELOPMENT: Developing their communication and language skills allows children to increase their confidence and talk about their own feelings and ideas. Children who find speaking and communicating with others more of a challenge may become frustrated and this will affect their behaviour.
- COGNITIVE DEVELOPMENT: The development of communication and language skills is closely connected to children's cognitive development. 'Cognitive' means acquiring knowledge through thought, experiences and the senses. Cognitive development is the development of intellectual skills or the ability to process information. Language is significant as it helps us to put our own thoughts together and think about the world around us.

Link it up

See Unit 2, A2 for tables showing ages and stages of development.

Factors that can affect language skills

A large number of factors may affect the development of a child's language skills (see Figure 6.1). The child's own natural ability plays a major role, but children are also influenced by their surroundings and the way in which they interact with others. Within an early years setting, adults should provide positive interactions with children as much as possible so that babies and young children are encouraged to communicate with others and to develop their skills in doing so.

The environment

Children are affected by their immediate environment and the noises around them. If they are unable to hear what is being said to them because it is noisy, or if storytime or singing is interrupted by something happening elsewhere, they are unlikely to be able to concentrate on what is being said. Young children can have short concentration spans, and distractions will make focusing even more difficult for them.

Figure 6.1: A variety of factors affect the development of children's language skills

The environment should be inviting for children – in other words, it should be ACCESSIBLE, colourful and with comfortable seating and temperature or ventilation.

Sensory needs

Young children start to experience the world with their senses from birth. If they have hearing loss or a visual impairment this will impact on their development. A child with SENSORY needs may already have been diagnosed as having a hearing or visual impairment, or this could yet be undetected.

Hearing-impaired and visually impaired children may have the support of hearing aids or glasses from a very early age if doctors are aware of their difficulty, so it is important that diagnosis takes place early. Sensory needs make it harder for children to pick up on some forms of communication, so ensure you look out for children who do not seem to be listening to or interacting with others, or who seem distracted.

Language differences

If children are learning more than one language, it may take them longer than children learning just one. They will be absorbing more information and making sense of two or more ways of communicating. You will need to work with parents and carers so that the children effectively develop their home language alongside English.

Interactions that support the development of children's language

When you are working with young children and supporting their development, you must remember that much of what they are learning is a direct result of what they see and hear around them. They will look to you to show them how to act and behave and also how to communicate. They will listen very carefully and copy what you do and say. Learning language will therefore be easier for children if those around them communicate as clearly as possible.

Tone and pitch of speech

When speaking to young children, your tone should be calm and clear. If those around them regularly use a loud or whiney voice with children, they will pick it up and copy it. You should alter your own tone and pitch when speaking to children to show expression and emphasise what you want to say so that they learn to do the same.

Syntax

SYNTAX means the set of rules and the sequence in which we put words together. For example, in English our sentences usually have a subject, a verb and an object, generally in that order (see Figure 6.2). For example, 'The cup is on the table.'

Link it up

For more on giving children instructions, see B5 in this unit.

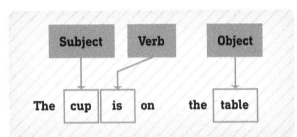

Make sure you communicate in a straightforward way, particularly if you are giving children instructions. Young children will seldom remember more than one instruction at a time, particularly if several instructions are given in quick succession. Gestures and props might help their understanding of unfamiliar **VOCABULARY**.

Figure 6.2:
Syntax tells us the arrangement of words and phrases to create well-formed sentences

What if...?

Ronnie is working with a group of children outside on an activity, and it is time to go in. He says to them, 'Go inside, take off your coats and put them on your pegs and then go and see Mrs De Souza so that she knows you're back.'

When Ronnie goes in, he finds that the children have taken off their coats but have not followed the other instructions. Why do you think this is?

Can you think of an example from your own experience in a setting, at school or elsewhere when confusion arose from a miscommunication?

The words used

When talking to children, choose words and phrases that are clear so they can understand you. For example, if you use an expression such as 'Shake a leg', meaning 'hurry up', it is unlikely that a young child will understand what you mean.

However, you should also explore new words with children when you can – for example, when they are learning about new things – so they can develop their vocabulary. Introduce new words by repeating them and giving an explanation in more simple terms. 'Can you help me put away the dressing-up clothes? Clothes are what we wear, like your jumper and trousers, or my skirt and tights.'

Semantics

SEMANTICS concerns the subtle meaning of words or phrases that could mean different things – for example, a pun or joke based on a double meaning. If you hear adults using this kind of phrase, you may need to explain it to children.

Use of receptive speech

RECEPTIVE SPEECH means the ability to understand what is being heard or read. Children who are developing their language skills will need support and explanations from time to time so that they can understand what is being said. When reading to children, make sure they understand any unfamiliar words and always be aware that you may need to explain things to them.

Use of expressive speech

EXPRESSIVE SPEECH is the speech you use to express what you want to say. Very young children can find it challenging to put their thoughts and feelings into words, or to put the words in the correct order. They may find this frustrating. Look out for this when supporting the development of children's language, but also remember that you should not interrupt children and speak for them. Allow them some thinking time so that they can have a go themselves.

Practise

1 Watch and listen to the way in which more experienced practitioners interact with children in the early years setting. Thinking about the aspects above, write down two ways in which they are supporting the development of the children's language through their own use of language.

2 Think about your own skills in communication.

- How well do you think you interact with children and others?

- Obtain feedback from at least one other person (another learner or someone in your workplace) about how effectively you communicate.

- Write down one way in which you could improve your skills so that you communicate more effectively.

A2 The role of the early years assistant in supporting children's communication, literacy and language development

A significant part of your role is to support other practitioners in developing children's communication, literacy and language skills, and to support the children directly.

Support early years practitioners in developing children's language skills

As well as the direct support you provide to children, you need to show how you support other early years practitioners in developing children's communication and language skills in a professional way. Communication and language are prime areas of children's learning and development, and practitioners will need to plan for activities and experiences that allow children to practise them. According to the EYFS Statutory Framework 2017:

> Communication and language development involves giving children opportunities to experience a rich language environment; to develop their confidence and skills in expressing themselves; and to speak and listen in a range of situations.

Here are some different ways you can support practitioners in your setting to develop children's language skills.

Preparation

Practitioners should make sure there are opportunities for children to speak, listen and use their language skills so that they can develop their understanding. Preparation for this will range from general day-to-day activities and resources, which are refreshed daily, through to specific preparation for special group activities and for individual children. To encourage communication, try to include subjects that particularly interest them.

Planning and observation

Planning will need to include plenty of opportunities for children to speak, listen and read, and to develop their other communication skills. Early years practitioners should always be on the lookout for new activities that will support the development of these skills. You should also use observation to look at how much the children use the activities and to find out which are the most popular.

Interaction

Adults should make sure they interact with children whenever possible. This is because children need to have the opportunity to practise their language skills as well as develop their relationships with others. Effective questioning when children are busy with activities is a particularly good way of doing this. Adults should make sure that they use OPEN-ENDED QUESTIONS. These questions take forward children's thinking as well as supporting communication.

Closed question: 'Are you enjoying doing that, Sam?'

Open question: 'Sam, what you are doing there?' (Such questions can then be extended.)

Feedback

Wherever possible, you should feed back in a positive way to children. This is likely to be verbal feedback, as you will be speaking to them at the time. Make sure you include phrases such as 'well done', 'that's great', 'good description' and so on, to encourage children as they develop these skills. You can also use feedback to drive further interaction – for example, 'That's a great description, Sam. I'd also like to hear what you think about the new water-play area.'

Engage in early communication with babies and children

Make sure that you communicate with children from an early age so they start to develop an understanding of how to interact with others. Here are some ways of doing this.

Appropriate facial expressions and tone of voice

Even very young babies will be able to focus on facial expressions although they may need some time to learn how to do this. You should look directly at children, using appropriate expressions and an appropriate tone of voice when you are talking to them, so that they start to pick up on what these mean. For example, if you are greeting a baby you might smile and say how good it is to see them, and you would use a specific tone of voice to do this. If you watch how adults communicate with babies in particular, you will notice that their tone of voice can be an exaggerated form of how they speak to an adult, or that they use a higher voice when speaking.

Body language

Make sure when communicating with babies and children that you are using the correct body language – get down to their level, face them and give them your attention so they are encouraged to communicate with you in response. Avoid putting your hand over your mouth, which makes you harder to understand, and try not to fold your arms as this can act as a barrier.

Body contact and eye contact

Always remain close to the child and give them eye contact so that communication is easier. You may need to put your arm around the child if you are comforting them. If you are telling them something important, you will need to face them and encourage them to look at you so you can ensure they have understood what you are saying. Remember that body contact and eye contact are also effective methods of communication on their own.

Recognition of personal space and boundaries

If a child is reluctant to communicate or turns away from you, this may mean they are too distracted or upset to listen to what you are saying. Although you may need to comfort children, you should recognise when they need space or time away from a situation to calm down. Unless the situation is dangerous for them or others, you should give them that space. In some situations, you should especially take care with personal space and be mindful of safeguarding issues – for example, do not put yourself in a situation where you are alone with a child. Remember also that children need their privacy and personal space in the same way that adults do, so don't insist on communicating with them if this is not appropriate in a given situation.

> **Link it up**
>
> See Unit 4, A3 for more on promoting dignity and respect through ensuring suitable levels of privacy during changing and toileting.

Support an environment that encourages communication and language development

The early years setting needs to be set up in a way that encourages communication and language development. Here are some suggestions for this.

- Appropriate lighting will encourage the use of literacy resources. An under-lit environment will be too dark; too much sunlight will be too bright. In both cases, children will struggle to look at books and will find something else to do. Make sure that lights are on when it is dark and that blinds are drawn on a sunny day.
- There should always be a quiet space or quiet areas for children who would like to share a book with each other or look at one on their own, or sit with adults to do so.
- Find activities to generate children's interest and interaction. Such activities tend to be those in which children have to explore or investigate something – for example, exploring which items stick to magnets. Adults can support this by addressing open-ended questions to the children as they carry out the activity, such as 'What are you doing?', 'Why do you think that is happening?' or 'Can you think of ways which might make it work?'

Link it up

See Unit 5, A3 for more on recognising that play provision promotes different areas of development – for example, through sharing books and rhymes and through puppet play. See also Unit 5, B1 for more on recognising how aspects of the environment stimulate communication and language skills.

- Stimulating displays can be put up showing children's work. These should be well labelled with questions, as well as the children's names, so that adults and children can talk about them.
- Activities to stimulate communication and language development can take place outdoors as well as indoors; for example, there is nothing to stop you having a quiet area outside for reading. You might also put up laminated questions to stimulate discussion. For example, 'How many steps are there?', 'Can you see any birds on the feeder?' and 'What shapes can you see on the ground?' are questions that can only be answered when the children are outside observing for themselves.

Practise

1 Each time you go into the setting, note down opportunities you have had for supporting children's communication and language development. How many might you have in any one session?

2 Make a list of the main factors practitioners should consider when assessing and observing children's communication and language development.

3 Create a short presentation explaining these factors and share it with the rest of the class.

Stimulating displays encourage children to engage with words and to want to decode them

Report any areas of concern

If you have any concerns about the communication and language development of a child in the setting, you should always speak to their **KEY PERSON** and the setting supervisor. You should tell others as soon as you can and give reasons for your concern so that you can discuss ways of helping the child as a team. You will need to give examples of what has happened to make you concerned, so it may be worth noting them down at the time.

> ### What if...?
>
> Melissa has a child in her setting called Ella who has been coming for over six months. She is 3 and Melissa has noticed that she often plays alone or alongside others but that she does not communicate with them. She seems to be 'in her own little world' and when it is time for the children to sit together on the carpet she does not participate or get involved.
>
> A nursery assistant has been asked to sit with her to try to engage her in conversation, but Ella has not been responsive to this.
>
> - What should Melissa do in this situation?
> - Why is it important that something more is done to help Ella?

A3 Approaches to communication for different ages/abilities

Children of different ages or abilities will need different levels and types of support. You will need to develop an understanding of the different approaches you can adopt to ensure each child receives the support they need.

Identify and use different methods of communication

There are different ways in which early years practitioners support children's communication and language development.

Non-verbal communication

All adults will use non-verbal communication and gestures to a certain extent, either alongside speaking or alone. This will help young children at the earliest stages of language development to understand what is being said. For example, if an adult is pleased or happy about something a child has done, they will smile and show that this is the case. If they are unhappy, they will frown and show it in their facial expression. A shake of the head can be enough for a child at the other side of the room to show them that what they are doing is not a good idea, while a 'thumbs up' for doing the right thing can be all the communication you need.

PECS

PECS (Picture Exchange Communication System) is one of the most popular tools used in early years settings. PECS is a set of very simple pictures that children can use to communicate what they want to say. Their choice of pictures is usually placed on a board to represent a sentence – for example, 'I want a drink.' (See PECS board image.)

PECS boards are also successfully used in many early years settings as a pictorial timetable, which helps children to see what is happening during the day. You may be able to find examples of such timetables in your setting. They are often used to support children who have special educational needs that include communication difficulties, such as those on the autism spectrum. However, they can benefit all young children.

If you have found that a child needs additional support in this area, you will need to be advised by others and in particular your early years SENCO. There are various commercial systems that you can be trained to use, as well as resources that can be produced in the setting.

PECS boards are a very useful tool to support communication

Makaton and sign language

Makaton and British Sign Language (BSL) are two methods of communication that may be used in early years settings. While BSL is used mainly to support communication for deaf children, Makaton is used for any child who has communication difficulties. It is similar to PECS in that it uses both signs and symbols to support spoken language. Children are encouraged to use gestures and other non-verbal communication and to gradually build up to using spoken words if they can.

Preparing language-based interactions

Although it can sometimes be difficult during a busy day, you should always try to prepare carefully the books, rhymes or other language-based interactions you are going to share with children. You may find, for example, that the book you plan to read or the game you intend to play with them is not age appropriate. If this is the case, children will not get the maximum benefit from them. See also 'Reading with children of different ages' below. Figure 6.3 shows the different types of language-based interactions and the text below explains them.

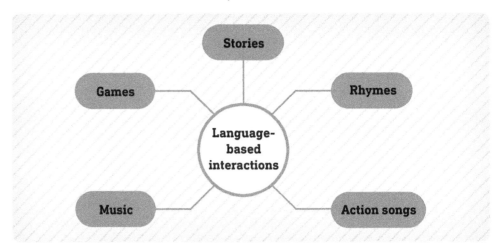

Figure 6.3: A variety of activities and interactions with children are language based

Games

Very young children tend to enjoy repetitive games or those in which they need to copy what you are doing, as these are predictable and develop their confidence. Older children will be starting to enjoy simple games, such as memory games, that will also encourage them to talk.

Stories

You should make sure if you are reading a story to children that it is appropriate for their age and stage of development. As you become more experienced, you will find that you have favourite books to which children respond positively and which you enjoy sharing with them.

Rhymes

Children will enjoy nursery rhymes from a very young age. Rhymes and songs should be used regularly with young children and you should start with very simple rhymes such as 'Pat-a-cake', or repetitive rhymes such as 'ten fat sausages'.

Action songs and movement

Examples of action songs include 'Five currant buns' and 'A sailor went to sea sea sea', which inspire children to carry out actions to the music. They encourage the development of communication and language as they require the children to 'fill in the blanks' and respond at a specific moment. The children will also need to know when to move to the rhyme or music by listening out. Action songs also support motor skill development.

Music

Music should be a key part of your day with young children. Even if you are not a confident singer or musician, you should encourage children to sing songs and listen to music or play instruments. This may mean using existing resources but can also be through instruments they make themselves or objects that are used to beat rhythms.

Practising reading and adapting activities

Practising reading with children of different ages

Reading and sharing books with children of different ages is an important part of supporting their language and communication development. It is something that young children should do every day as it is a good way of ensuring they have focused adult time. Most children are keen to share books when they are given the chance.

All pre-school children will be learning about how to hold a book and turn the pages carefully, that print carries meaning, and that it runs from left to right. Table 6.1 shows how children's focus on books develops stage by stage.

Table 6.1: Children's reading development in the early years

Stage	Reading activity
6–12 months	Children will enjoy looking at picture books with adults. You can point to different illustrations or photos and tell them what they are looking at
12–18 months	Children will enjoy having picture books with simple rhymes and singing games read to them
18 months to 2 years	Children will still enjoy reading simple books. By 2 years, they may be able to say a few nursery rhymes and may join in as you read to them
2–3 years	Children will be able to remember and repeat favourite texts with you and will like their predictability. They will continue to enjoy the closeness of reading with an adult
3–4 years	Children will be able to say favourite texts at the same time as the reader and tell you off if you miss anything out! At this stage you can occasionally start to follow the text with your finger to show the child that the print relates to what you are saying
4–5 years	Children may be able to retell you longer stories. They will enjoy going to the library to find new books and will continue to enjoy familiar stories and rhymes

Adapting activities where necessary

Depending on the age of the child you are reading with, you will need to adapt the way you approach the activity. With very young children, remember that they will not be able to concentrate for very long, so don't try to extend the session if they want to stop. Older children may be stimulated by books and will want to discuss what is happening in a story. In the case of non-fiction books, they may want to talk to you about their own experiences. You should be able to run with what they would like to talk about as this will enrich the child's language experience.

What if...?

Sanjay is using a story sack (a bag of props to accompany a story book) to read a book with Jilly, who is 2 years and 6 months old. The book is called *The Pig in the Pond*, which has a number of animals in it, and the story sack includes small figures of the animals. Jilly is enjoying looking at the animals and is making an animal sound for each one after taking it out of the sack. She has become distracted from the story and just wants to look in the sack and play with the toys rather than carry on with the book.

- What might Sanjay do in this situation?

- Give reasons for your answer.

STEP BY STEP | READING WITH AN OLDER CHILD (4–5 YEARS)

- ☐ Comfortable, accessible, quiet area
- ☐ Limited distractions
- ☐ Appropriate lighting
- ☐ Appropriate book for child's age/stage of development
- ☐ No time limit

STEP 1

Open the book so that both pages are clearly visible both to you and the child. Allow the child to hold it if they would like to. Read slowly to allow the child to take in what is happening. If the book contains repetition, give children the chance to join in if they can.

STEP 2:

Encourage the child to turn the pages carefully and show them how to do this if necessary.

STEP 3:

Point things out and question the child while you are reading the text. If it is a non-fiction book, relate what you are reading to the child's own experience.

STEP 4:

Talk about the book when you have finished. Ask the child what they have enjoyed, how they felt when reading and what they think of the different characters.

Children whose home language is not English

In your setting you are likely to have some children whose home language is not English. You will need to know how to support them positively as part of your role. A child's home language is very important both culturally and as part of their identity, and you will need to work with parents and carers to ensure that this is developing as expected.

Children should have opportunities to develop their home language in play. If there is more than one child sharing a language, they may well speak their home language while playing. However, the EYFS guidance states that they should also have 'sufficient opportunities to learn and reach a good standard in English language... ready for Year 1.' It also states that adults working with young children should assess children's progress in English, so it is important that they do this.

You should make a point of interacting regularly with these children in a positive way so that they have plenty of opportunities to develop their English skills and extend their vocabulary. If you have any concerns about their progress in English, you should speak to your supervisor so that the setting can discuss this with their parents or carers.

Practise

Ask whether you can work with a child whose home language is not English in your setting. Talk to their key worker and find out whether there are any areas in which the child needs specific support or whether they would just benefit from more communication opportunities in English.

- Where you can, work with the child in different situations to support their English – for example, during snack time, singing, when they are carrying out activities alongside other children or when speaking with their parents about what they have been doing.

- Read with the child and talk with them about what is happening, asking open questions where possible.

- Adapt activities if necessary to support the child's understanding and ensure that activities are enjoyable and meaningful.

Skills and knowledge check

☐ I can explain the difference between speech and language.

☐ I can name one way in which language skills affect children's emotional development.

☐ I can ensure that the environment supports the development of communication and language skills.

☐ I have practised using appropriate language and tone of voice with babies and children of different ages.

○ I know why it is important for children to learn to communicate.

○ I know how to use songs and rhymes to support language development.

○ I know why it is important to engage with children whose home language is not English.

○ I know how to prepare different language-based interactions to use with children.

B Support children with different communication needs and abilities

B1 Communicating with children of different ages

You will need to learn to develop your skills in communicating with children of different ages, through careful planning of activities and through ensuring that you use different strategies. As you work closely with other practitioners you will be able to look at the way in which they assess language and communication development. Through this you will strengthen your own skills in this area.

Observe how experienced practitioners assess language development

As part of your work placement, you will have daily opportunities to watch experienced early years workers interacting with babies and children. The EYFS requires that observations are carried out in all areas of learning and, as a prime area, communication and language are particularly important.

Practitioners may note down specific words or phrases that are said by children, record when they first start to join in with singing or action rhymes, and note whether they can listen attentively and follow instructions. They may use a checklist to look at the MILESTONES the children have achieved, or assess children simply by interacting with them and getting to know them. It is through interacting with babies and children and developing positive relationships with them that their communication skills will be developed.

Plan your approach to communication

You may be working on a focused or non-focused activity with a specific child or group of children in order to develop their communication skills using a plan or the setting's schedule. You should be aware of the communication opportunities that are available in each activity so that you can meet the setting's requirements. Schedules should set out the routines and activities that will be taking place during the setting at any one time, and this should guide you in choosing your approach.

Routines will support the development of language. As children get to know what happens at different times of the day, they will start to associate events with the language that goes with them – for example, at snack time they may learn the names of different foods and the language of sharing.

Communication opportunities may take many forms, as already listed in learning aim A, through activities such as games, singing, stories and other speaking and listening activities. When planning your approach to communication, it may be helpful to compile a checklist to refer to. You could consider some of the following questions.

- Exactly what do I need to do?
- Which children am I working with and do they have any specific needs?
- Have all the children been included in the activity?
- What will I need?
- How long should I spend on it?
- What should I do if the child/children are not able to do the task or if they complete it quickly?
- Do I need to record anything or feed back to other staff?

Practise

Observe an experienced practitioner working with a pair or a small group of children playing a game. Look particularly at the way they:

- encourage all children to participate
- model clear speech and language for the children
- ensure that the game is fun and engaging.

Think about the way you interact with children. Can you use any of these strategies to support the development of their communication skills?

Link it up

For Unit 7, A1 you will need to show continuous reflection and use feedback from others to identify areas to improve.

The importance of working closely with parents and carers

The EYFS emphasises the importance of working closely with parents and carers in order to support all areas of learning and development. You should therefore take every opportunity to develop good relationships with them. Although you may find this easy to do with some, it may be more challenging with others and these are the ones to whom you should perhaps devote more energy. For example, there may be some parents or carers who do not engage with the setting or do not want to talk to staff. You will need to work with other staff to encourage interaction as it will be better for the child if support at home and support at the setting complement each other.

It is important for children to see that you have positive relationships with their parents and carers and can communicate effectively with them. This helps both sides as well as supporting the development of children's language, particularly when children speak English as a second or additional language. Your setting may hold special events such as book weeks or reading meetings to support parents and carers in choosing suitable books to read with their children at home. It may also provide other information about how best to support their children in the earliest stages of learning to read. You may need to encourage some parents and carers to respond to invitations or events. As you become more experienced, make a point of speaking as much as you can with parents or carers of key children, so as to develop this relationship.

Link it up

See Unit 3, B2 for more on recognising and interacting with different caregivers and meeting and greeting them; and C1 for more on supporting colleagues in working in partnership with parents.

What if...?

Little Bees nursery has a group of new parents who have not been engaging with staff. This is partly because the new parents' evening was cancelled as so few people had said they would come. The setting has a parents' rep who has said she will help if needed.

- How could you and other staff encourage the new parents to become more involved?
- What could the parent rep do to help?

Being an effective role model

When you are interacting with babies and young children, you are acting as a role model for language. In other words, you are showing them how to use language through what you say and how you say it. Adults often repeat things to young children so that they have longer to absorb information and to hear the correct way of saying it. When children answer, the adult may also repeat what they say back to them, particularly if they are just learning to put a sentence together. Look at the following:

> Adult: 'I'm going to get the table ready for snack time. Would anyone like to help me?'
>
> (Annie, aged 2, goes over to adult)
>
> Adult: 'Would you like to help, Annie? Here are some plates.'
>
> Child: 'Annie help.'
>
> Adult: 'Oh, thank you. Are you going to help me, Annie?'
>
> Child: 'Yes.'
>
> Adult: 'That's great! Can you put these plates on the table for me, please?'
>
> Child: 'Plate on table.'
>
> Adult: 'Yes, put the plates on the table, thank you, that's wonderful.'

As you can see, the adult is repeating what he is saying both to model the correct language and to reinforce what he is doing so that the child understands. The adult will also be able to gently correct the child while still encouraging them, for example by adding the plural to plate, and emphasising the s, as in the last line.

You can also see that he is teaching the child about the process of conversation, which is that one person speaks and the other listens, and then they swap over. Most adults in an early years setting will do this without even thinking about it, but you need to check that you are. Although the example above is only a few lines, a lot of information is being sent and received.

Making language-based activities fun and engaging

There are lots of different ways in which you can make language-based activities fun. Stories, songs and games are a great way of supporting language development as they encourage children to take turns and wait for one another as well as talking about what is happening. They are also a good opportunity for having fun with young children, who have a natural sense of humour and usually respond positively to jokes that arise as part of what you are doing with them. This will help to engage them in activities and make them more likely to want to repeat the experience.

Another way to engage children is through the use of props. Story sacks and puppets, for example, draw children in straight away by giving them something visual to hold while you are working with them.

B2 Suitable resources to support literacy

Literacy resources encompass much more than books. You will need to be able to identify appropriate materials, know where they are kept and know how their use fits in to your setting's agreed way of working.

Identify appropriate reading materials

As you will be working with children of different ages in the setting, there should be a variety of reading materials available to read with them. Generally speaking, you should make sure that books are appropriate for the age and stage of the children – for example, don't try to read longer story books to babies, or books that are too simple to older children. You would make an exception, though, if a child has a particular interest or has brought something to the setting that they want to share with you. Reading materials may come in different formats – for example, feely books, pop-up books, noisy books, card books, stories, information books and magazines. Children should be encouraged to bring and look at any of these that interest them so that their enjoyment of reading can be nurtured.

Do the books you read with children match their age and stage and reflect their interests?

What if...?

Jamie, aged 4, has been diagnosed with autistm spectrum disorder. He enjoys learning about trains and has brought a magazine that has details of a number of different models. Despite the fact that the magazine is 'too old' for him, he has read it with his mum and can tell adults in the setting all about the different trains in detail. One of the assistants has said to Jamie that the magazine is 'too difficult' for him to read in the book corner and told him to put it in the home box.

- Why is it important for Jamie that adults in the setting talk to him about his interest and look at the magazine with him?

- How might the assistant's comment have caused Jamie distress and put him off reading the magazine?

As you become more experienced, you will be able to identify more easily the kinds of materials that are best for the children you are working with. Reading materials should also be available for children to choose for themselves, and there should be quiet, comfortable areas for them to look at books together or on their own.

Link it up

See Unit 5, B3 for more on resources and equipment for play and learning activities and how to select stories and rhymes that are age/stage-appropriate.

Know where resources are kept and how and when they are used

You will need to know where literacy resources are kept in your setting. Remember that this does not just mean books and reading materials for children of different ages. You may have resources such as:

- large letter tiles
- alphabet charts and puzzles
- key words
- letters made of different materials such as sponge or wood
- story or rhyme CDs
- interactive literacy resources on computers
- interactive boards or tablets.

What literacy resources can you find in your setting other than books?

There are many other resources that will all support literacy development in different ways. Remember also that literacy resources should be kept both inside and outside and that children should have access to them at all times as far as possible. When storing resources, mark or label them clearly so that all adults and children can find them easily. Keep them tidy so that you can encourage the children to do the same.

How and when resources are used will depend upon the setting and how they plan for **ADULT-LED** and **CHILD-INITIATED** activities. For example, some resources may be accessible to children so that they can self-select them at any time. In other cases, specific resources may only be put out for particular adult-led activities. Plans should always be accessible so that all adults can refer to them – for example, they should be routinely put on the same wall or in the same file, and it should be clear on the plans which resources are needed.

Using the setting's agreed way of working

You will need to consult your setting's Literacy Policy so that you are clear about the setting's preferred way of working when reading with children. There may be guidelines or a simple set of instructions such as those in the Step by Step in A3. You should also check that the materials you use have been agreed by the setting – for example, if you have brought in your own book to read with the children.

Practise

Ask your setting manager if you can carry out separate observed literacy activities over several sessions so that you can practise your skills at supporting literacy. You will need to be able to work with the setting's plans and show that you:

- can find and use the resources needed
- follow the setting's agreed way of working
- use appropriate communication strategies when interacting with children who have different communication needs
- use some of your own ideas to enhance the activity, if possible, and stimulate children's interest.

Using appropriate communication strategies for children with different needs

It is important to follow the setting's policy on working with children with different needs when you are carrying out literacy activities. This may include adapting your approach to communication and choosing particular resources to support children's learning. You should be aware of who these children are so you can ensure there are no barriers to their learning. They may include:

- children with sensory difficulties
- children who speak English as a second or additional language
- children with a **LEARNING DISABILITY**.

Children with sensory difficulties

Children who have sensory difficulties may have a visual or a hearing impairment. In each case, this will mean that they find it harder than other children to communicate without additional support and/or resources. Children's senses need to be stimulated from an early age to develop the pathways in the brain that support communication, and adults will need to give children with sensory needs additional support to develop these skills.

If you are working with a child who has a sensory impairment, you will need to ensure you have their attention when you are communicating with them. A simple gesture will help, such as holding their hands so they know you are communicating with them, although this will not always be possible unless you are close by. In addition, you should make sure that you encourage eye contact where possible and talk through what is happening so that you reinforce the language and give children additional time to process it.

Children who speak English as a second or additional language

There are many advantages to speaking more than one language, and you may have a number of children in your setting who do this. These children will need to develop their home language to help them associate with their own home environment and culture, but they may also need support in the development of English. It is helpful to find out their level of development in both their home language and English so that you can help 'fill the gaps' by working on suitable activities with them.

For those who are at the earliest stages of learning English, make sure you speak slowly and use vocabulary that is simple to understand so they have time to listen and process what you are saying. If you are reading with them, check they have understood by asking them questions about the text as you go. Bilingual texts are also available to support reading in two languages.

Children with a learning disability

Children who have a learning disability may take longer than other children to develop the cognitive skills needed to think in an abstract way, use their memory and work things out. This may also affect other areas of their development and in particular language and communication skills, as these are what we use for thinking.

As with children with other differentiated needs, they are likely to require more time than other children to process language and to think about what is being said. If possible you should repeat what you say so they have time to take in the information.

Developing activities and objects that generate children's interest

When you are developing activities to support literacy and stimulate communication, you will need to use activities and objects that capture children's interest.

If you are using resources that are new to them, it is always worth giving them some time to 'play' with the new items before you start. Otherwise, it can be difficult to get them to focus on what they should be doing.

Link it up

For more on communication strategies for children with sensory difficulties, see B6 in this unit.

Link it up

Go to B3 in this unit to find out more about how to support children with English as an additional or second language as well as the kinds of resources that may be helpful.

Link

For more on general communication strategies, see A3 and B5/B6 in this unit.

A good way of generating children's interest is to engage their senses by asking them to describe what they can see, hear, feel and smell. Figure 6.4 shows some practical ways to stimulate children's senses and engage them in activities.

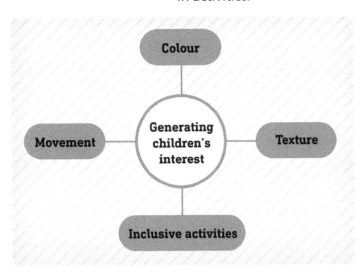

Figure 6.4: You can use many resources to stimulate children's senses

Colour

Very young children can be stimulated by bright colours or enjoy talking about the effect colours have on different things. Often when painting they may choose colours that are not 'correct' because they want to see what it looks like – for example, blue grass or purple trees. This is a good opportunity for you to talk with them about the effect colours and light have on things or ask them to describe what they can see. Colourful objects can be very stimulating for children but don't just use plastic toys – use natural materials and objects too.

Texture

Looking at textures simply by providing different materials is another good way for children to engage in discussion and use descriptive vocabulary. Look at items that are hard, soft, bumpy, shiny, grainy and so on.

Inclusive activities

You should make sure you provide activities and objects that are **INCLUSIVE**. If you have a child who has special educational needs, for example, you must make sure they are able to use the resources and activities you have provided.

You should also make sure that resources and activities are culturally inclusive – for example, by reading books from different cultures or talking about items from other countries. These can be excellent opportunities for talk. Make sure when planning to use activities and resources that you do not include any that may be offensive to a particular religion or ethnicity.

Movement

Some young children will not be able to stay in one place for long, so resources and activities that encourage movement may keep their attention for longer. Examples of this might be asking them to bounce a ball on the ground on chalk-drawn letters and seeing if they can identify the sound of each letter; or playing an instrument while they are singing a counting song.

Practise

Ask your supervisor whether you can provide some objects to talk about with children that will generate their interest and encourage their language skills.

- Ask the child/children whether they know what each object is.
- See if they can describe each object to you.
- Note down what they say, particularly any effective vocabulary.

B3 Communication strategies for special educational needs (SEN), English as a second language (ESL), English as an additional language (EAL)

You may need to use different communication strategies for some children in the setting – for example, those who have special educational needs or who speak English as an additional or second language.

Where children have special educational needs, these may be caused by many different factors and affect them in many different ways. However, here you will be thinking specifically about how special educational needs may affect children's communication.

- Physical or sensory needs, such as a hearing or visual impairment, will mean the child needs support to access the curriculum. They may need to have a hearing loop in the setting or wear a hearing aid, and may need to sit close to adults during learning activities.
- A **LEARNING DELAY** may mean that the child has difficulty communicating because they take longer than normally developing children to process language or to express themselves.
- Social or emotional needs may mean that the child is reluctant to speak due to anxiety. They may be what is called a 'selective mute', which means they only speak to adults they are familiar with, or only speak to their peers but not to adults.

In all of these situations, children will need additional support. Early years workers will need to seek advice from the SENCO and the child's speech and language therapist as well as their parents and carers.

Children who are learning to speak English as a second or additional language will take longer to learn to speak than those learning one language. They will be tuning in to and understanding a different set of rules as well as listening to different speech sounds. They may be at different stages of learning English – some may be reasonably fluent, while for others the setting may be their first experience of their second language.

If their fluency is good, you may need to remind yourself from time to time that English is not their first language and check that they have understood everything. It can be easier for them to miss some aspects of what is said. Always be aware of the speed at which you speak to them and the kind of vocabulary you use, and try not to speak in very long sentences. You may then need to make sure they have understood you by asking them to repeat back what you have said.

Know about the role of relevant professionals

If you notice that an ESL/EAL or SEN child is not making any progress over time, you should speak to others in the setting to find out whether this has been discussed with their parents and with other professionals. If they are bilingual, it is important to find out whether they are making progress in their home language.

If it is decided that there are concerns, the child will be referred to one of several professionals (see Table 6.2) for an assessment of their language skills. There are a number of different professionals who may be involved; most will come from outside the setting.

Table 6.2: Professionals who support communication, literacy and language development

Professional	Main role
Special educational needs co-ordinator (SENCO)	This professional may be based in your setting or support a group of local early years settings. They will talk to staff and advise them on ways of working with all children who have communication difficulties or other special educational needs. They may provide strategies to help within the setting and at home or refer to another professional such as a speech and language therapist
Speech and language therapist	A speech and language therapist will work with children to assess and support those who have problems processing or expressing language. Children will usually be referred to a therapist and after a wait will be allocated a block of six sessions with follow-up work for parents and carers to do at home
Educational psychologist	An educational psychologist will visit the setting and assess children if they have been referred by the SENCO. They will usually give the child a series of activities to do in front of them so that they can work out their precise area of difficulty. They will then speak to parents and the early years team to work out a way forward, including targets to work on together
Hearing support services	Hearing support services are usually based within the local authority or health trust. They will work with schools and early years settings to support children who have or who may have a hearing impairment so that they can develop their communication and language skills. This will be through the provision of resources, advice and training

Link it up

Refer to Unit 1, A2 for policies and procedures in early years settings and understanding the role of other professionals. Also link to Unit 3, C1 for supporting colleagues in meeting children's needs in early years settings.

Tools to measure and identify communication difficulties

As well as the professionals listed in Table 6.2, there are other tools and training available to equip those who work with children to support children's language development. One of these is the Every Child a Talker or ECAT programme, a national system to measure and encourage the development of early language.

A lead practitioner is sent for training and then co-ordinates ECAT in their setting through a series of activities to support communication needs. The training is designed to increase knowledge of children's early development in language so that practitioners and parents can better support children. Other systems also exist and your setting may have different programmes in place to measure, identify and support communication difficulties.

The importance of early detection

As you are working with babies and very young children, you need to be aware of the importance of finding out early about any areas of development that may be delayed. Action can then be taken and strategies put in place as soon as possible.

Link it up

Remind yourself of the development stages outlined in Unit 2, A1.

What if...?

Gina is 2 years and six months. She speaks Italian at home and although she has been in the setting for four months, she has not started to speak any English. She is very 'clingy' with adults in the setting and needs lots of reassurance in most situations, even familiar ones.

- Why is it important to find out whether there is a problem?
- How can you help Gina in the meantime?

Communication and language are prime areas of learning, and problems here will affect other areas of development. Children who speak English as a second or third language will typically speak later than others. However, if you have any concerns, you should always speak to your early years SENCO and outline your reasons.

After referral, children will be put on a waiting list and this will vary between local authorities. Your early years SENCO will be able to tell you about the average wait in your area to see different professionals. It is likely that your SENCO will meet with the team, including the child's key person, and set some targets that they can work on in the meantime.

Working with a key person to support children

You will need to show how you work alongside a child's key person to help them develop their communication and language skills. If you need to support a specific child, you should be given advice and help to do this so that you are very clear on what you need to do.

Usually the child will have specific targets to work on, which have been set by the early years SENCO or by another professional. You should make sure that you understand exactly what the targets mean and what strategies you need to use to help the child move towards them. If you have any concerns about this you should always speak to the key person or early years SENCO to make sure you are supporting the child effectively.

Practise

Ask your early years SENCO whether there is a child or children to whom you can give additional support to develop their communication and language skills. You will need to work alongside their key person and understand exactly what is needed to help the child meet their targets.

Link it up

See Unit 5, C2 for more about the individual play and learning needs of children, how early years workers observe and assess, and how support can be adapted to meet these needs. See also B6 in this unit for ways of adapting how you communicate to support children.

B4 Verbal/non-verbal communication strategies

When you are working with young children, you will need to use different verbal and non-verbal strategies to support communication and language, and to encourage the children to use them too.

Using visual cues and props and providing different interactions

One aspect of the EYFS requires the provision of 'enabling environments'. In other words, children's physical surroundings and the adults around them should both support their learning, directing them so that they can find things out for themselves. They should also be encouraged to interact with others in different ways – for example, by asking questions, through working as a team or by giving you a commentary on what they are doing.

Using visual cues and props means making use of anything in the environment that enhances meaning and enriches the children's learning experience; these may be either verbal or non-verbal.

Link it up

See A3 in this unit on providing different interactions for children.

Visual cues

When we are learning language we also rely on non-verbal cues to help us understand what people are trying to communicate. These can include simple eye contact, a nod or shake of the head, body language, or raising our eyebrows to show surprise. If you watch more experienced practitioners, you will notice they often use exaggerated gestures when communicating with children to ensure they get their message across. It is likely that you will also need to use these to back up what you are saying and to make language more meaningful to children.

Children should also be starting to find relevant visual cues to help them understand the displays or print around them. You may need to point these out when children are new to the setting so that they start to look out for them and learn that print in the environment carries meaning. This might include looking for their name on a cup or peg, or a sign with a question to get them thinking, such as 'How many steps up to the door?' or 'What can you see on this table?'

There should also be displays that link to stories or rhymes or work that children have done so that they can see a visual connection to the language used.

Props

In early years settings there should be a role-play area to support children's communication and language development. This will represent environments such as shops or the home, and children should be free to explore and develop their speech, language and communication skills using the area. Adults may supply specific props so that children can recreate situations they want to copy from their own experience. You may also be able to ask parents for props. For example, a parent who is a hairdresser may be able to provide props for a role-play hairdresser's salon.

Puppets and soft toys are also often used to support children's communication development. Children can sometimes find it easier to talk to a puppet or soft toy than to another person. Used by a familiar adult, they can encourage children to talk about how they are feeling or what they think about situations in the setting. If you would like to use this method with a child, you should speak to another adult in the setting about the best way to approach it with your particular case.

What if...?

Jaz has been working at Little Trees nursery for six months and has noticed that the role play-area is never changed. It is kept as a 'home corner', with the same props, so that this is the only situation the children can recreate.

- Should Jaz say anything about this?
- Why is it important for adults to change the role-play area on a regular basis to include alternative situations?

Practise

Find out whether you can be responsible for setting out props in a role-play area. This can be any scenario that fits in with the setting's plans. Observe how the children use the props and how these support the development of their communication skills.

Encouraging children's use of different methods of communicating

Some children will need to be encouraged to communicate more than others. In addition to using props you may need to use other methods when supporting children who are shy. Modelling the use of language and communicating with others are the most important ways as children will be able to see you using language in context. However, you will also need to encourage children to do the following things.

How can puppets and soft toys encourage children to communicate?

Use appropriate language and pace when talking – you may need to ask children to slow down when they speak. Sometimes small children become anxious to 'get the words out' and this can cause them to muddle their words. You may also need to support them if they use incorrect vocabulary in the earlier stages of learning to talk. If you correct children's speech or help them use full sentences, do it gently by repeating back the correct form of what they want to say rather than telling them they are wrong. (See the example in B1 in this unit of a child helping an adult to lay the table.)

Use correct body language and eye contact – again, modelling the correct body language and level of eye contact is helpful, but you may also need to talk it through with children so they understand what is appropriate in different situations.

Use different types of interactions – for example, using open-ended questioning, using commentary so that children are encouraged to talk through what they are doing, or encouraging them to take part in interesting activities that encourage speech and language.

Develop children's confidence by looking at books with them – this is important as it helps to build children's vocabulary as well as supporting their confidence through their knowledge of what will happen next. They are likely to join in with familiar repetitive text and enjoy listening to stories with their peers.

B5 Methods of providing guidance/clear instruction

Passing on clear guidance to the children in your setting is very important, as is following instructions from your supervisor. You will need to develop the skills to enable you to do these things.

Providing clear guidance to children

As already discussed, you must make sure that you are very clear with children when you are communicating with them, particularly if they have SEN, ESL or EAL requirements. With all children you should get down to

Getting down to the child's level and making eye contact helps to reinforce any instructions you give them

the child's level and make eye contact. You should listen and respond carefully to what they are saying. You should also develop positive relationships with them through the way in which you communicate, so that they will be keen both to respond to you and to initiate conversations themselves.

When you are giving them instructions or guidance, be careful that you don't give too much information as this can be difficult for young children to process quickly.

If you are working with a group on an activity, a smaller group is better if at all possible, so there are fewer distractions for the children.

CHECKLIST **PROVIDING GUIDANCE AND CLEAR INSTRUCTIONS TO CHILDREN**

☐ Make sure you are fully prepared for the activity and know what you are doing; check resources and plans so that you do not need to leave the children at any point

☐ Check that the immediate environment is suitable and not too hot, cold, noisy or busy for them to listen to you

☐ Greet the children individually if possible and by name so that they are involved straight away

☐ Make sure the children are quiet before you speak – never speak over them

☐ Check that the children are looking at you

☐ Give them your full attention and expect theirs

☐ Speak clearly and in short sentences using appropriate language

☐ Give simple instructions, one at a time

Following supervisor's instructions when communicating with children of different needs and abilities

You must make sure you follow the instructions of your supervisor, the early years manager or SENCO if you are communicating with children who have different needs or abilities. It may be that they have specific equipment, targets to work on or other issues that you need to know about. If you need to write these down and refer to them while you are working with the child, you should do so. However, you should be aware of **CONFIDENTIALITY** and only use the information when you are working with the child or children within the setting.

Confidentiality means that any personal information you learn about children in your setting should only be shared with other professionals. You must not talk about it with anyone outside the setting, as it is provided on a **'NEED-TO-KNOW' BASIS**.

Practise

Ask your supervisor to give you an activity to work on with children. Using the 'Checklist' guidance above, give the children clear instructions to carry out the activity.

B6 Ways of adapting your behaviour in response to the needs of the child/group

It is important to remember young children's age and stage of development and any needs they may have when you are communicating with them. You should think about additional strategies that support them and you may also need to adapt how you speak to ensure you communicate effectively.

Using appropriate strategies to promote communication development

Allow time for the child to express themselves

Always give children time to think through what they are saying and let them finish it themselves. If you regularly interrupt or provide the words for them, they will start to rely too heavily on adults rather than attempting to speak themselves.

Use of questions

When you are doing activities with children, effective questioning is very important. Make sure you ask children what they think as you go along so that you extend their learning, rather than telling them things and preventing them from thinking for themselves. Effective open-ended questioning is particularly important as it encourages the development of children's learning and can make a real difference to their experience. Remember that you are not there to do the task for the child but to support what they are doing.

Respect

You are acting as a role model for children. You should therefore show respect – for example, waiting for them to finish speaking, not interrupting what they are saying, and paying attention to them. In this way you will also be encouraging them to do the same for others.

Giving positive feedback

When you communicate with children, you give them positive feedback simply by listening to them and responding to what they say – by smiling, nodding and valuing their contribution. You can extend this by actively commenting on what they have said in a positive way with things like 'That's interesting,' or 'Oh, what a good idea!' If you ask a question linked to what they have just said, you further encourage them: it shows you listened, thought about what they said and want to hear more from them.

Adapting your own methods of speech and communication to meet the needs of others

Adapting your methods of speech and communication means changing the way you communicate in order to help your listener. You will have to do this regularly when working with children with special needs as they will not always be able to understand or communicate with you in the same way as other children. This may be for a number of reasons.

Needs

Children may have special educational needs or a disability that means they need additional support to help them with communication and language. You should have been told if they have specific equipment such as a hearing aid or if you need to communicate with them in a particular way.

Link it up

See Unit 1, D2 for more on developing inclusive practice in early years settings and encouraging communication methods suitable to children's needs.

However, if you think this is the case but you have not been told about it, you should speak to the child's key person or the SENCO to find out.

Preferences

You may be using words the child is unfamiliar with, or they may respond best to adult support in a small group or one-to-one. If they don't seem to be responding to you, ask them how you could help as this may be all that is needed.

What if...?

Gemma is on work experience one day a week in a small nursery. She knows that Jake, aged 4, has some communication difficulties but she has not been told what they are. She is finding it difficult to develop a relationship with him, especially as she is not in the nursery very often.

- What might help Gemma to communicate with Jake?
- Why is it important that she is **PROACTIVE** in this situation?

Abilities

The children you are working with will all be of different ages and will have different abilities. You will find that some are more able than others when communicating with you. If they are finding it hard, think about some of the strategies discussed here, such as slowing down, using simple language and making instructions very clear so as to give the children a chance to think and to process what you are saying.

Practise

Work with your SENCO to look at the communication needs of a child in your setting. Discuss ways to adapt how you communicate and use language with them in order to meet their needs. Set out how you are going to do this.

Skills and knowledge check

☐ I can think about my own communication skills when I am supporting children's language development.

☐ I can work closely with parents to support children's communication skills.

☐ I can make language-based activities fun and engaging for children.

☐ I can use appropriate communication strategies when interacting with children who have different communication needs and abilities.

☐ I can adapt my methods of communication to suit the needs and abilities of the child.

○ I know where to find literacy resources in my setting that support communication.

○ I know why it is important to detect any communication problems as soon as possible.

○ I know how to develop positive relationships with children so they are encouraged to respond and initiate conversations themselves.

○ I know how to give positive feedback to a child when communicating with them.

Ready for assessment

For this unit, you will need to show that you can promote the communication skills of children. You will need to carry out two assessment activities.

1 Observe an experienced practitioner supporting children's communication, literacy and language skills.

2 Provide support in an activity that you have carried out with an experienced practitioner to support the development of children's communication, literacy and language skills.

This means you will have to provide evidence that you have worked alongside an experienced practitioner to observe and carry out a communication and language-based activity that supports the development of children's language skills. Your evidence may come from the plan itself, the observation record, photographic or video evidence, and your learner log.

You should also make sure you have completed Unit 6, Section B of form CPLD 1 in your Work Placement Assessment Portfolio of Evidence. Complete the self-assessment form and include ideas about the different skills you have developed when completing the activities for this unit. Make a note of things you could do to keep improving these skills.

The following checklist is to help you think about how you can prepare for the tasks and to remember key points.

1 Observe an experienced practitioner at work

- Before you observe them, ask the practitioner to talk through the plan with you. Keep it with you as you observe the activity so that you can note things down and write down any questions you want to ask them later.

- Find out about the needs of the children and how the practitioner will adapt the way they communicate with them if necessary.

- During the observation, look at how they use facial expressions, body language and non-verbal communication and whether this is effective.

- Note the children's responses and any strategies that work particularly well or not so well.

- Look at how the practitioner adapts their communication and language when talking with different children.

2 Supporting children in a communication-focused and language-based activity

- Ask an experienced practitioner to observe you using their planning.

- You will need to work with at least two children who have different communication needs or abilities. Make sure you know what these are and whether they have any communication targets so that you can support them effectively, making sure this is on the plan. If you have any ideas, ask whether these can be included too.

- The activity could be reading, singing, circle time or a game.

- Make sure the environment is suitable and that you minimise distractions as far as possible.

- Set up the activity and make sure you have the plan with you.

- Carry out the activity, making sure you use a range of communication strategies to support the needs of the children.

- **ANNOTATE** the plan afterwards, noting down whether the activity was successful in meeting the needs of the children.

- Remember that this will need to be signed off and dated by an experienced practitioner.

- Make sure you complete the relevant sections of your Placement Experience Assessment Portfolio of Evidence.

You may also be able to gather evidence for other units through this activity, for example Unit 7 on reflecting on practice.

WORK FOCUS

HANDS ON

For this internally assessed unit, you will need to show that you are able to make the link between the knowledge you have gained and the skills you are showing as part of your work placement. There are also some transferable skills to practise, which relate to this unit and that could help you to gain employment as an early years assistant.

1. Communication

- Show how you communicate effectively with others, both when working with children and as part of the early years staff. Remember to use positive facial expressions and body language as well as thinking about how you can communicate clearly.

- Develop your confidence when communicating with others in different ways and think about how you do this in different situations, such as with parents, colleagues and children of different ages.

2. Preparing for work

- Plan activities carefully and review what you have done afterwards to develop your awareness of your own practice.

- When carrying out activities with children, show how you are applying your knowledge and understanding of their communication skills so that you can relate this to your interactions with them.

3. Demonstrate thinking skills

- Show that you can assess situations quickly so that you can adapt how you communicate with others. Remember that some children may have communication issues which are as yet undiagnosed.

- Use **INITIATIVE** when working with children and show that you can think independently, but *do check* if there is anything you are not sure about.

Ready for work?

Look at the examples below. In each case, outline how you might support these children effectively going forward. Then look at the suggestions below. Do they match your ideas?

1 Selina is 3 years old and has just started at the setting. She does not speak to others at all although her parents say that she speaks at home. Your supervisor has told you that it is important you do not try to force Selina to speak.

2 Milan is a quiet child aged 2 years and 6 months who lacks confidence. You are working alongside his key worker to develop activities that will promote his communication skills.

3 Romero is 4 and speaks English as a second language. His parents only have a little English.

1

A Speak to your early years SENCO or Selina's key worker to find out as much as you can about her through information from parents and th speech therapist. They will be able to say whether she has been in situations like this before.

B The setting should discuss how adults will manage the situation and how to approach communication with Selina. (It is likely that she has selective mutism, which is a condition caused by anxiety.)

C Follow advice about how you should communicate with Selina.

2

A As well as working effectively alongside Milan's key worker, suggest the kinds of activity that might help him. You could include singing and action rhymes, stories and simple picture books as well as encouraging him to play alongside others on activities that interest him. The use of props may also encourage Milan's communication skills.

B Ensure that the environment is set up so as to encourage him to communicate. Use positive feedback when you respond to him.

3

A Make sure you are aware of any additional needs Romero may have and speak to his key worker to find out whether other professionals have been involved.

B Find out about Romero's interests so that you can talk to him about things that interest him.

C Make sure you speak clearly to him and try not to include too much information at once.

D Speak to Romero's parents as much as possible to form positive relationships with them and if necessary find out if there is anyone who can translate when speaking to them.

7 Developing Professional Practice in Early Years Settings

Imagine if we never stopped to think about the work we have done and how well we did it. How would we improve and develop new skills?

In this unit you will learn how to plan for your personal and professional development. You will understand how to use evidence from your reflective practice to clearly identify your personal qualities, strengths and areas for development. You will then be able to use your findings to help you plan for your personal and professional development.

How will I be assessed?

This unit is assessed internally by your tutor. It is a synoptic unit, meaning that it brings together the skills and knowledge you have gained throughout the course. You will use the outcomes of your reflective practice as evidence to complete a comprehensive skills audit. This will identify areas for further development in your skills, knowledge and professional practice.

Evidence for this unit will be gained from your work placement and from your Placement Experience Assessment Portfolio of Evidence, which you have created from studying all the units in this qualification.

You may need to provide additional evidence such as:

- An information booklet or presentation detailing what reflection is and why it is important.
- A completed document (from your Placement Experience Assessment Portfolio of Evidence) that shows your knowledge and understanding, skills and practice.
- A presentation, written report or other method that discusses the methods of reflection that you have used to identify your strengths and areas for development.

Assessment criteria

Pass	Merit	Distinction
Learning aim A: Explore how reflective practice of own work supports self-development		
A.P1 Identify ways that reflective practice is used to support personal and professional development in early years practice.	**A.M1** Describe how appropriate methods of reflective practice are used to monitor and improve personal and professional development in early years settings.	**A.D1** Evaluate different methods of reflective practice used to develop personal and professional practice in early years settings.
A.P2 Identify appropriate methods of reflective practice with reference to a range of roles and responsibilities in early years settings.		
Learning aim B: Carry out reflection on professional practice skills and in supporting children's communication, literacy and language development		
B.P3 Demonstrate appropriate reflection on own professional practice, knowledge and skills when working in early years settings.	**B.M2** Demonstrate appropriate and detailed reflection on own professional practice, knowledge and skills and support of children's communication, literacy and language development, with reference to relevant examples.	**B.D2** Demonstrate appropriate, comprehensive and insightful reflection on own professional practice, knowledge and skills and support of children's communication, literacy and language development, with reference to detailed examples.
B. P4 Demonstrate appropriate reflection on own knowledge and skills when supporting children's communication, literacy and language development.		
Learning aim C: Carry out reflection on skills, knowledge and practice of supporting children's physical care needs and children's learning through play		
C.P5 Demonstrate appropriate reflection of own knowledge, skills and practice used when supporting children's physical care needs.	**C.M3** Demonstrate appropriate and detailed reflection on own knowledge, skills and practice used when supporting children's physical care needs and learning through play with reference to relevant examples.	**C.D3** Demonstrate appropriate, comprehensive and insightful reflection on own knowledge, skills and practice used when supporting children's physical care needs and learning through play with reference to detailed examples.
C.P6 Demonstrate appropriate reflection on own knowledge, skills and practice used when supporting children's learning through play.		
Learning aim D: Review knowledge, skills and practice gathered to support own professional development as an early years assistant		
D.P7 Review own knowledge, skills and practice to identify current strengths and areas for improvement for an early years assistant.	**D.M4** Present a detailed skills audit with reference to strengths, areas for improvement and further training needs for an early years assistant.	**D.D4** Present a comprehensive and insightful skills audit with in-depth reference to strengths and areas for improvement and relevant training needs for an early years assistant.
D.P8 Present own skills audit that identifies further skills and training needs for an early years assistant.		

A Explore how reflective practice of own work supports self-development

A1 How early years practitioners use reflective practice

What is meant by reflective practice and why is it important for you to carry it out?

Importance of continuous reflection

Reflective practice means looking back at your actions within the workplace. Regular, meaningful reflection helps you to identify what you have learned and what you need to change. By continuously reflecting on your work you can make sure that your professional behaviour is of the highest quality and that you are providing the best possible outcomes for the children you work with. Reflective practice can help you improve both your skills and knowledge.

Early years practitioners use reflective practice to:
- ensure their working practice supports the healthy growth, safety and welfare of children
- ensure that they are always developing themselves personally and professionally
- consider the effectiveness of teamwork and the use of common goals in the setting
- consider different perspectives and approaches to their work
- support professional behaviour
- understand whether effective learning experiences are taking place
- ensure that quality is consistently improved.

There are also benefits to you of reflection.
- It will increase your self-awareness and highlight what you do well, which in turn will boost your confidence.
- It will give you a better understanding of others.
- It will encourage you to become more engaged within the workplace.

Reflective practice should be recorded to enable both you and your supervisors to monitor your progress. This will support important discussions about your personal and professional development and provide you with examples that you can use for a future job role or promotion. It is important to remember that reflection is not a one-off activity.

Using reflection to develop your own job role or career

Reflection will allow you to learn from past mistakes and plan so that you can respond to future changes or situations more effectively, helping you to fulfil your personal and professional goals in the long term.

Early years settings usually provide effective learning and development opportunities but what they offer may not always meet your needs.

For example, you may wish to gain new or further experience of working with children of different ages or with children who have specific learning needs. Taking ownership of and responsibility for your personal development will help you develop in line with your chosen career path.

Here are some ways in which you can support your professional development.

- Seek advice and guidance from people whose skills or career you would like to imitate.
- Attend workshops or training courses on offer.
- Find a **MENTOR** (someone, ideally an experienced practitioner, who can guide and advise you).
- Undertake **WORK SHADOWING** (observing a work colleague closely as they carry out their role in the setting).
- Find time for guided reading and online study.
- Update your knowledge regularly.

Practise

From time to time, check out job adverts for early years assistant roles or a role you may be interested in applying for in the future. Compare the job specification with your own knowledge, skills and experience. Is it similar or do you need to take up further training or develop additional skills?

Developing your knowledge, skills and practical competence

A skill is something you are good at doing, either because you have a natural talent or because you have practised it over and over again.

Your knowledge is developed through education, training and researching current issues related to the sector – for example, Early Years Foundation Stage (EYFS) updates.

When you apply them together in the workplace – for instance, your knowledge of children's development and your organisational skills – you will be showing practical competence.

By reflecting on your skills and knowledge, you can identify your strengths and weaknesses and develop a realistic plan to improve weaker areas.

PRACTICAL COMPETENCE means that you are capable of doing your job properly. It comes from experience in carrying out your daily activities within the work setting. One way of developing your competence is to mirror the good practice and behaviours of colleagues and other professionals. If you spend time thinking about the effectiveness of other people's skills and behaviours, you may be able to copy them.

The key areas for reflecting on to identify skills, knowledge and practical competence are:

- activities you carry out with the children
- how you work with other professionals
- your role as part of the team
- how you engage with parents.

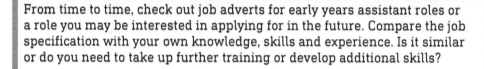

Link it up

Refer back to Unit 1, A1, B1 and C3, to remind yourself about EYFS statutory guidance.

Link it up

Go to Unit 5, B2 for more on supporting learning through play.

Practise

From your portfolio of evidence, select examples of activity plan write-ups and evaluations for different ages and different activities.

Reflecting on these examples, you can identify your level of knowledge and understanding of child development across the age ranges by asking yourself the following questions:

How did I use my knowledge of child development to:

- make sure that the activity met the play and language needs of the children?
- plan activities appropriate to the children's age and stage of development?

In what ways do similar activities vary between ages to meet the children's different needs such as painting activity.

As part of the EYFS requirements, planning of activities should detail how an individual child's needs are being met as part of the whole-group activities. Your knowledge of child development will support your planning of developmentally appropriate activities. Your evidence for Unit 5 in your portfolio will have lots of different examples to show how you have done this.

Using reflective practice to change behaviours

Reflective practice can help not just individuals but early years teams to identify what needs improvement and which changes are valuable. If we do not reflect, we can become trapped in outdated practice and rely on unchallenged ideas, attitudes and expectations. This can lead to a poorly motivated workforce with limited or out-of-date knowledge and skills.

How can I do this in practice?

There are many ways in which you can use reflective practice to change the way things are done in your setting. For example:

- Asking a colleague or a manager to observe you working and to tell you how they view your practice. Nobody likes being observed but if this is done well it can be very beneficial to all concerned.
- Use parent questionnaires to find out essential information that will help the setting meet a child's individual needs. This could include information about their cultural or religious beliefs around food and nutrition. Their feedback may provide you with information you had not previously thought about.

Reflection can inform more than just your personal practice. For instance, by taking part in meetings that reflect on group practice in the setting and sharing your views and experiences with others, you will be contributing to the development of your colleagues' and the setting's overall skills and knowledge.

How others can support your reflective practice

Your tutor, assessor and your work colleagues can also support your reflective practice and continual personal and professional development. They can provide you with feedback, identify areas for development and can support you in developing a plan to meet identified areas.

Example 1

Your tutor may say: "Your assignment showed that you were able to identify some areas of the children's development during the collage activity you provided for 3-year-olds. You have included some good information, however you could have expanded further on how the activity promoted their language skills.

- Did you talk to them about their pictures?

- Were you actively listening to them, asking open questions in return?

- Did you encourage them to extend their vocabulary such as asking them to describe the textures of the materials they were using?"

Example 2

Your supervisor may give feedback following your induction period when you were adjusting to your new role:

"You are showing that you have settled well into the room routine and are developing positive relationships with your colleagues and the children which is great to see. However, you now need to become more familiar with the procedures for providing feedback to parents. I have arranged with your room manager to discuss and clarify this procedure with you during your next weekly progress meeting."

Using feedback from others to identify areas to improve

It's normal to feel anxious about receiving feedback, but other people can give you a different perspective on your personal and professional weaknesses. It is important to be open minded, to accept praise alongside **CONSTRUCTIVE CRITICISM** (feedback that helps you to improve) and to show your ability to listen and learn from others.

For example, during your time in placement, your assessor will have directly observed your practice, making judgements on it and providing you with feedback. You may have used this already for your personal reflection activities.

Consider how the plans you create for play and learning opportunities show your understanding of the essential ways in which children learn, develop and make progress. Reflection and feedback on your own planning skills and knowledge will help you make sure that the children are learning effectively.

Seek opportunities for feedback with your mentor or a colleague who is responsible for overall planning. You will need to think about what opportunities you have provided for children to:

- explore, investigate and try new experiences
- remain engaged and build up their resilience by repeating activities to overcome difficulties they may experience
- problem solve and apply their own ideas and strategies.

Plans should reflect EYFS requirements for the long, medium and short term, physical behaviour, communication and language, and specific areas like literacy and mathematics.

Speaking and listening with children on a daily basis will influence the view they have of the world around them. Think about the feedback that you have had about your communication with children from your assessor and colleagues as they observe you. How well have you adapted communication styles to suit different ages? For example:

- Babies aged 0–12 months: Have you used positive facial expressions, face to face interaction, pitch and tone in your voice when responding to them?
- Toddlers aged 12–36 months: Have you expanded on their few word responses and helped build their sentences, given them one instruction at a time, used routines such as nappy change to talk through the sequence, and responded to them pointing at something?
- 3–5-year-olds: Have you supported children's memory and recall, for example, "what did you do at the weekend", help them make connections between the spoken and written word, for example, labelling a chair, given them time to talk to themselves to support their engagement in an activity?

Practise

1   Think about your involvement with planning activities for the children. Look at examples of the children's activities that you have supported, reflect on their background, how they have evolved, and discuss these with your colleagues. Following their feedback what can you suggest to improve future activity plans?

2   Discuss with your colleagues how you might expect the children to respond and behave when they interact with their parents, grandparents, carers etc. Reflect on examples of how your communication styles have adapted to suit different age groups.

Continuing professional development (CPD) that reflects changes in the early years sector

You need to find ways to engage with early years sector changes in response to new and updated early years frameworks, government legislation and local authority requirements.

For example, the Early Years Foundation Stage (EYFS) statutory guidance and accompanying development matters framework can feel daunting at first, but attending a training seminar or workshop with colleagues can give you a better understanding of how they relate to and impact your everyday practice.

Local authorities may also facilitate initiatives or training events for settings in their locality that you should attend to develop your skills and knowledge around specific elements of practice, such as understanding your Local Safeguarding Children's Board (LSCB) procedures.

Examples of safeguarding changes could be:
- EYFS (2017) Safeguarding and Welfare Requirements
- Working Together to Safeguard Children 2015.

Your supervisor or manager should keep you informed of these and ensure you have access to relevant training and information gathering opportunities specific to your role and responsibilities.

Using challenging situations to improve your practice

Challenging situations can and do occur within the workplace, and it is important that you deal with them swiftly, effectively and professionally. For example, children can feel unhappy and misbehave because they are hungry, tired or unwell, or there may be other reasons not so easily identified.

Although it is important to follow the setting's policies and procedures in these instances, you must always reflect on them to identify what you have learned. This will make you think about the experience, its outcome, and your thoughts, feelings and understanding of it. Through reflection you can formulate different or new approaches in the future to help you improve your practice, such as adapting your communication method or style to respond to the changing needs of children.

> ### What if?
>
> Harriet is a happy 3-year-old who has been coming to the nursery for two years. She has recently been diagnosed with a deteriorating visual impairment. Identify three ways in which you would adapt your communication style to ensure that Harriet continues to feel a valued member of the nursery.

A2 Application of reflective practice

In this section, you will find out about different methods of reflective practice to support your personal and professional development.

Self-reflection

One simple method is to use evidence from your daily activities to support reflection. Self-reflection will:

- enable you to take personal responsibility for improving your professional practice
- provide you with a balanced perspective of your practice
- highlight your strengths and areas for development
- enable you to think about why you chose particular ways of working and consider alternatives
- help you introduce new knowledge into your practice.

> ### Example: Self-reflection
>
> Demonstrating your care for children's personal care needs is important. Reflect on the following statements.
>
> 1 I am able to adapt my practice to meet the children's developmental needs and parental preferences, providing a safe, warm and encouraging environment.
>
> How do you do this? Consider, for example, use of safety features, giving reassurance, routines, work with parents.
>
> 2 I use the sleep routine as a learning opportunity and to develop a positive and trusting relationship with the children.
>
> How do you do this? Consider, for example, interaction, providing comforters, praise and encouragement.

Practise

Think about a time when you gave support to children during planned play, where you led the play and chose the resources. Now think about an activity you supported that was **CHILD-INITIATED**, where the child chose what to play and the resources to use. Then answer the following questions:

1 What did you do that was the same during the two activities?

2 What was different? Why was this?

3 How did you extend the children's language and thinking skills?

4 What learning opportunities arose and how did you use them?

5 What does this tell you about your personal and professional practice? What changes would you make to improve the routine next time?

Link it up

See Unit 3 A1 for suggestions on how to keep and what to record in your diary.

Using your daily log for reflection practice

During your time in your placement you will have been encouraged to keep records of your activities so that you can reflect upon them in a daily log or diary.

To enable meaningful reflective practice, it should be a record of your learning journey and how you are reacting and responding in different circumstances. It will help you to remember and recall your past experiences so that you can learn and benefit from them.

An important point to remember is that the logs should also contain evidence of your professional behaviours such as time keeping, identifying and maintaining your role and responsibilities and how you ensure you comply with Equal Opportunities policies and procedures.

Your daily log is likely to include:

- General information about an activity – timings, details of what happened, background, the outcomes
- Observations – what you noticed about the children, individually or group, and your colleagues
- Reflections – thoughts, feelings, your view on what happened
- Theory – what sense you can make from the situation. Link your thoughts to your notes to support your understanding
- Questions – ask yourself and colleagues questions, you may find answers, be given information to help you resolve queries or questions, or information on how to develop something further
- Evaluation – a judgement of the situation, the positives and negatives, what action you need to take?
- Conclusion – what you have learned and how it has improved your practice, behaviour, your role or your part within the team, what development activities you need to seek out.

Figure 7.1: Top tips when keeping a log

| 1 Write something regularly, daily is ideal | 2 Remember to date your entries | 3 Ensure you maintain confidentiality and follow procedures | 4 Your conclusion should be based on the evidence in your log |

Equal opportunities

Equality affects every aspect of your daily practice. A key principle to remember is that equality is not about treating everyone the same, but treating everyone with equal concern. All practitioners continually seek to do this to the best of their ability, and reflection plays a vital role in helping to do it better.

Practise

When reflecting in your log, ask yourself the following questions to identify whether you have met equal opportunities requirements.

1 Did I adapt the activity to suit the needs of the children in my care?

2 Am I consistently warm and welcoming to all adults I greet in the setting?

3 Am I respectful of the opinions of my colleagues?

Link it up

Look back at Unit 1 D3 to refresh your knowledge of equality legislation and policies.

Physical care routine write-up

An important part of your role is to support children towards developing independence in self-care, an awareness of their health needs and making healthy choices. To be effective in this, you need to make a record of any physical care routines that you support during your working day. You can use these write-ups to reflect on your work. This will ensure that you are continually working towards creating a safe and secure environment to enable children to build their skills towards an independent life.

Link it up

Recap the use of personal protective equipment in Unit 4, A2.

Routines include:

- providing healthy, nutritious snacks and sociable mealtimes
- supporting dressing, washing and/or bath-time
- toileting and nappy changing
- supporting and encouraging periods for rest and sleep
- looking after skin, teeth and hair.

Practise

Look at the example of a physical care routine write-up below. Now choose a different care routine you are familiar with and using the same format as given in the example, identify how well you have supported children. Remember to consider the following questions.

1 How familiar are you with the policy and procedure related to that routine?

2 Identify two skills and two behaviours that you have demonstrated from carrying out the routine?

Figure 7.2: Example of a nappy change routine write-up

Date 3rd January	Time 10.15
Location Saplings bathroom	Aim of routine physical care
Age of children 13 months	Number of children/adult/child ratio one-to-one

A general description of the routine
Mum had identified that baby has a nappy rash and supplied specific cream to be used on rash area, and that baby cries when nappy is changed as they are sore. Requested two hourly nappy changes

Describe your role in implementing the routine
Reassured and comforted baby throughout routine
Followed parental request by using supplied treatment cream for rash and own supplied wet wipes
Ensured my colleague supervised me during the routine so that I was not left alone
Ensured that I had all items needed for nappy change close to hand
Used supplied disposable apron and gloves (personal protective equipment-PPE)
Changed baby on designated mat using anti-bacterial spray before and after routine
Disposed of soiled nappy, double bagged and disposed of in designated clinical waste bin
Washed mine and the baby's hands with soap and water following routine
Returned baby to the room
Put soiled clothing into a disposable bag and put into baby's bag to go home (without rinsing)
Washed my hands thoroughly
Recorded routine on specified chart

Describe the learning opportunities for children which arose in the routine
I drew the baby's attention to the fish mobile suspended from the ceiling in nappy changing area, sang "one, two, three, four, five, once I caught a fish alive.....", played "this little piggy went to market" with their toes, I chatted and smiled a lot to them. I made sure I gave them eye contact, used rise and fall in my voice and gave lots of smiles

Why is the routine important for the children and the setting?
I had one-to-one interaction and they had my full attention
It helped to build a caring and trusting relationship between the child and the family
It helped to build the baby's understanding of what is happening at the time and what happens next
It promoted the baby's verbal and non-verbal methods of communication

Describe the skills required to carry out the routine
Took my time so that it was not rushed even though we were busy
I made sure the routine was specific to the baby
I responded to the baby by chatting and smiling
I told the baby what I was doing throughout the routine
I remained professional throughout, I did not pull a face when I took the nappy off even though it smelt quite a bit so it wasn't a negative experience for the child

Signature of supervisor to prove implementation (please make sure you get the routine sheet signed by your supervisor to prove that you played an active role in the routine)

Signature	Date
Jennie Hands room leader	4 January 2018

Feedback from others

The perspective of others we work with is a valuable tool for reflective practice. Reflecting on the views of peers, tutors, supervisors and others will provide a lot of insight.

Feedback is a two-way process that is designed to enhance your learning. It can be formal, for example, following an observation of your practice by an Assessor or informal such as from a colleague you were working with during an activity.

A two-way process means that you have a discussion around the feedback in order for you to make sense of it and use it to help you plan improvement activities with specific targets in mind.

Example 1

You have received feedback from your room supervisor following a team meeting:

"I was very pleased that you were well prepared for the meeting and put forward your ideas and suggestions for the Autumn term themes enthusiastically, however try not to get side tracked when offering them as we have limited time for the meeting, have confidence and do not be afraid to ask your colleagues or me any questions on things you are unsure of...."

Example 2

You have received feedback from your designated health and safety colleague:

"...you have followed the risk assessment sheet well for your planned outdoor activity, however, I have arranged to have a brief one-to-one meeting with you tomorrow to further explain the procedure on how to make your colleagues aware of your findings and how to consider different perspectives to reduce the risks you have found, so that you really understand the importance of carrying out risk assessments....."

Techniques for observations of practice

There are several techniques that you can apply to observations and you can use the evidence gained for reflective practice. You work alongside your colleagues everyday while in your setting, but have you ever considered taking the time out to actually observe their practice?

Non-participant observation

Non-participant observation is when you observe a colleague implementing an activity (for example, from a distance) without you becoming involved in it, therefore not influencing anyone's actions. Table 7.1 outlines some advantages and disadvantages of non-participation observation.

Advantages	Disadvantages
• observe with your own eyes	• people can act differently when they know they are being observed
• observe body language and communication methods used	• watching from a distance may result in inaccurate information
• make judgements	• time consuming/inconvenient to the person you intend to observe
• open-minded to different ways of working	
• better understanding of situation or person	• you may not have a depth of knowledge of what you observe and may make a biased judgement (subjective)
• person being observed is aware their practice is being observed (known as overt)	

Table 7.1: Advantages and disadvantages of non-participation observation

Following this method, you will need to analyse the information that you have gained. What does it tell you about the person, their behaviour, responses and reactions? How might your practice change as a result of this activity?

Practise

Discuss with your mentor, supervisor or colleague what opportunities there are for you to carry out a non-participant observation of a colleague during literacy or play activities. If possible, carry one out, analyse your findings and make a note of actions you need to take to improve your own practice.

Narrative observations

You can also use narratives of children's play activities to understand child development theory.

EYFS requirements stress the importance of regular assessments on children in the setting. Observing what their interests are, what they choose to do, their preferences and resources they enjoy will help you to gauge children's needs more accurately and plan to meet their next steps more effectively.

Practise

Using a narrative observation of a child at play in your setting, what does it tell you about the child's stage of development? Write your thoughts down then refer back to the work you did on child development to check how knowledgeable you are in child development theory. If you were inaccurate, refresh your knowledge by revisiting the relevant section in this book.

Witness statements

A witness statement is a written and signed record of your practice activities that relates specifically to criteria in your Placement Experience Assessment Portfolio of Evidence. It can be carried out by any practitioner in the setting who has witnessed you carry out an activity and can be for any of the activities you carry out. It will be a record of your skills based on their professional judgement. It is a valuable tool that you can use to measure your actions alongside the skills and behaviours required for a particular role or activity.

Either you or the witness must list the assessment criteria for which the activity provides evidence and clearly describe the activity. This will enable your Assessor to judge the validity of your activities if it is to be used as evidence for your portfolio.

Figure 7.3: Example of a witness statement

Learner name	*Tom Green*
Qualification	*BTEC Level 2 Early Years Assistant*
Unit number and title	*Unit 4: Supporting children's physical care needs*

List the assessment criteria for which the activity provides evidence

Task: *preparing and serving snack routine*

Description of activity/skill witnessed

Tom prepared a morning snack as part of his role requirements for the day. He followed correct procedures for checking on the dietary requirements of the children present. He competently followed health and safety procedures, using PPE, correct chopping boards, correct hand washing procedure throughout. Tom offered a good range of fruits to promote healthy eating.

However, it would have been even better if Tom could have created a more sociable environment for the children by sitting down with them with a plate of fruit and eating and chatting to the children, developing children's language and personal development with his interactions.

Witness name	JENNIE BLOGGS	Job role	Room leader
Witness signature	J. Bloggs	Date	3/11/18
Learner name	TOM GREEN		
Learner Signature	Tom T. Green	Date	3rd Nov 18
Assessor name			
Assessor Signature		Date	

Routine write-ups

Routines are something that you carry out on a regular basis. They help to create order and structure in your life. In early years settings, they help children to understand time and time management, and to become settled and comfortable.

Writing up routines allows you to reflect on the similarities and differences between those for children of different ages and ability groups. Write out the routine for the age group or groups you had experience with and compare those to the routines of age groups you didn't work with. What were the differences and similarities and consider why you think that might be?

A routine write up could include:

- Preparing resources for play and learning, such as mixing paint, maintaining sand
- Maintaining a safe environment, such as tidying away resources and equipment, checking equipment for damage before, during and after play activities
- Maintaining a stimulating environment, such as interacting with children during snack/mealtimes, creating wall displays using children's work
- Supporting children's learning in activity areas, such as small world/role play, table top activities, outdoor play or independent/free play.

See Appendix 1 of the Portfolio of Evidence for a template

Practise

You will have carried out many care routines with children of different ages throughout your placement. Choose two examples of care routine write ups from your Placement Experience Assessment Portfolio of Evidence and ask yourself the following questions to identify how you have adapted your practice between the age groups.

1 How does the typical day's routine vary between the age groups?

2 How is time managed between longer periods of active learning with shorter routines such as snack time?

3 How does the routine ensure that the day remains flexible to accommodate children's changing interests?

Records of activities

As you carry out your daily activities, new learning opportunities will naturally arise. However, to provide the best possible outcomes for children your focus should be to actively develop your skills and understanding and not just carry out activities because you have been told to. If you regularly review records of your experiences, positive or negative, it will provide you with a balanced perspective.

As we explored earlier in this unit, it can be helpful to jot down activities in a weekly diary such as:

- how you have supported colleagues in the planning process and
- what you did to support the implementation of those activities whilst safeguarding the children.

This may be time consuming but you, the setting and the children will reap the benefits if you make the effort, and it will help the setting and you to implement the EFYS appropriately.

When reflecting, do not be too hard on yourself when things didn't go to plan, the important thing to remember is that you identify the causes and improve in the future.

Models of reflective practice

There are several well-known models of reflective practice that you can use to support your continual learning.

Kolb's Learning Cycle

Kolb's Learning Cycle is based on the idea that we learn from everyday experiences of life and activities that we carry out. It supports the idea that reflection is a central part of learning. His theory is that the learning process follows a cycle or pattern and has four stages: Experience (do something); Reflect (think about what you did); Conceptualise (make changes based on what happened), and Plan (how to make those changes next time).

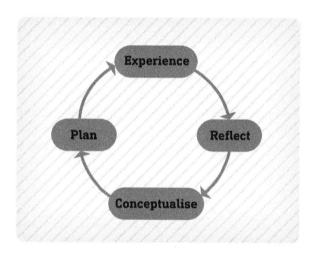

Figure 7.4: Kolb's Learning Cycle (1984)

Gibbs's Reflective Cycle

This model of reflection includes six stages and encourages you to think in a methodical way. You need to think about each experience or activity and consider each stage of the cycle for meaningful reflection: Description (what happened); Feelings (what your thoughts and feelings were); Evaluation (what was positive and negative about the experience); Analysis (what sense you can make of the situation); Conclusion (what else you could have done), and Action (if it happens again, what you would do).

Figure 7.5: Gibb's Reflective Cycle (1988)

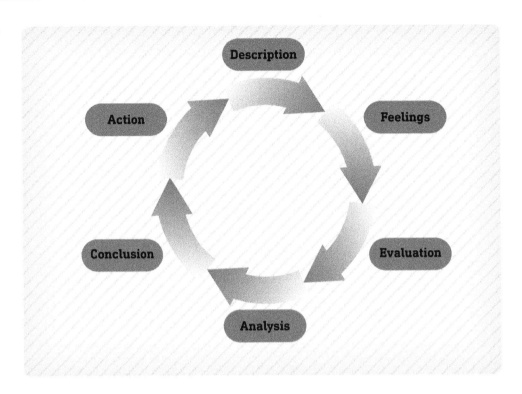

Rolfe et al.'s (2001) Reflective Model

This cycle is based on three simple questions: What? So what? Now what? The principle is to describe the experience that you will be reflecting upon, make your observations about that experience then finish with the changes you would make in the future. Figure 7.6 gives examples of some of the questions you could ask yourself and Table 7.2 an example of what you might generate using the model.

Figure 7.6: Rolfe et al.'s Reflective Model (2001)

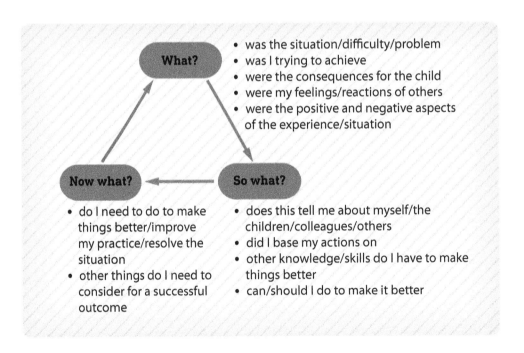

Table 7.2: Example of Rolfe's et al.'s Reflective Model

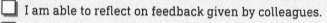

What?

I was asked to set up and implement a leaf painting activity using the children's hand prints. The objective was to create a family tree using their hands for the wall display. The consequences for the child were to gain sensory experience, self-expression, independence and enjoyment. I was looking forward to the activity because it was one that I had suggested during the planning meeting. It was positive that all children engaged with the task, but my attention focused on one child more than the other two and one child decided to paint up their arm and over their sleeves and I told them off.

So what?

This tells me:

That the children like to explore and require more focused attention than I had originally anticipated.

That I am not fully aware of the children's developmental stage of what is acceptable and unacceptable behaviour.

That my reaction and response to the situation may have been inappropriate as a result of my lack of knowledge in child development theory.

Now what?

I need to consider all the individual needs of the children within the group prior to starting the activity.

Adapt my practice to meet those needs in a way that is fair to the group as a whole.

I need to refer to the child development booklet to make sure I understand the level of support required.

I will ensure that I can access colleague support when working with a group, allowing me to give appropriate one-to-one focus within the group, whilst the others are being appropriately supervised.

Link it up

Go to Unit 5, B1 for a variety of ways you can support children's play in the environment and C1 for supporting planned play and learning activities.

Skills and knowledge check

☐ I am able to reflect on feedback given by colleagues.

☐ I am able to explain the benefits of self-reflection.

☐ I can define "knowledge and skills".

☐ I can explain the term "practical competence".

○ I understand why reflective practice is important.

○ I can identify three methods of reflective practice.

○ I can explain formal and informal forms of feedback.

○ I can identify my own strengths and areas for development using SMART targets.

B Carry out reflection on professional practice skills and in supporting children's communication, literacy and language development

B1 Reflecting on knowledge and skills when demonstrating professional practice

For your final assignment, you will need to show how you have reflected on your knowledge and skills in your work with children.

Link it up

Unit 1 A1 gives details on policies and procedures in the setting.

Policies and procedures

There are policies and procedures in place to ensure the well-being of all those connected with the setting, for example, families, children and staff.

A policy contains the main principle of what the setting aims to achieve and a procedure gives clear instructions and guidance as to how things should be done in a particular situation, for example, responding to a disclosure made by a child. These documents must be regularly reviewed by the manager of the setting (at least once a year) and adjusted to reflect any changes in law or guidance.

For completion of this unit you will need to provide evidence demonstrating how you have implemented policies and procedures in accordance with the settings requirements and best practice.

Look through your Placement Experience Assessment Portfolio of Evidence for relevant examples such as:

- a witness statement explaining your participation during a fire drill
- a reflective log showing how you have set up the environment for children's play
- an assessor observation of your practice clearly demonstrating your ability to support children's physical care needs based on what you have learned about their individual needs.

There will be other forms of evidence specific to your portfolio so take the time to update it regularly, revisit the information within it and think about how your practice has developed in line with your increasing knowledge. Your portfolio of evidence should be able to demonstrate the skills you have acquired as a result of the knowledge you have gained.

Practise

One of the most important documents in your setting is the Safeguarding and Child Protection Policy, which will encompass the health, welfare, safety, well-being and development of children.

Refer back to your Placement Experience Assessment Portfolio of Evidence for examples of work documents, reflective logs or record keeping that demonstrate how you have applied your knowledge in practice. For example: accident form, risk assessment, a child's daily diary.

1 Why is the completion of these forms necessary?

2 Identify two examples of the consequences of poor record-keeping.

Practise

Select one of your completed learning through play activity write-ups and answer the following questions.

1 Why is it important to identify proposed learning outcomes, such as links to the EYFS?

2 What information did you use to identify and meet the individual needs of children during the activity?

3 How have you used the information from your activity evaluation to improve future practice?

Demonstration of professional standards of conduct

The parents of the children you work with place an enormous amount of trust and confidence in you so it is very important that you behave and present yourself in a professional manner at all times and follow professional standards of conduct. Children also observe, copy and learn from you so it is vital that you are a positive role model for them.

Feedback from a colleague or your own account of your professional behaviour contained in your Placement Experience Assessment Portfolio of Evidence can help you evaluate the strengths you possess and potential areas for development.

Personal presentation style

Your setting will have its own policies and standards of how you should present yourself and behave at work. Your setting's policies will always comply with equality and diversity requirements. For example, the dress code will respect cultural head wear.

The policies and standards may cover:

- the dress code
- keeping personal and professional life separate
- using your common sense and initiative
- modelling positive and correct language for children
- staying safe and healthy.

You should have a high standard of personal hygiene and wear clean and tidy clothing suitable for joining in activities with children. It is vital you adhere to the setting's policy on this and consider the role that you are in. Not complying with the setting's requirements can result in you being sent home to return in more suitable clothes. Bear in mind that if you consistently disregard policy, disciplinary procedures may follow.

Link it up

Unit 1, A2 looks at safe working practices and safeguarding procedures. Unit 1 B2 details policies and procedures for keeping children safe.

Continually revisit Unit 2 A2 to develop a working knowledge of different areas of child development.

Link it up

Look back at Unit 3 A1 to remind yourself about professional standards of conduct.

Professional and positive approach to work

In any work setting, your behaviour reflects the level of professionalism and attitude you have towards your role. Showing respect, politeness, empathy (the ability to understand and share the feelings of another), DIPLOMACY (dealing with people in a sensitive and tactful way), tact and sensitivity are all ways you can foster a positive approach to the working and caring environment.

Example

Dexter is two-years-old and is very busy at a painting activity. His mother arrives early to collect him and is impatiently waiting for you to get him ready to go home. She notices he has paint on his sleeves and complains that his top is new and you have ruined it. From your professional development you know you must act in a calm and understanding manner to the parent's complaint.

1 Why is it important to remain professional?

2 How can you support the parent to encourage a positive outcome?

Developing positive organisation and timekeeping skills

Organisation is all about keeping things in a sensible order. Using good organisation skills in the workplace will mean that you are able to achieve your everyday responsibilities and tasks, build positive relationships with colleagues and become a reliable and proactive member of the team. It may also reduce your stress levels as you will feel more in control and relaxed in the workplace.

You are also an ambassador for the setting and the impression that you give to parents/carers and visitors may affect their attitude to the setting as a whole.

To be organised you need to prioritise and structure your commitments and tasks. You will already have used many effective strategies to help you in your Placement Experience Assessment Portfolio of Evidence for Unit 3. These can include:

- Record of hours sheet: provides evidence of your placement hours and keeps you informed of your time-keeping requirements.
- SMART target record: helps you to focus on specific areas for professional development such as time management skills and encourages you to consider how this can be achieved.
- Evidence of meetings with your placement mentor: in these meetings you can discuss your progress to date and seek support, for example, being unable to complete tasks on time.
- Reflective log or diary: collating your own evidence about your induction process and demonstrating your understanding of codes of conduct through your everyday practice.

In Unit 3 you will have learned about the crucial role of personal organisation and time management in maintaining a positive environment for children and colleagues.

Practise

Reflect on the strategies you have used to help you organise yourself, for example during your work placement.

1 Have you ever been late for work? If so, how did it affect the children, the routine or your colleagues' attitude to you?

2 What were your findings for the case study in Unit 3, A2, with Liza, the nursery assistant working at Meadows Nursery?

3 What effect could your poor organisational or timekeeping skills have on parents/carers in the setting?

Link it up

Go to Unit 3 A2 for more information on strategies for positive organisation and time-keeping skills.

Look back at Unit 3 A2 Table 3.2 page 93 to refresh your memory about setting SMART targets.

Communication with colleagues and visitors

As human beings, communication is key. You will have noticed that the way you communicate with your friends and family is different to how you communicate in the workplace. Effective communication skills within the workplace are important in supporting good practice.

Practise

Unit 3 B1 gives more details on communicating with colleagues and Unit 3 B2 looks at how to communicate with visitors.

1 Can you find a witness statement in your Placement Experience Assessment Portfolio of Evidence that demonstrates your skills in communicating with visitors?

2 What skills have been identified in the witness statement?

3 What are your areas for development?

Demonstrating effective communication skills

Practitioners may be excellent in what they do with the children but if they are unable to communicate effectively with each other it can have a negative effect on children, staff and all connected with the setting.

Reflect on the ways you communicate with your colleagues, carers and other professionals. Keep a record of your own contribution in one-to-one or group meetings in a diary or ask for a copy of minutes from meetings or feedback from a colleague.

Can you find evidence in your Placement Experience Assessment Portfolio of Evidence for the following?

- Listening and responding positively?
- Asking questions and clarifying your understanding?
- What other methods can you identify as good practice in your setting?

Adapting communication skills to individuals and situations

There are times when you will need to adapt your communication skills to the needs of individuals and specific situations. It is important that this is done appropriately. You will need to make sure that you remain polite, respectful and professional at all times.

Reflect on an emotional situation that you were involved with, such as when a parent was upset at leaving their child at the setting for the first time or you had a disagreement with a work colleague.

Staff meetings provide the opportunity to analyse and reflect on your practice.

- What were your feelings at the time?
- How did you manage those feelings whilst dealing with the situation?
- What communication skills did you demonstrate?
- How would you react if a similar situation arose again?

Respecting confidentiality

Maintaining confidentiality is vital when you communicate with others, whether you are talking casually to someone directly in the setting or formally in written communications. All information that is to be shared must comply with the setting's confidentiality policy.

You will have collated evidence for Unit 1 A4 and Unit 3 B1 to demonstrate how you manage confidential information on a daily basis. Can you identify written evidence in your Placement Experience Assessment Portfolio of Evidence to support this?

Look for evidence of:

- How you have stored information securely
- How you have shared sensitive information on a need to know basis
- How you have maintained anonymity of children in your Placement Experience Assessment Portfolio of Evidence.

What if?

You are in a local restaurant with your family one Friday evening and a parent from your setting comes over to your table and begins to express her views about which child she felt had bitten her child the day before.

1 What would your immediate response be and why?

2 What would be the implications for you, the child, the parent and the members of your family?

Discuss your response to this scenario with your mentor/supervisor and discuss what alternative response you could have given in that particular situation and why.

Link it up

Unit 1 A4 covers maintaining confidentiality when sharing information and Unit 3 B1 looks at respecting confidentiality.

Written and spoken English, IT skills, literacy and numeracy

Demonstrating a good standard of written and spoken English, IT skills, literacy and numeracy are essential when working with young children.

As a role model you should use the correct vocabulary and grammar at all times when speaking and your written work should be clear, legible and concise. Reflect on the following to identify your strengths and areas for development.

- How effective were you when writing notes following children's observations?
- What has your assessor said about how you communicate with children and adults?
- How have you annotated the wall or table-top displays? Did you use the correct spelling and punctuation?
- Find examples from your practice and course of study where your numeracy skills have been used.

Link it up

Unit 6 B1 covers role-modelling clear speech and language when communicating with children and Unit 3 B1 gives more detail on using IT skills and demonstrating good spoken and written English.

Professional conduct with visitors

Early years settings are busy places, they often have visitors at the door or the telephone seems to ring continually. Have you had to answer the door or the telephone when you were in the middle of doing something?

- What was your attitude and reaction in this situation?
- Did you follow procedure or were you a bit short with them because you were busy?

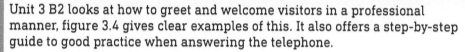

Practise

Unit 3 B2 looks at how to greet and welcome visitors in a professional manner, figure 3.4 gives clear examples of this. It also offers a step-by-step guide to good practice when answering the telephone.

Next time you answer the phone ask a colleague to give you feedback on your communication skills and telephone manner.

Responding to parental requests

Working closely with parents is an essential part of your role to ensure that you provide the best possible outcomes for the child and continuity of care. Parents are the children's main carers and know their children best, so any changes to their child's routine or care, for example, starting the weaning process, will be far more effective when you work in partnership.

- How do you respond to parents in your setting?
- Do you actively listen to them, clarify their request and check your understanding?
- Are you polite and respectful?

Reflect on your interactions with parents, then observe experienced colleagues and compare their interactions with yours. What do you need to do to improve your practice or mirror colleagues' good practice?

Link it up

Unit 3 B2 details how to respond to parental requests.

Impact of inappropriate communication

There can be severe consequences in response to inappropriate communication. Look back Unit 3 B2 and your responses to the scenario with Tanya on page 110 to remind you.

Now look back at your practice and consider the impact of inappropriate communication in the workplace.

- What could the effects be on other parent's and children's confidence in the setting?
- How can situations be misinterpreted?
- What kind of errors may occur?

- Do you have examples from your practice to support your answers?
- If you saw two colleagues having an argument in the corner of the baby room, what might your response be and why?

Partnerships with parents ensure high-quality, consistent care

Supporting colleagues in meeting children's needs

By now you will have recognised that having good organisational skills, using your initiative and showing appropriate professional conduct contributes enormously to the quality of care and service that is provided.

Practise

For the following examples, reflect and identify one different skill and one piece of knowledge that you have learned or developed in the process of supporting colleagues.

1 when welcoming children and visitors

2 observing children during play activities

3 preparing resources.

For example, taking part in team meetings:

Skill – I clearly communicated my ideas and suggestions for the autumn term planning.

Knowledge – I informed Sally that Todd had pulled himself to a standing position in his cot today as she is his key person.

Having worked as part of a team you will know that efficiency, mutual support, sharing knowledge and experience, and working flexibly together are the main benefits of working with others. Consider the following daily routines and for each one give examples of your own contribution to effective teamwork. Look through your Placement Experience Assessment Portfolio of Evidence to help you do this. You may have evidence in the form of witness statements, routine write ups and feedback from assessors.

- Helping to prepare and maintain clean and safe environment
- Meeting children's hygiene needs
- Supporting colleagues during play activities or outings.

Contributing to record-keeping

Throughout your practical experience, you will have kept records. These should always be clear, concise, accurate and legible. You must understand how to organise and store information appropriately in order to support both your colleagues and the effective running of the setting. You must also comply with legislation such as data protection and confidentiality.

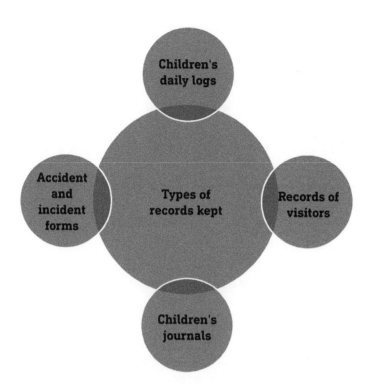

Figure 7.7: Examples of types of records kept in the setting

Practise

Take a look at records in your setting that you may have contributed to, such as nappy change reports and children's journals. Write down the potential consequences of poor record-keeping and information handling on:

- a child's health, safety and wellbeing

- the setting's future Ofsted report.

What do they tell you about your understanding of the importance of good record keeping?

B2 Reflecting on knowledge, skills and practice when supporting children's development

Applying your knowledge of policies and procedures

In Unit 1 you were introduced to some key pieces of legislation designed to promote and uphold the rights of every child. The United Nations Convention on the Rights of the Child 1989 clearly sets out a legal framework for children's rights worldwide. Amongst the key articles rights include "the right to an education enabling them to fulfil their potential" and "the right to be listened to and express their opinions".

Such legislation informs the policies and procedures of any setting and is communicated to practitioners to ensure everyone upholds those rights.

You will have been asked to read these policies and procedures to ensure you have the interests of the children at the heart of everything you say and do. Applying your knowledge of these rights can involve giving children choices, and making sure they can be heard and understood. It can also mean allowing them free flow access between the indoor and outdoor play environment, and allowing reception class children to devise their own rules of play using verbal and non-verbal methods of communication.

Using knowledge and skills to communicate with children

Effective communication skills are central to all areas of your practice.

Look back at your Placement Experience Assessment Portfolio of Evidence for Unit 6 to identify your effective practice in communicating with children in a variety of situations. This can include:

- a signed record of your observation of a colleague communicating with children
- a plan you have devised for a language-based activity.

Use of appropriate methods to communicate with children

In Unit 2 you learned about the ages/stages of development in young children, and that the rate of development can vary from child to child and be influenced by many factors, for example, a child's ability to talk can be affected by a lack of stimuli.

Knowing the children you work with and understanding their individual pattern of development will help you to adapt your communication methods to meet their individual needs. Having written play-plans will provide you with a regular opportunity to think about the adaptations you need to make when communicating with individual children. Evaluating these will help you to reflect and ask if your methods were appropriate or if future adaptations need to be made. Look through your Placement Experience Assessment Portfolio of Evidence for evidence of this.

Interactions to support language development

In Unit 6 you will have learned and had time to practise your interactions with children, specifically their language development. You will have learned that pitch and tone in your speech is crucial in ensuring your communications with children are positive.

Think about how this has developed over time. For example, you may have shouted across the room before working with children as that is how you may have communicated with your peers. Think about how that has changed now. Are you now at their level? Do you give eye contact when speaking? This is clear evidence of progress over time.

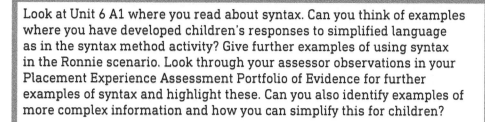

Practise

Look at Unit 6 A1 where you read about syntax. Can you think of examples where you have developed children's responses to simplified language as in the syntax method activity? Give further examples of using syntax in the Ronnie scenario. Look through your assessor observations in your Placement Experience Assessment Portfolio of Evidence for further examples of syntax and highlight these. Can you also identify examples of more complex information and how you can simplify this for children?

Overcoming barriers to communication

During your working practice you will most probably have come across barriers to communication. These could be due to environmental factors, sensory impairments, speech difficulties or children whose first language is not English.

Now that you have spent time with children, use the table below to identify strategies you have used to ensure barriers to communication are removed or minimised. One example has been completed for you.

Table 7.3 Communication strategies

Barrier to communication	Activity	Adaptations
Environment	*Story time*	*Story time is in the story tent in the quiet corner to reduce noise level and visual distractions*
Sensory impairment		
Speech difficulties		
English as an additional language		

Using verbal and non-verbal communication

Look back at your assessor reports about what they have said about your engagement with children using both verbal and non-verbal communication. Identify examples of the following:

- use of facial expressions
- eye contact
- hand gestures
- body language.

Can you identify two other examples of verbal or non-verbal communication in your Placement Experience Assessment Portfolio of Evidence

Do you think you have enough evidence for your final assignment? If not, then take the chance now to do some new activities to generate some more. If you are unsure if you have enough, seek your supervisor's advice, or from another colleague, perhaps one who has recently completed this qualification, if possible in your setting.

Link it up

Unit 2, Aim A2, covers child development theory.

Supporting colleagues

Supporting your colleagues in planning and observing children's interactions is important if you are to provide consistency and effective support for children's language and literacy development.

Refer back to your daily log, witness statements and assessor observations to identify the ways in which you have supported and been involved with observing the children's interactions and how the information you have gathered has supported the planning of language and literacy activities.

Creating environments that encourage communication

Now you have gained valuable experience working in an early years environment, you will undoubtedly have seen both good and bad examples of play environments. As you are aware, much time and consideration should be given to the set-up and location of activities to ensure they are inviting, stimulating and with minimal distraction. For example, story time should be in a quiet area.

Practise

To help you reflect on your practice experiences and to assess what you know, compile a "5 Top Tips" list for creating an activity area that encourages communication and language, for example, a role play scenario.

Link it up

Look back at Unit 6 A1 to remind you about factors in the environment.

Unit 5 B1 gives detailed information on creating stimulating and enabling environments.

Reading with children of different ages/stages

You will have spent many hours during your placement reading stories to children of different ages. You will have recognised by now that different types of books appeal to different ages/stages: hardback/fabric feel books for babies, sound books for toddlers, and stories with alliteration for preschool children.

Look back at the different types of evidence, such as witness statements, where you have been observed reading to children. What does the feedback tell you about your communication skills? Did you adapt your pitch and tone of voice to your audience? Did you keep the children engaged in the story?

Practise

Take a look at the different play environments in your setting and identify further opportunities where you can participate in reading activities with the children. These could be:

- books in Braille and other languages
- pictorial displays and home language signs.

What additional sources are in your setting?

Observing practitioners

A crucial skill in your ongoing professional practice is learning from others. You can do this by watching your colleague's interactions with children during communication, language or literacy-based activities, for example, show and tell.

Practise

Carry out a non-participant observation on a colleague during story-time. Think about:

- Where is the practitioner in relation to the children?

- How were they holding the book?

Now add three more techniques that you have identified that demonstrate effective communication with children during story time.

Supporting others in communicating effectively

As you develop and enhance your own communication skills through experience and observations of colleagues across the age ranges, you will in turn become a model of good practice yourself. Think about the advice you might offer to a new student at the setting about interacting with the children of different ages/stages and needs.

Examples of what you might say about the skills needed and the techniques to use are shown in Table 7.4.

Table 7.4: Skills and techniques

Skill	How to.....
Give your full attention	Use eye contact where appropriate to ensure you give full attention
Listening	Be patient and try not to interrupt, nod and smile

Practise

Make a list of 10 key skills a practitioner should use to communicate effectively, that the student could refer to for guidance. Remember to include barriers to communication.

Encouraging language use for babies and children

As a role model for children your communication skills are key. Children will learn from what you do. Reflect on how you have interacted with babies and children and consider what strategies you have used, for example, allowing time for children to express themselves.

Practise

Imagine you are sitting on the floor with an 11-month-old baby in your care who is posting objects in a bucket.

1 How will you engage and encourage the baby to communicate verbally?

2 What non-verbal methods could you use to engage the baby?

As children develop they are more able to express themselves verbally. You will have seen many examples of this in practice, such as a child returning after the weekend and telling you about their visit to the zoo or a child giving a detailed account of an argument between two friends.

Think about a similar example that you have been involved in. What was your role during this communication? How did you share the information given to you by the child?

Skills and knowledge check

☐ I can demonstrate how to maintain confidentiality in everyday practice.

☐ I am able to maintain an up-to-date portfolio of evidence.

☐ I can make changes to communication and language activities following reflection.

☐ I can demonstrate a good standard of English when displaying children's work.

◯ I understand what is meant by the term "syntax".

◯ I know what information to record in my daily log.

◯ I understand the importance of adhering to the setting's code of conduct.

◯ I know how to record health and safety information in accordance with the policies and procedures of the setting.

C Reflect on skills, knowledge and practice of supporting children's physical care needs and children's learning through play

You will have gathered evidence of your practice through completing other units and producing your Placement Experience Assessment Portfolio of Evidence. You must now use this evidence to show how you have supported children's physical care needs and their learning through play.

C1 Reflecting on knowledge, skills and practice when supporting children's physical care needs

Throughout your work placement, you will have developed skills that support children's transition from total dependence to becoming independent individuals. You will also have knowledge of policies and procedures that can support you in giving the appropriate care at each stage of development.

Table 7.5 gives some examples of a range of skills needed for different care routines and age groups. It acts as a reminder of safe practice.

Table 7.5: Care skills by age group

Routine	0–12 months	Toddlers (1–3 years)	Older children (3+)
Feeding	Provide close contact to bottle-feed baby, holding baby in arms, with lots of eye contact and facial expressions used. Support spoon-feeding during weaning stage, sitting at eye level to make eye contact, baby strapped into chair. Provide one-to-one attention throughout routine.	Child may need strapping into chair. Offer finger foods but close supervision is needed. Introduce appropriate size of spoon and fork to support emerging independence when eating. Provide closed cups for drinking.	Child can eat independently and make own choices based on food preferences. Promote healthy choices. Child should be seated at a table with other children, creating a sociable environment. Supervision is required but in a small-group situation.
Washing	Use individual cloths to clean hands and face.	Children need to be assisted in the bathroom – putting soap on their hands, turning on the taps and washing/drying their hands.	Child can wash hands independently in the bathroom. Demonstrate hand-washing routine for the children to copy.

In all cases, it is important that practitioners are knowledgeable about the relevant health and safety legislation and that they are able to apply it in practice.

Practise

Look at your Placement Experience Assessment Portfolio of Evidence.

1 What have your assessor and supervisor or manager noted in their observation and reports about your ability to follow health and safety codes of practice?

2 Compare their assessments of your practice during care routines with your reflection activities. Are you able to identify similar outcomes?

3 You could talk to the person responsible for health and safety in your setting to discuss ways in which you could improve.

Link it up

In Unit 4 A3 you looked at supporting physical care needs and in Unit 1 B2 and Unit 3 B2 you learned about food hygiene requirements.

Supporting care routines

Care routines are an important part of a young child's day. You should view them as shared activities and not as a list of jobs you need to get through. If you hurry through them the children will not learn and develop from the experiences that feeding, cleaning, dressing and preparing for sleep provide. For example, giving close, warm and unhurried interaction whilst bottle feeding a baby will support their emotional development.

Reflect on your everyday practice and routine write-ups. What do they tell you about your caring skills?

Observing and supporting others

Do you observe your colleagues as they carry out their care routines? Do you mirror their good practice?

Practise

Reflect on hand-washing, toilet and dressing routines that you or a colleague carried out.

1 Identify two ways in which children's language and communication was supported.

2 How did you recognise and support their likes and preferences?

3 What are the consequences for children if the routine is hurried or negative?

4 Look back at your routine write-ups. How have you progressed from when you began your course of study to where you are now?

Following procedures and guidance

When everyone in a setting follows procedures and guidance it makes sure that activities are done in the same way to support children's physical care needs. This ensures compliance of the EYFS statutory requirements and legislation (the law).

Practise

Reflecting on the care routines you have carried out, evidence you have gained for Unit 4 in your Placement Experience Assessment Portfolio of Evidence, and what you have learned about policies and procedures in Unit 1, answer the following:

1 Give two EYFS requirements for child:staff ratio for children under two years.

2 Name two different routines where you used PPE and the types you used.

3 Write down the importance of keeping records of children's care routines.

Promoting dignity and respect

It is a child's right to expect privacy, dignity and encouragement and support to become an independent person. You have dealt with children's physical care needs on a daily basis, so you will know how important it is to uphold those rights at all times and in all places.

Maintaining privacy and dignity

Reflect on your routine write-ups and other evidence from Unit 4 about maintaining children's dignity during toileting and nappy changing. Ask yourself the following questions:

- Did I inform the child about what was about to happen?
- Did I provide comfort and reassurance when children were upset?
- Did I carry out the routine within a sensible timeframe to maintain their dignity?
- Did I make sure the children were familiar with the layout of the bathroom to build their confidence?
- Did I offer children a choice of potty to use where appropriate?

How confident are you with how you maintain children's privacy and dignity?

Promoting children's independence

We all know that when children dress and undress themselves it can be a slow process and sometimes you may have felt that it was easier and quicker to intervene to save time, particularly if you are "busy". However, actively encouraging children's independence is a vital part of your role.

Link it up

Unit 4 A3 gives detailed information about promoting dignity, respect and encouraging independence.

Practise

Reflect on how you have supported children's independence with their dressing and undressing routine.

1 Was the routine carried out in an appropriate environment?

2 Was sufficient time allowed for this routine?

3 What level of assistance did you provide to a child when putting coats or shoes on? Could they have done more for themselves?

Look back at what your assessor has said about how you promote and encourage independence on their observation reports. What do you need to do to improve? What advice have they offered to support improvements to your practice for this routine?

Demonstrating awareness

You will have learned that your setting's policies and procedures are a reflection of the EYFS statutory requirements.

Practise

What do the requirements say in their welfare guidance regarding children's personal, social and emotional development (PSE)?

1 Look back on your reflection activities and the different types of evidence you have gathered and identify examples of how you have met those requirements, such as:

- demonstrating respect (for example, offering choices)

- providing emotional security (such as empathy and reassurance)

- promoting confidence (for example, praising their efforts and achievements no matter how small).

2 Identify why building positive relationships is important and support how you have done this with examples from your practice.

Link it up

Look back at Unit 4 A3 to remind you of the ways you can promote PSE during physical care routines.

Supporting others in ensuring safety

It is everyone's role and responsibility in an early years setting to provide support and maintain an environment where children can learn, grow and develop in safety.

Carry out the tasks in the Practise feature below to help you reflect on your teamwork activities in maintaining a safe environment.

Practise

Look at the evidence gathered in your Placement Experience Assessment Portfolio of Evidence, diaries, witness statements and workplace documents relating to how you followed policies and procedures in maintaining the health, safety and welfare of children.

For example:

- completing risk assessments on indoor and outdoor environments

- dealing with visitors to the setting

- your response to accidents and incidents.

What have your assessor and supervisor said in their observation reports about your ability to follow procedures or how you work as part of a team in maintaining a safe environment?

Can you identify how you have improved over time?

Link it up

Unit 1 B2 gives information on policies for evacuation and Unit 4 B1 Table 4.7 identifies Do's and Don'ts for carrying out evacuation procedures.

Supporting others to maintain cleanliness and hygiene

It is important that you understand the relationship between keeping things clean and the spread of germs and related illnesses. The risk of cross infection in early years is high and your role in maintaining a "clean" environment is vital in reducing that risk.

If you follow your setting's procedures you will meet those requirements. It is also your duty to encourage others to engage in and promote high standards of hygiene.

Practise

The statutory safeguarding and welfare guidance in the EYFS details responsibilities of settings in maintaining a healthy environment. Using your Placement Experience Assessment Portfolio of Evidence, such as diaries and routine write ups, identify an example of each of the following:

- infection control
- waste disposal
- sterilisation procedures.

Link it up

Unit 4 B2 gives information on infection control and table 4.9 gives examples of sterilisation methods.

Setting up and tidying away activities

Setting up and tidying away resources and equipment for the numerous daily activities you carry out is part of your role and can seem never-ending. However, it is necessary to ensure you provide a safe, stimulating and organised environment where children can play and learn.

To help maintain a safe and enabling environment it is good practice to encourage the support and help of the children where appropriate.

Practise

Look back at Unit 4 B3, Table 4.10 for a good practice guide for storing children's belongings.

Now reflect on your own practice, for example, daily log/diary, assessor observation, witness statement, feedback from colleagues. Consider the following points of good practice.

1 Have you ensured that storage boxes or equipment are labelled or have pictures on for children to easily identify where things belong? For example, coat pegs have photos of the children they belong to.

2 Have you encouraged older children to act as role models for younger children?

3 Have you offered children a clean wet cloth to help you clean down the tables at an appropriate time in the process?

Preparing snacks for children

When preparing snacks for children you will need to have considered:
- how you can encourage children's awareness of healthy eating
- your level of knowledge of the range of food intolerances/allergies of the children you care for
- how to recognise potential signs and symptoms of allergic reactions
- religious and cultural variations in food preparation and choices and how the setting's procedures ensures that these are respected
- portion sizes that are appropriate to the child's stage of development.

Practise

Look back at your experiences and evidence from your Placement Experience Assessment Portfolio of Evidence, for example, activity plans, routine write-ups and witness statements that show how you have supported and maintained the health and safety of children during snack routines.

1 Compare feedback from your colleagues, assessor or others to measure your level of progress and ability.

2 From the evidence, can you identify three actions you could take to improve your practice?

Supporting children during meal and snack time

If you have a positive attitude and create relaxed, sociable and engaging meal and snack times it will encourage positive responses from the children.

Reflect on the times you have been responsible for preparing and serving a healthy snack routine and identify:

- How you introduced different and unfamiliar foods and encouraged positive responses, for example, what language/ facial expressions did you use?
- Were you a positive role model for acceptable behaviour at the table, for example, by using good table manners?

What if

Tim is in charge of snack time in the pre-school room he works in. He is keen to go on his break so hurries the children along, not giving them time to make choices or chat to their friends as they eat. He hovers over them saying "come on I need to clear up".

1 Do you think Tim is a positive role model to the children in his care?

2 What is the impact on the children of his actions?

Link it up

Unit 4 C3 looks at opportunities for promoting choice and independence

Promoting children's choice and independence

How would you feel if you were never offered a choice or seem to have no control over anything you do? The response is likely to be "frustrated". The same feeling also applies to children. It is a vital part of your role to encourage children to be self-sufficient and independent. You must continually reflect on your actions and evaluate your skills and knowledge to ensure you are following best practice.

Practise

1 Identify two examples from your practice for each statement below, showing where you have encouraged children's choice and independence:

- when involving children in talking about healthy foods

- in encouraging use of cutlery

- when and how you have joined in with the children during mealtimes.

2 For each statement, identify two different areas of development that you have also promoted. This will help you to check your knowledge of child development and how you use routines as learning opportunities.

C2 Reflecting on knowledge, skills and practice when supporting children's learning through play

By now you will understand the benefits of learning through play, such as how it can encourage communication, support intellectual development and help to build relationships. Reflection will help you determine how well you support children to enrich and extend their learning through play.

Link it up

Unit 5 A1 and A2 have more detailed information on exploring play and learning provision.

Applying your knowledge

To effectively support children's development, you need to have an understanding of the stages of children's development from birth to five years and knowledge of the setting's policies and procedures. You will gain this by continually reflecting and improving your practice.

To help you reflect on what you know about EYFS requirements in planning activities, follow the example below for each of the seven areas of learning:

- include a range of ages 0–5 years
- name an indoor and outdoor activity
- identify one policy and one procedure that relates to those activities.

Example: linking policies and procedures into practice

EYFS area of learning	Activity	Policy/procedure
Understanding the world (3–4 years)	Making winter bird feeders outdoors Where I live – creative indoor wall display of our town	Policy – health and safety Procedure – risk assessments

1 Have you given different examples of policies and procedures for each area of learning to show a depth of understanding?

2 What does this tell you about your knowledge of the range of policies that affect activities you carry out with the children?

Types of play

Indoor and outdoor play environments and activities for young children should be integrated and allow free flow between them to give you the opportunity to observe children at different types of play in each environment. It is important that you understand the categories of play and how children can be supported, both indoors and outdoors.

Link it up

Unit 5 B1 has examples of types of indoor and outdoor play

Practise

Reflect on your observation notes of children at play indoors and outdoors.

1 Identify similarities and differences in how the children use the indoor and outdoor spaces:

- during role play
- during sensory play.

2 Explain any similarities or differences you have identified.

3 Identify three other types of play and write down how the activity can support children's imagination and problem-solving skills.

Understanding the stages of play

The stages of play are important to children's development and they should all involve creativity, fun and exploration. The different ways that children play and who they play with can tell you a lot about the progress they are making and will enable you to plan effectively to support their development.

Practise

Look back at your activity write-ups and your observation notes of children at play. Highlight examples of the following:

- Solitary play
- Parallel play
- Social play.

For each stage of play identify an activity to encourage a child's learning and development. Choose different examples from those in your Placement Experience Assessment Portfolio of Evidence.

Link it up

Unit 5 A2 provides information on stages of play.

The importance and benefits of play for children

Play is a vital part in every child's life, letting them enjoy their childhood as well as promoting their physical, personal, social, emotional and intellectual development. Play helps children make sense of the world around them through exploring or mimicking what they see.

Practise

Look back at any activity plans you may have created for your Placement Experience Assessment Portfolio of Evidence and your observation of your colleagues.

1 What have you learned about the relationship between play and learning?

2 What is the importance of providing play and learning to support different areas of development?

Recognising and understanding the benefits of play will enable you to provide and support a balance of enjoyable, structured and free activities that will promote children's holistic (whole) development.

Link it up

Unit 5, A3, looks at the relationship between play and learning.

Observing different forms of play

Observing different forms of play across all areas of children's development is a fundamental part of a practitioner's role and should always be approached with sensitivity and respect.

From the observations carried out and recorded in your setting, you will know by now that children are observed to gain more information about:

- interests
- likes/dislikes/preferences
- what motivates them
- how they talk and interact with other children
- which activities/areas they choose
- how they are developing
- how they have responded to an activity
- patterns in behaviour
- friendships and attitudes.

Practise

Information on children's development can be gained as children play. Look at the three play activities below and link these to areas of children's development.

Look back at Unit 5 to help you.

- Role play

- Outdoor bikes and trikes

- Playdough

How can you use the information from observing children to inform activity planning and learning experiences?

Supporting others to create stimulating environments

Planning that promotes children's development will be ineffective if the physical environment does not support it. By now you will have gained valuable experience in setting up play and learning activities, both indoors and outdoors and in planning and maintaining play areas.

In Unit 5 you learned about what is needed to create an enabling and stimulating environment. The Practise activity in B1 encouraged you to evaluate your effectiveness in setting out appropriate resources and equipment. What did it tell you about your skills? Perhaps you have photographs of wall or table-top displays you have been involved with. What was the feedback from parents and carers?

Reflect on times when you have used your initiative while setting up or when responding to children's requests for resources.

Link it up

Unit 5 B1 gives you information about providing an enabling and stimulating environment. C1 suggests ways to support children in their play.

Contributing to play and learning curriculum plans

In Unit 5 you learned about the purpose and structure of planning for children and the ways in which this can be done. The EYFS gives specific guidance on the prime areas of learning and development and it is your role to develop plans that reflect those requirements.

Have you been involved with planning meetings or in discussions with colleagues about your ideas and suggestions for activities? Refer back to the setting's planning documentation.

- Identify how the plans link to the EYFS?
- Identify the differences between short, medium and long-term plans.
- What have you learned about the reasons for the three types of plans?
- Identify your contributions to planning in your setting.

Speak to your supervisor about becoming more involved in planning to develop your understanding of how children learn through play.

Link it up

Go to Unit 5 B2 for more information on play and learning curriculums.

Identifying resources for play and learning activities

It is a part of your role to:

- select and use appropriate indoor and outdoor resources
- identify risks and potential hazards related to age/stage of development
- prepare and organise resources to engage children in activities
- support independence.

Link it up

Unit 5 B3 describes resources for play and learning.

Identify evidence from your Placement Experience Assessment Portfolio of Evidence to show how well you have carried out these requirements. Assessor observation reports, daily logs, feedback from colleagues and examples of risk assessments are all valuable tools for reflection. Discuss with your assessor or supervisor how you can develop your knowledge and skills further.

Supporting children's play opportunities

By now you will have developed a variety of skills to support children's play opportunities, for example patience, flexibility and being adaptable. You will also need an understanding of what is meant by child-initiated, adult-led and child-led play.

For example, when you reflected on child-led play did you

- let children follow their impulses and instincts?
- support them without interrupting?
- give them sufficient time to explore and become engrossed in their play?

Carry out the Practise activity to identify relevant skills that you have used to support play in different contexts.

Link it up

Have another look at fig 5.3 in Unit 5 C1 to remind yourself about supporting play in different contexts.

Practise

Look back at the What if? activity in Unit 5 C1.

1. What does it tell you about what you know about supporting adult-led activities?

2. Compare the skills you have identified in your reflection between child-led and adult-led activities. What are the differences and why do you think that might be?

3. Write down your role and responsibilities in observing children's play and learning opportunities. Give two reasons why this should influence your practice.

Approaches to supporting child-initiated and adult-led play

Through working with babies and young children you will have learned that child-initiated activities can come about in different ways.

- Child-initiated: a child selects their own resources and engages in their own activity, for example, a toddler playing with a toy farm animal and tractor. The child puts the driver into the tractor and moves it around, then swaps the driver for a farm animal to drive the tractor.
- Adult-led: a group of children are given a watering can to water the seeds in their pot, one begins to pour the water into the mud to make a puddle. In this way, the play has developed from the adult's intention for the activity.

Reflect on your understanding of child development, your relationships with the children and how you observed and supported them as they played. Give examples of your approach in supporting the following activities: literacy; mathematics; language and communication; and social and emotional. For example:

- child-initiated: I ensured the children had easy access to a broad range of mark-making materials so that they could explore during free flow time should they choose
- adult-led: I set out the planned hospital role-play scenario and acted as a patient to support the children's social skills.

Why is it important that you follow children's interests when planning a balance of adult-led, child-led and adult-initiated activities?

Planning activities with colleagues

Evidence from observing children and identifying their needs, interests and progress will inform how you and your colleagues plan activities. Reflect on what you have learned from your setting's planning procedure.

- Have you used evidence from your observations during planning meetings with your colleagues?
- Were the discussions in planning meetings based on children's needs and interests?
- How and where are these needs/interests recorded on the plan?
- Is the plan a working document? Has it been placed in the care setting so that practitioners can easily use it as a point of reference? Can it be adapted and modified to support children's play and development needs?

Link it up

Go to Unit 5 C1 for guidance in supporting children in their play and C2 for adapting support.

Look back at Unit 5 Aim C for guidance in supporting children in planned play and learning opportunities.

Practise

Identify evidence of how you have contributed to and supported the following:

- assessment of individual needs
- procedures for sharing information
- methods of recording specific needs
- supporting and extending activities.

Skills and knowledge check

☐ I am able to evaluate learning and development plans to inform future practice.

☐ I am able to reflect on my own effectiveness in supporting children's play plans.

☐ I can demonstrate what information should be recorded in a routine write-up.

☐ I can demonstrate I am following equal opportunities policies when supporting children's play.

○ I can name two policies that I follow when supporting children's physical care needs.

○ I understand the importance of promoting healthy eating.

○ I know how the EYFS welfare guidance is used to support children's personal, social and emotional development.

D Review knowledge, skills and practice gathered to support own professional development as an early years assistant

D1 Review own knowledge skills and practice

In this section you will reflect on your progress and identify your own professional development needs.

Identifying strengths and areas of development

Remember that in an early years setting you are always learning, and your continued reflection will help you to identify your strengths and the areas you need to develop. The following examples are areas where your current skills and knowledge compare to the requirements of your role. You can use the methods of reflection identified in A2 of this unit for evidence of how you have met these requirements and what you need to improve.

Policies and procedures

It is important to review your reflection activities in relation to policies and procedures. To help you identify gaps in your knowledge, ask yourself where you are now compared to where you need to be.

> **Practise**
>
> From your Placement Experience Assessment Portfolio of Evidence select a copy of a physical care routine write-up that you completed early on in your placement and one completed towards the end, such as a handwashing procedure. Look closely at how you implemented the routine in the early example and compare this to the later example.
>
> 1 How has your role developed during this period of time?
>
> 2 Identify how your skills have improved.

> **Link it up**
>
> Go to Unit 1 for policy and practice. Go to Unit 4 and C1 of this unit for physical care needs.

Children's development and learning

To ensure that you provide high quality, developmentally appropriate care you will need to review your reflections from activities such as:

- planning, setting up and maintaining a stimulating environment
- using opportunities to encourage children to count
- supporting child-initiated play
- supporting knowledge and understanding of the world, for example, a construction area
- using routines to enhance learning
- responding to children's needs to support emotional development.

Link it up

Go to Unit 2 for more information on child development, Unit 5 for learning through play and Unit 6 for language, literacy and communication.

Look back at evidence between working with babies and children aged up to four years. How does the care and learning environment differ between the ages?

Professional practice skills

There are many examples from your practice that you can draw on to identify your level of professionalism. For example, reflect and evaluate your skills in:

- your personal presentation
- your ability to receive and follow instructions
- using your initiative
- timekeeping
- relationships and how you communicate with other team members.

What if?

Esme is a Level 2 student at Perch House pre-school. She is constantly late each morning and very often forgets the time on her lunch break which affects break times for her colleagues. Her lack of time-keeping has come to the attention of the nursery manager who has asked to speak to Esme in person.

1 How can this affect her potential job opportunities?

2 What impact can her actions have on the team she currently works with?

Link it up

Go to Unit 3 for more detailed information on professional practice.

Children's physical care needs

Your daily activities will have largely involved supporting children's physical care needs in a variety of ways. How confident are you about your skill set and practice now?

Look back at previous experiences and reflections to evaluate your skills in the following examples:

- feeding and caring for babies
- supporting independence at snack times
- promoting good hygiene practice
- following a babies sleep routine and keeping relevant records.

Here is an example of how you could use Kolb's reflective cycle at snack time.

- **Experience:** What do you plan to do? Promote independence at snack time for three-year-olds.
- **Reflect:** What actually happened? Children were offered a selection of chopped fruits to choose from and milk or water to drink. This enabled them to make choices.
- **Revise:** What do you need to change? Children were offered choices and preferences but opportunities were few, limiting their level of independence.
- **Plan:** How will you make changes happen? Ensure snack time allows for children to select and prepare their own fruits under close supervision and provide small sized jugs so the children can pour their own drinks. Ensure there are cloths on hand so they can 'mop up' any spillages. Offer a washing-up bowl and towel nearby for them to wash their own utensils to promote self-sufficiency.

Link it up

Go to Unit 4 for more detail on children's physical care needs and C1 of this unit for reflective practice on supporting those needs.

Children's learning through play

Play underpins the EYFS, supporting both learning and children's holistic development. You have learned about the benefits of play and observed those benefits in action as you watched children play.

Your reflections and evidence in your Placement Experience Assessment Portfolio of Evidence will provide you with a wealth of feedback on how competent you are in supporting children's development through the play and learning activities you have been involved with.

Look back at your Placement Experience Assessment Portfolio of Evidence for examples such as:

- art and craft activities to develop imaginative skills
- story time to support literacy
- finger play rhymes to support expressive art
- jigsaws to promote problem-solving skills.

Look at the EYFS learning and development requirements – Learning Goals, the prime and specific areas. Does your practice reflect these requirements?

Communication, literacy and language

You will by now have some understanding of why communication, literacy and language (CLL) is so important to babies and young children, i.e. it gives them the power to express their own thoughts, wants and needs.

To determine how effective you have been in supporting children, you need to reflect on what use you have made of the opportunities during everyday activities, routines and conversations to encourage children to speak, communicate and practice literacy skills. For example, have you used sign language, or could this be a further training activity?

Opportunities to promote CLL could include:

- personal care routine
- tidy up time
- show and tell
- role play
- general conversations such as, "what did you do at the weekend?"
- story time
- name cards on tables at snack/mealtimes
- annotated table-top displays
- item in setting with a label on it, for example, "chair"
- circle/song time.

What areas do you need additional support or training on?

Link it up

Unit 5 explores how children learn through play and C2 of this unit looks at reflection when supporting children's learning through play.

Link it up

Go to Unit 6: Supporting children's communication, language and literacy development

D2 Identify development needs with reference to the early years assistant role

You will carry out a skills audit to identify professional development and training needs for an early years assistant.

Identify the skills needed to work as an early years assistant

All children need a safe, caring and positive environment in which to learn, grow and develop, and they all have many and varied needs. By adapting the type of support you provide to meet those differing needs you will help children to reach their full developmental potential (Table 7.6).

Table 7.6: Examples of some of the skills required for an early years assistant when working with children

Babies 0–12 months	Children with special needs	Children who have English as a second/additional language
• Support an individual sleep routine • Patience to allow babies to repeat activities • Offer close physical contact and affection • Encourage, listen and respond to their communications	• Work in partnership with parents and other professionals if special support or equipment is required • Support children to make friends • Encourage independence	• Keeping them safe when they do not understand verbal instructions • Recognising and understanding when children have "silent" periods and how to respond

Practise

Research, discuss with your work colleagues or reflect from your own experience to identify what additional skills are required for working with children in the examples given in the table.

Identify additional skills and training

Working with more experienced practitioners at your placement can help you to identify key gaps in your knowledge and skills you need to improve.

The process by which you can assess and evaluate your skills and knowledge is known as a skills audit. From that process, weaker areas can be specifically targeted for further development, to ensure that you continually have the essential skills required of an early years assistant.

Assessing your skills mainly falls into two areas:

- behaviour – how something is carried out, for example, attitude, conduct etc.
- technical skills – how you actually carry out an activity, for example, changing a baby's nappy safely.

Use the examples in the skills audit in Figure 7.8, which have been taken from real job descriptions, or those from a real job description that you have found online to audit your skills. You could even approach a local setting you might wish to work for in the future, explain who you are, what qualification you are doing and ask them for a current or previous description.

Figure 7.8: Example of a skills audit that can be applied to all aspects of a practitioner's role

Duties and responsibilities	My skill level now			
To work as a member of a team to provide a safe, caring, stimulating environment for children at all times, in line with the EYFS.	1	2	3	4
To provide a wide variety of activities for the children suitable to their individual stages of development.	1	2	3	4
To actively participate as part of the nursery under the direction of the team leader to provide safe, high-quality education and care to children 0–5 years of age.	1	2	3	4
To ensure that children's records, such as learning diaries/next steps and individual folders are kept up-to-date.	1	2	3	4
To ensure the maintenance of adequate standards of cleanliness and hygiene for the children attending the nursery. This includes changing nappies and toilet training.				
To record accidents/incidents on the correct forms.				
To build up relationships with the parents in order to ease the transition between home and setting for the child.	1	2	3	4
To manage own workload and plan time effectively.	1	2	3	4
To take responsibility for own professional development.	1	2	3	4
Key 1 = have no experience, need training 2 = basic skills, need additional training 3 = demonstrating some competence, may need some training 4 = competent in this area				

Practise

Discuss with your supervisor/mentor etc., what skills (technical and behavioural) are required by an early years assistant for the examples given above.

Then carry out a skills audit to assess your own skill level against the activity requirements to identify any additional skills or further training needed.

Sources of further training and development

As you progress through your career, you will no doubt take some form of additional training or study for further qualifications, alongside continually developing your knowledge and skills as you work. Identifying what you need to do to achieve your aims will help you to make your training more effective and allow you to meet any new requirements for your role.

As well as reflective practice, there are a range of additional training and development opportunities available to you, both inside and outside the workplace. Not only will you gain new knowledge to share with your colleagues, but training courses and events are also a great opportunity to network with other professionals and to discuss good practice. You may even feel that, by sharing examples of your practice, you are helping others to develop theirs – a great confidence booster! By attending, you will always learn something new, even if it is only to confirm that you are already following best practice.

Figure 7.2: Take every opportunity to develop yourself

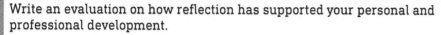

Evaluating the effectiveness of your reflection

Throughout your learning journey and practical experience you will have been continually reflecting in a variety of ways, for example, daily logs, routine write-ups, feedback from tutors, discussions with colleagues and peer observations.

If reflection is done well it will help you identify what your strengths and areas for development are, and highlight your personal qualities. In this way, reflection can help to support your personal and professional development.

Carry out the Practise activity to evaluate how effective you feel this process has been for you.

Practise

Write an evaluation on how reflection has supported your personal and professional development.

Structure your evaluation following these steps:

1 Overview: Provide an explanation of what reflection is, its importance and the methods used.

2 Focus: Detail the reflective cycle/s that you have used, such as Gibbs, Kolb, Rolfe and explain why you chose them.

3 Evidence: Discuss both positive and negative aspects of the reflective process and support these with evidence, for example, diaries, witness statements, assessor feedback.

4 Draw conclusions: Has the reflective process identified your strengths and areas for development to help you plan how to improve?

Skills and knowledge check

☐ I am able to use reflective practice to identify my own training and development needs.

☐ I can demonstrate a professional approach when communicating with adults.

☐ I can identify three sources of support available to me for my own professional development.

☐ I can identify three skills an early years assistant needs when working with babies.

○ I understand how evaluating reflection outcomes can support my development.

○ I understand what is meant by the acronym "PECS".

○ I can explain three methods of reflection.

○ I understand the benefits of completing a skills audit.

Ready for assessment

You will need to create your own detailed skills audit identifying your strengths, areas for development and own training needs.

You will need to have gathered evidence from your Placement Experience Assessment Portfolio of Evidence, for example reflection activities, assessor observations, activity and routine write-ups and evaluations, supervisor feedback, witness statements, daily logs/diaries and your own accounts of events. You must be able to show how you have evaluated your chosen methods of reflection and identify with examples from your Placement Experience Assessment Portfolio of Evidence how you have used it to develop your skills, knowledge and practice over the duration of your course.

You may be asked to create an information booklet, write a report or carry out a presentation that discusses your methods of reflection.

The following activities will help you to collect evidence for assessment.

- Identify two different examples of reflective practice from your Placement Experience Assessment Portfolio of Evidence that demonstrate your skills, knowledge and practice in supporting children's communication, literacy and language development.

- Look back at your reflection activities relating to children's physical care needs. Can you identify two examples of how reflection has developed your knowledge and skills?

- Identify one example where reflection has shown up an area for development when supporting children's learning through play. Explain why you think you need to develop this practice further.

WORK FOCUS

HANDS ON

As an early years assistant there are some important skills that you will need to practise to identify your strengths and plan for your progression.

1. Work skills

- Choose three of the key responsibilities of being part of an effective team and write down two possible consequences of not carrying these out.

- Choose your three best personal qualities. Describe how each one has had a positive impact in your setting.

2. Reflection

- Look back at your reflective logs/diaries and identify three examples of how your practice has improved as a result of your reflection.

- Reflect on how well you have engaged with parents and what you have learned from them. How can you improve your communication?

3. Planning for progression

- Seek a local early years assistant role that is being advertised and that might be of interest to you. Compare the role requirements against your own skills. What does this tell you?

- Identify an interest or hobby that you pursue outside of the setting and reflect on how that can support your progression.

Ready for work?

As an early years assistant, you will need to demonstrate a range of skills and behaviours that support a positive environment. Can you find the words from the list below in the word search?

```
K  I  B  B  H  U  V  P  S  G  I  D  Z  S  E  L  V  O  E  A
I  R  A  I  T  M  K  O  S  D  K  V  E  L  O  Y  S  T  F  N
I  T  O  X  Q  A  J  Z  E  X  W  N  Z  A  P  D  A  G  S  T
M  U  G  W  P  J  U  R  R  H  C  P  H  T  E  W  F  S  B  I
G  V  Z  O  M  S  Y  O  G  O  G  P  P  S  C  R  E  V  D  D
Y  D  S  N  M  A  Z  B  O  C  C  I  I  F  O  Z  G  L  K  I
N  O  F  J  F  S  E  D  R  N  J  N  Z  O  M  Y  U  N  P  S
F  M  K  F  J  Q  H  T  P  X  A  A  O  E  M  X  A  J  U  C
R  P  S  A  T  P  Y  I  X  G  U  F  Y  P  U  P  R  F  E  R
G  E  V  F  E  T  O  S  R  V  C  Y  J  I  N  O  D  O  D  I
A  V  Y  R  S  N  C  O  Y  D  P  H  K  K  I  H  I  S  O  M
J  I  G  E  J  R  R  O  B  P  I  T  Q  U  C  P  N  U  F  I
U  T  N  F  A  B  E  L  B  A  T  P  A  D  A  P  G  U  Y  N
V  R  V  L  M  A  L  A  G  E  R  U  N  G  T  N  D  O  O  A
H  O  E  E  R  M  I  I  E  K  N  D  Y  S  E  C  D  E  V  T
U  P  E  C  G  P  A  C  Q  F  M  M  I  Y  K  A  G  R  V  O
A  P  Q  T  S  Z  B  T  R  A  M  S  C  Z  N  N  H  L  N  R
S  U  N  I  T  E  L  T  I  Y  L  A  R  Q  C  C  L  K  S  Y
I  S  H  V  G  B  E  G  R  L  E  I  T  R  J  I  X  W  H  L
J  M  O  E  H  L  O  A  X  M  C  O  W  V  Q  Q  C  B  L  B
```

RELIABLE
ADAPTABLE
TEAMWORK
PROGRESS

REFLECTIVE
ORGANISED
SAFEGUARDING
ANTIDISCRIMINATORY

SUPPORTIVE
COMMUNICATE

Can you find any additional work-related words or acronyms?

Answers to Assessment practice questions

Shown below are suggested answers to questions in Assessment Practice features in Units 1 and 2. Where Assessment Practice features require you to carry out your own research or give individual answers or opinions, no answers are provided.

Unit 1

Assessment practice 1.1

Learner's own research task, but an example answer is shown here:

1 ⋅ There are 45 articles in the United Nations Convention on the Rights of the Child. The main features are that *every* child has the right to life, survival and development. Each child should be listened to and be able to express their opinions. Each child has the right to be raised by, or have a relationship with, their parents. Children should be protected from abuse and neglect and have the right to an education.
2 The purpose is to support the care, education and development of children worldwide.

Assessment practice 1.3

Suggested answers:

1 This goes against my setting's mobile phone policy, which says that mobile phones must be locked away to safeguard children.
2 I would report my concerns to my designated safeguarding lead, as it is important to highlight any safeguarding concerns and not ignore them.

Assessment practice 1.4

- Burn on stomach, bruise on buttock.
- If I had a concern I would report this to my designated safeguarding lead.

Assessment practice 1.6

- Priya was not following COSHH regulations.
- The child's eye might become sore or inflamed, he may even have to go to hospital.
- The HSE might investigate Priya; she may be fined or the pre-school could be closed down.

Assessment practice 1.7

Policy or procedure could be any one of:

Health and Safety	Food hygiene
Emergency evacuation	Ratios
Fire Safety	Safe moving and handling
First aid	Supervision

Second question: learner's own research.

Assessment practice 1.8

- Any five potential hazards from:

glass bottles	gates left open
syringes	wet and slippery equipment and surfaces
cigarettes	broken equipment and apparatus
plastic bags	animal faeces (especially in uncovered sand pits)
broken fences	pools of gathered rain water

- It is important I always check the environment before children play outside so that any hazards can be noted and reported to my supervisor so the area can be made safe.

Assessment practice 1.9

1 Anaphylactic shock.
2 I would alert my supervisor or a senior staff member straight away. An ambulance may need to be called.

Assessment practice 1.10

- He has asthma. He is choking.
- I would alert my supervisor or a senior staff member straight away and follow their instructions.

Assessment practice 1.11

- Indirect discrimination is shown because only dads are invited to the picnic, so this is discriminating against gender.
- Direct discrimination is shown to Danny as he is being excluded from the picnic due to the fact that he has autism.

- Danny and his dad might feel offended, angry or upset that they have been excluded.
- Children without fathers might feel left out and disappointed that they cannot attend.

Assessment practice 1.12

- Dual-language books; an interpreter.
- I can help to make Ana feel included in the setting by learning some key words in her home language. I could find out what she is interested in and offer activities to help her feel at ease. I could use a visual timetable to help support her routine. I could make sure resources are labelled with pictures. I would offer her lots of reassurance and support, getting down to her level and communicating clearly.

Unit 2

Assessment practice 2.3

1 At two years old, Emma should have around 100 words, although this is an average. Even if she is not speaking, she may respond when adults or other children try to interact with her and you should be able to tell if she has understood, for example when she is offered a drink or snack; children will understand before they start to speak clearly. Remember that Emma is learning two languages and is likely to take a little longer to start to speak; however, every bilingual child is different. See if her parents can get her hearing checked in case this is an issue. Monitor Emma's progress and note down any words she uses in the setting. Talk to her parents about the progress she is making in Spanish as time goes on and keep records of what you and they are doing to encourage her to speak. If there is no further progress after several weeks you may need to seek professional help.

2+3 You should talk to Emma as much as you can in English about what you and she are doing, providing a commentary so that she links the words to the activities. Always speak clearly and get down to Emma's level so that she can see your facial expressions which will help her understanding.

You should read to Emma in English and talk to her about the book, pointing things out and involving her if you can. If she reacts by speaking, using gestures or showing emotion, make sure you respond in turn to encourage this.

Sing with Emma, on her own or part of a group, as children will often respond to music and rhymes and this may encourage her to start to sing, enjoy and then to remember the patterns in words.

Assessment practice 2.3

1 Yes, you and the setting should be concerned about Sami for several reasons:
- Breakfast is very important for young children. If he has not had anything to eat, he may become tired and irritable. He will also find it more difficult to focus on the activities in the setting and enjoy his surroundings.
- The setting may wish to talk to Sami's mum about the importance of her son having breakfast. If she is finding it difficult to manage financially, she will find it hard to support her child and may need support herself, both emotionally and practically. The setting may recommend local groups, social services and food banks who may be able to help her and give advice and support. These may be groups such as:
    Gingerbread, a support group for single parents (www.gingerbread.org.uk)
    Citizens Advice Bureau for guidance and advice on a range of problems (www.citizensadvice.org.uk)
    Barnardo's for help with parenting issues and through providing local networks for parents (www.barnardos.org)
- If Sami wears dirty clothes it may also mean he does not wash every day. As a result, his personal hygiene will suffer and he may be more prone to illness and infections. He may also pass illness and infections on to others in the setting.
- The nursery manager may have a meeting with Sami's mum to discuss the concerns of the setting and to show that they are approachable so that she feels that she can ask them for help if needed.

2 On an individual level, you could:
- speak to his mum each day and ask her how she is. Be friendly and introduce her to other parents. Talk to her about what Sami has been doing and make sure she knows about any setting events so that she feels involved and part of the setting.
- keep an eye on Sami and check on him every day. Talk to him about his interests and activities in the setting so that you are approachable for him.
- talk to Sami about the importance of washing his hands, and of personal hygiene, especially after using the toilet. You could do this as part of a group so that you are not singling him out.

Glossary of key terms

ACCESSIBLE: available to all

ACCIDENT: an unexpected event, causing harm or damage to property or an individual

ADULT-LED: guided by an adult

AIRBORNE INFECTIONS: infections that are carried through the air and inhaled

'ALL ABOUT ME' RECORD: information completed by parents/carers that gives you an overview of a child's development to date and a record of discussions with parents about topics and themes that interest the child

ALLERGENS: substances that the child is allergic to, such as plants, perfumes, soap, detergents and clothing

ALLERGIES: a medical condition that causes you to react badly or feel ill when you eat or touch a particular substance

ANAPHYLACTIC SHOCK: a severe allergic reaction in which breathing may become difficult and the tongue can swell up

ANAPHYLAXIS: a response of the immune system to a substance resulting in symptoms including skin irritation, altered heart rhythm and restricted airway

ANNOTATED: notes added, with comments

ASTHMA ATTACK: when asthma symptoms suddenly become much worse

ATTACHMENT: a close relationship

ATYPICAL DEVELOPMENT: development in one or more areas that is not following the normal milestones at expected times

BACTERIAL INFECTIONS: infections caused when germs enter the body

BASIC NEEDS: the essential things in life (food, water, shelter, warmth, love)

BRITISH VALUES: the sector values that early years settings have a duty to follow

CARDIOPULMONARY RESUSCITATION (CPR): an emergency first-aid procedure to be used when someone's heart has stopped or they stop breathing

CHILD-INITIATED: chosen by the child

CODE OF CONDUCT: a document setting out the way you should behave

COGNITIVE DEVELOPMENT: development of the mind for thinking, using memory and working things out

COMMUNICATION: the way in which we pass information to one another

CONDUCT: the way you behave

CONFIDENTIALITY: only sharing personal information you learn about children in your setting with other professionals

CONSTRUCTIVE CRITICISM: feedback that helps you to improve

CONTINUING PROFESSIONAL DEVELOPMENT: continuing to develop personally and professionally

CONTINUITY OF CARE: ensuring you are adopting the same approach to meeting children's physical care needs in the setting as at home

CONTINUOUS PROVISION: activities and resources that are available to children all the time in an early years setting

CONVULSIONS: when the body goes stiff and jerks

CRADLE CAP: yellow scaly patches on a baby's scalp

CROSS-CONTAMINATION: spreading germs from one place to another

DATA: personal information held in the setting

DESIGNATED CAMERAS: cameras that are for use in the setting only

DESIGNATED SAFEGUARDING LEAD: the person who has further training on safeguarding issues and to whom you should report any concerns

DIPLOMACY: dealing with people in a sensitive and tactful way

DIRECT DISCRIMINATION: treating a person less favourably because of their protected characteristics

DISCLOSURE: the process whereby previously unknown information is revealed

DISCLOSURE AND BARRING SERVICE: the organisation that carries out the record-checking process to ensure that people who work with children do not have a criminal record

DISCRIMINATION: treating people unfairly because of their protected characteristics

DIVERSITY: the visible and non-visible differences between all of us

EARLY YEARS FOUNDATION STAGE (EYFS): government guidance that sets standards for the learning, development and care of children from birth to 5 years old

ECZEMA: a very dry skin condition that itches intensely, causing red patches or even breaks to the skin

EMOTIONAL ABUSE: this occurs if someone is treated in a way that can upset them and damage their mental health

EMOTIONAL DEVELOPMENT: development of the way in which children learn to express and deal with their feelings

EPI-PEN: a syringe holding adrenaline to relieve symptoms of anaphylactic shock

EQUALITY: treating children with 'equal concern'

EVACUATION: the removal of everybody from a setting

EXPRESSIVE SPEECH: speech you use to express what you want to say

FACILITATIVE: when something is made easier or easy

FASTING: going without food , usually for religious reasons

FEBRILE CONVULSION: a fit that can happen when a child has a fever

FEVER: a temperature above 37.5 °C

FINE MOTOR SKILLS: small muscle movements

FOOD CONTAMINATION: when food contains high levels of bacteria

FOOD INTOLERANCES: cause you to react badly or feel ill when you eat or touch a particular substance

FUNGAL INFECTIONS: infections that usually affect a child's skin, for example ringworm

GENDER REASSIGNMENT: changing from male to female, or vice versa, also known as a sex change

GLOBAL DEVELOPMENTAL DELAY: not meeting expected milestones across all the areas of development

GROSS MOTOR SKILLS: large muscle movements

GROWTH: the increase in a child's physical size

HARM: injury

HAZARD: something that may cause harm to an individual

HEURISTIC PLAY: play where children explore and discover for themselves

HOLISTIC: treated as a whole thing

IMMUNISATION: when your body has learned how to protect itself, so you are now immune to a disease

IMMUNITY: protection from a disease

INCLUSIVE: accessible to everyone

INCUBATION PERIOD: the time between catching an illness and showing the signs and symptoms of it

INDIRECT DISCRIMINATION: treating a group of people less favourably because of a certain protected characteristic

INFANT: a child under 12 months old

INFORMATION HANDLING: managing people's personal or sensitive information

INITIATIVE: the ability to do things without waiting to be asked

IRRITANTS: substances that irritate the skin

KEY PERSON: an individual who has overall responsibility for a child's daily wellbeing and acts as a point of contact for the parents

LANGUAGE: the code or sounds you use to communicate through speech or sign language

LANGUAGE DEVELOPMENT: development of speech and communication skills

LEARNING DELAY: when a child has difficulty communicating because they take longer than normally developing children to process language or to express themselves

LEARNING DISABILITY: a disability that affects a child's ability to learn

LEARNING JOURNAL: an individual file for a child that includes photographic and written evidence showing the child's responses to activities and experiences in the setting

LOCAL SAFEGUARDING CHILDREN BOARD: the statutory body that works to safeguard children in an area

LOOKED-AFTER CHILDREN: children who are under the care of the local authority

MANDATORY: something that has to be done

MANUAL RECORDS: paper records

MENTOR: someone, ideally an experienced practitioner, who can guide and advise you

MILESTONES: points in the recognised pattern of development that children are expected to reach at particular times

NATIONAL SOCIETY FOR THE PREVENTION OF CRUELTY TO CHILDREN: a charity that has the legal power to intervene if a child is in danger

NEED-TO-KNOW BASIS: only sharing the facts that people need to know, and nothing else

NEGLECT: a pattern of failing to meet a child's basic needs

NOMINATED FIRST AIDERS: staff who have a current paediatric first-aid certificate

NON-VERBAL COMMUNICATION: communicating using facial expressions, gestures and body language

NUCLEAR FAMILY: a family with two parents, usually a father and mother, and their child or children

OFSTED: the Office for Standards in Education has the role of inspecting childcare settings in England

ONLOOKER PLAY: watching other children as they play but not joining in

OPEN-ENDED QUESTIONS: questions that don't limit the answer to 'yes' or 'no'

PALMAR GRASP: holding a crayon in the palm of the hand by gripping it

PARALLEL PLAY: play that takes place alongside another child

PARASITES: tiny creatures that live in the child's body, making them feel ill

PARTICIPATORY PLAY: when children take part in play

PERSONAL PROTECTIVE EQUIPMENT: equipment and resources provided by your place of work to ensure you and others are protected from hazards and harm in the workplace

PHYSICAL ABUSE: this occurs when an injury is caused to someone by another person acting aggressively towards them

PHYSICAL DEVELOPMENT: development of the body

PHYSICAL DISABILITY: limited movement of one or more limbs

PINCER GRASP: using index finger and thumb to grasp objects

PRACTICAL COMPETENCE: being capable of doing your job properly

PREJUDICE: an opinion that is not based on actual experience or reason

PROACTIVE: making things happen

PROFILE: a place where information about a child is recorded

PROTECTED CHARACTERISTICS the differences between people in a diverse society

RECEPTIVE SPEECH: the ability to understand what is being heard or read

RECOVERY POSITION: the recommended body position for an unconscious but breathing casualty

REFLECTION: looking back at something, often yourself and your practice

REFLEXES: automatic movements that we cannot control

REGRESSING: when children behave in a way they used to when they were younger

RELIEVER INHALER: an inhaler used to relieve asthma symptoms quickly

RISK: the likelihood that something will cause harm to an individual

RISK ASSESSMENT: a written document listing the potential hazards in your setting so that measures can be put in place to lessen the risk of accidents and harm

SAFEGUARDING POLICIES AND PROCEDURES: the methods used to protect children from harm and abuse

SEIZURES: when the body goes stiff and jerks

SELF-RESOURCING AREAS: low-level storage boxes or shelves from which children can select objects and resources whenever they wish

SEMANTICS: the subtle meaning of words or phrases that could mean different things

SENSORY: relating to the senses of touch, taste, smell, sight and sound

SENSORY DISABILITY: impairment of the senses such as hearing, sight or touch

SEPARATION ANXIETY: being anxious when separated from a trusted adult

SEXUAL ABUSE: this occurs if someone is persuaded or forced to take part in sexual acts

SIBLING: a brother or sister

SIDS: sudden infant death syndrome

SOCIAL DEVELOPMENT: development of friendships and learning social skills

SOCIAL FACTORS: situations in family or home life, such as poverty, social exclusion, domestic violence, substance abuse, poor parenting skills

SOLITARY PLAY: the process of playing alone with toys

SPACER: a hollow container to help young children use an asthma inhaler

SPECIAL EDUCATIONAL NEEDS CO-ORDINATOR (SENCO): a teacher who works closely with children who have additional needs, and offers support and advice to their families

SPEECH: the physical act of talking and the way in which we do this

STATUTORY: required by law

STATUTORY DUTY: a legal requirement

STEREOTYPING: defining a person by their characteristics

STERILISED: a process which kills bacteria that can cause diarrhoea and vomiting

SYNTAX: the set of rules and the sequence in which we put words together

TRANSITIONS: moving from one area to another in the setting

TRIPOD GRIP: holding objects between the thumb, index and middle fingers

VACCINATIONS: injections or nasal sprays containing vaccines

VACCINES: products that are introduced into someone's body to help them develop immunity

VERBAL COMMUNICATION: communicating using words

VIRAL INFECTIONS: infections that can spread from person to person, such as measles, chickenpox and flu

VISUAL AIDS: pictures or images to make meaning clearer, such as picture and word cue cards

VOCABULARY: words

VOCALISE: use the voice

WEANING: the process of starting a baby on solid food

WHISTLEBLOWING: when concerns are reported about fellow practitioners

WORK SHADOWING: observing a work colleague closely as they carry out their role in the setting

Index